THE POLITICAL IDEAS

OF THE GREEKS

AMS PRESS
NEW YORK

THE POLITICAL IDEAS
OF THE GREEKS

WITH SPECIAL REFERENCE TO EARLY
NOTIONS ABOUT LAW, AUTHORITY, AND
NATURAL ORDER IN RELATION TO
HUMAN ORDINANCE

By
JOHN L. MYRES

O.B.E., M.A., Hon. D.Sc.; Fellow of New College, Oxford;
Wykeham Professor of Ancient History; Fellow of the British Academy
and Vice-President of the Society of Antiquaries of London

THE ABINGDON PRESS
NEW YORK   CINCINNATI

Reprinted from a copy in the collection of
the University of Florida Libraries
Reprinted from the edition of 1927, New York
First AMS EDITION published 1971
Manufactured in the United States of America

International Standard Book Number: 0-404-04549-9

Library of Congress Number: 71-137278

AMS PRESS INC.
NEW YORK, N.Y. 10003

CONTENTS

FOREWORD

THE request of the publisher that I write a foreword to this book is a compliment which I little deserve. Doctor Myres requires no introduction to any public familiar with current studies in history and archæology. Though not a prolific author, when he writes he has much to say that deserves the attention of scholars.

These lectures deal with the political ideas of the Greeks. The reader will not find in them a description of their political institutions, which have for us a deep interest as the first to embody the ideals of liberty under law that dominate our modern world. Books of that character exist and exercise a legitimate appeal; but they are at best unsatisfactory and may prove misleading, because they present of necessity a picture far from complete. Ancient Greece has been well called a laboratory for the creation and testing of political institutions; but of the many constitutions devised and tried those of Athens alone are sufficiently known in detail to permit one to assess their worth.

The world is inclined to value institutions

too highly, perhaps because of their solidity and apparent permanence. They have been likened to the bones of the social organism, the solid frame that persists in the ceaseless metabolic process; but institutions are themselves subject to inevitable changes of accommodation no less effectual because gradual and concealed by a brave outward show. When they prove to be perdurable it is because the spirit and ideals which animate them are renewed from age to age.

Behind every institution stands human character, the character of an individual, of a race, of an age; and character is molded by ideas, perhaps the least destructible of all things known to man. Once conceived and taken to the heart, an idea appears to be ineradicable; but it joins with others and in this union begets ideals of conduct by which man judges his fellows, even if he does not himself conform to them. It is in ideas, therefore, that society is rooted.

Nowhere else do our sources permit us to penetrate so deeply into the governing social ideas as in ancient Greece, where they may be observed in the process of defining and grouping themselves into those elemental forms which even to-day constitute, as it were, the materials whereof political institutions are builded. The structures erected with them

6

have undergone many a change, have, indeed, been at times quite demolished; but the constituent ideas persist and enter into ever new combinations. In them, whatever revolutions may come, we have the strongest guaranty of a life of freedom under law. In studying these elements of the social consciousness we recognize at once our kinship with our fellows who live under different institutions and our debt to those ancient Greeks who created once for all the formative ideals without which life would seem to us little worth living.

For the serious student of organized society the sketch of the evolution of these ideals here given by Doctor Myres will have an uncommon interest. It is not for me to pass judgment on the merits of these lectures; but I am confident that others will appreciate, as I do, the scientific spirit and the penetrating insight of the eminent scholar who presents in this volume a labor of love.

W. A. HEIDEL.

Wesleyan University.

WESLEYAN UNIVERSITY

GEORGE SLOCUM BENNETT FOUNDATION

LECTURES
For the Promotion of a Better Understanding of
National Problems and of a More Perfect
Realization of the Responsibilities
of Citizenship.

First Series—1918-1919. STEPS IN THE DEVELOPMENT OF AMERICAN DEMOCRACY. By Andrew Cunningham McLaughlin.

Second Series—1919-1920. THE UNITED STATES AND CANADA. By George M. Wrong.

Third Series—1920-1921. THE VALIDITY OF AMERICAN IDEALS. By Shailer Mathews.

Fourth Series—1921-1922. THE IDEALS OF FRANCE. By Charles Cestre.

Fifth Series—1922-1923. THE POLITICAL AWAKENING OF THE EAST. By George Matthew Dutcher.

Sixth Series—1923-1924. THE RECENT FOREIGN POLICY OF THE UNITED STATES. By George H. Blakeslee.

Seventh Series—1924-1925. ECONOMIC LIBERALISM. By Jacob H. Hollander.

Eighth Series—1925-1926. THE POLITICAL IDEAS OF THE GREEKS. By John L. Myres.

PREFACE

THE first duty of a lecturer on the George Slocum Bennett Foundation is to express his gratitude to the Trustees for the opportunity of submitting some portion of his work for the friendly consideration of colleagues and students in the Wesleyan University; for the welcome and memorable experience of an all-too-brief sojourn among them, and conference with them on matters of common concern, in the happy surroundings of their life at Middletown; and for undertaking the publication of this volume through The Abingdon Press.

His next duty—and it is a peculiar pleasure—is to acknowledge the unfailing help and wise counsel of one whose own work has covered much of the ground of these lectures, and whose writings have suggested the treatment here attempted of some of the chief questions here discussed. To have Professor Heidel's encouragement in undertaking this course, and his personal assistance in revising the drafts, completing the literary references, and correcting the proofs, has been a good fortune which his readers can appreciate, but only his friends will realize in its abundant humanity.

And then, there is the proper business of a

preface, to explain the subject of the lectures, and the treatment of it which has been attempted. To the ancient Greeks—as to the "Chosen People" of Israel—the modern world owes some of its most vital ideas, in politics and in morals. To those who are making most use of these great heritages, the question, how they acquired them, may well seem less important than the use to which we are putting them. But if we are to make intelligent and sympathetic use of other people's ideas, it is at all events useful, and indeed only fair, to put ourselves in their place, and appreciate what they were trying to do, and how their experience led them to a theory of life as well as to the lives they actually led. Now, both the Hebrews and the Greeks had this exceptional fate, that, while they arrived at fresh and significant results in their practical dealings with their surroundings, each people created a literature in which their experiences are recorded and their aspirations expressed with exceptional frankness and clarity. Their greater men seem to have realized that what they were doing was also worth recording, and that their thoughts were worth discussing; that their history and their philosophy alike were of more than passing significance, and, indeed, marked a fresh stage in the advancement of knowledge.

PREFACE

But these experiences were in the first instance special; they occurred in a period of history, and among geographical surroundings, which defined the task and limited freedom of choice and action. In particular, their times and their circumstances alike were exceptionally difficult, obscure, unprecedented. If necessity be the mother of invention, both Hebrew and Greek owed their rare originality to unusually insistent need.

It is only recently that fresh sources of information, documentary and archæological, have made it easier to understand how Greek society came to be constituted as it was, and consequently what were the special experiences, political and social, out of which Greek institutions and the Greek view of life emerged; and to trace these inventions and discoveries back into the "Dark Age" which precedes Greek civilisation, far enough to throw some light on their sources. Fundamental Greek discoveries of this kind are the notions of a Natural Order among the events of nature and the doings and experiences of man, capable of being formulated, through accurate observation and exact reasoning, as a guide for conduct; of Authority, as the personal initiative of gifted individuals, accepted as beneficial by their fellows; of Justice, based on reasonable interpretation of Custom, as the security against misuses of such initiative; of Law, as an agreed description of normal conduct among reasonable and humane people; and of Freedom, as the fruit of self-mastery, in the citizen individually and in society at large.

Each of these conceptions has had abiding and fruitful influence, and most of all on our modern world on both sides of the Atlantic. Their value, far from being exhausted, is indeed only gradually being revealed. We are ourselves exploring many dark places in human experience, where Greek thinkers and men of action have been before us, and have recorded what they found and how they fared.

To describe the main features of Greek experience in these matters it has not been necessary to employ more than a very few Greek words, which have no exact English equivalent because our own forefathers had not quite the same questions to discuss. And these necessary terms have been carefully (perhaps over-fully) explained. But to facilitate reference to the principal literary texts, and to enable those who read Greek for themselves to verify the quotations translated in the text, the more important phrases are printed in the original Greek, by way of commentary. It should, however, be quite easy to follow the argument without them; and in this respect, as in their

PREFACE

general plan and diction, the lectures have
been printed almost as they were prepared for
delivery. The point of division between the
last two lectures has, however, been shifted, for
better balance of their contents after replacing
some paragraphs omitted in the lecture room
for reasons of time.

JOHN L. MYRES.

LECTURE I

GREEK POLITICAL EXPERIENCE: ITS MEANING AND VALUE

MAN is always trying to live well. If he fails to do so under any given conditions, it is essentially for one of two reasons. Either external nature is so hard and wild that the possibility of living well and fully is cramped, so that man either fades out or becomes literally brutalized and lives on sufferance, precariously, or—and this is commoner—under the given conditions two ways of life are open to him, either toward a fuller and larger, or toward a meaner and narrower existence; upward (as we say) or downward; and he does not choose to go up. If he does choose the fuller and larger, and usually also the more arduous way, he is in a fair way to realise that supreme end—living well, a good life.

Now, it may be that in man, perhaps even in all things at bottom, there is some ultimate will-to-do discernible among the reasons, as we call them, why what is done is done just so. But if we are to discern such will-to-do, we must be competent to separate those other reasons and estimate the force and cogency of

15

each. And until we have done that, such initiative, even in man, may well elude us, and we are left with little more than a primary distinction between two groups of reasons why things happen as they do; between all those reasons which are external and make up that which is Not-Us, and those which are, in fact, our own "make-up," our Will-to-Do.

Both groups have changed historically in time and within human memory, just as both groups vary locally as we observe them in space. This sequence of changes in the "make-up" in this or that group of men we call his or their "past"; and the expressions of such "make-up" in this or that group of men, living in these or those surroundings, we call their "culture"; that is to say, the way they look after themselves and one another, and the way they look *at* that which is not themselves. For "culture" is not a state or a condition only, but a process; as in *agriculture* or *horticulture* we mean not the condition of the land but the whole round of the farmer's year, and all that he does in it; "culture," then, is what remains of men's past, working on their present, to shape their future.

THE LEGACY OF THE PAST

Now, the commonest reason why man fails

of the choice to go up, to win through his difficulties, is the quality of his "past." Without knowing something of this it is not easy to form any estimate at all of the value of any human achievement, except upon some such hypothesis or abstraction as the "economic man" of certain writers of the nineteenth century. On the other hand, if we do know something of the past of any man or group of men, we have not only some indication of the meaning of their present conduct but some measure of guidance as to what to expect of them.

And this is no less true of ourselves. Sometimes, looking back into our own nearer past, we realise how large a part in determining our conduct then has been played by all that "past" of ours which lay further back still. More rarely, and with closer self-knowledge, we may take "time by the forelock," as the saying goes, and make our own acts of choice with a certain measure of foreknowledge, how they will work out in events and how they will affect and modify our own "make-up."

To form opinions of this kind presumes either innate ability to see things as they are, to know men's "make-up" as we know their natural surroundings—and this is where the seer is rightly credited with a gift of prophecy —or else such experience of actual situations

as may train any natural ability of the first
kind which may be in our own "make-up";
and, this being the commoner chance of the
two, the need is more general for what in aca-
demic phrase we call "history" and "geography" in our normal scheme of such training;
not insulated contemplation either of events
abstracted from their situations, or of situations void of events (as some of us remember
it), but interdependent studies of historical
geography and, no less, of geographical history.

This was needful enough when the culture
which we call "European" was still confined to
that continent, and mainly to the western half
of it; and it was the merit of men so differently
constituted as Bodin, Machiavelli, Raleigh, and
Hobbes that they realised that need and tried
to meet it. It is no less valuable now, when
that culture has ceased to be either geographically or socially or politically "European" and
is acclimatising itself to distant regions and
alien surroundings, in the transatlantic New
World of North America; in the transequa-
torial world of antipodean continents, an
Australian Commonwealth, a South African
Union, a Latin South America; and in the
transpacific Old World of Japan, China, and
Malaya. Formed in the narrow cradle of the
least of the continents, between the Mediter-

ranean and the Baltic lake-regions, secluded long from the greater and older East by rivals and aliens, Saracen, Ottoman, Muscovite, frustrated of its crusading hope by the spasms of its own growing pains, and of the fruits of Viking pioneer work, by the premature union of the "three crowns," it experienced the discipline of the Renaissance and the Reformation, before its temper and character were matured and the great occasions came.

THE GIFTS TO MANKIND OF HEBREW AND GREEK

On either side of the cradle of that civilisation, of which we are the trustees, stand two guardian angels—or shall we say fairy-godmothers?—the genius of the Greek and of the Hebrew. Each of these has brought us its own gift; and the gift of each is, if not a solution of life's riddle, at all events the last word of experience and insight from a whole cycle of human achievement.

Hebrew philosophy—and by philosophy I mean that body of beliefs, principles, conclusions (for in different aspects they are all of these) which are the Wisdom, the "view of life," of a people, as of a person—is a subtly, compounded essence of the Wisdom of the Ancient East, of that group of regions within

19

which Egypt and Mesopotamia are the most significant in their material accomplishments, and successive Semitic-speaking overflows of the population of pastoral Arabia seem to have been the *primum mobile* in thought as in action.

Greek philosophy—in the same broad sense of the Greek outlook on the world—"an exact steersmanship for charting man's life," as Heraclitus' philosophy[1] is described to us—is in the same way the Wisdom of the Mediterranean region, or, rather, of those Mediterranean coastlands which harboured, and permitted to flourish, Greek city-states, and those other societies, of kindred origin, whose maturity was dominated more or less consciously by Greek ideas and customs. We shall see later how even so characteristically Italian an achievement as the Roman system of law owes its vitality and organic coherence to its acceptance of Greek principles of jurisprudence.

ANALYSIS OF THE RIVER VALLEY CULTURES OF THE ANCIENT EAST

I hope I need not do more than characterise briefly the correlation between the greater phases through which the main current of human culture has passed and the well marked geographical regions within which each successive phase has originated and developed, nor the intimate interdependence of each with its geographical surroundings.

In the Riparian (River Valley) cultures of the Ancient East we have for the first time as main physical conditions a perennial water supply traversing alluvial and therefore irrigable land, under subtropical climate, on a sufficient scale (though necessarily ill-shaped for intimate co-operation of each with all) to permit the maintenance of a considerable population, over and above the actual cultivators, available to supply their non-agricultural needs, and to do other things as well. Food supply, thus adequately assured, permitted leisure and reflection, as well as industries and arts, including the supreme art of manners—so indefinable, and yet so fundamental a bond in any society.

Corresponding, as main achievement, to these main physical conditions, we have (1) highly *organised production* and peripheral exchange of commodities with neighbouring regions; (2) *organised defence* against external raiders, comparatively easy in Egypt, where the desert guards both sides of the valley and man has only to guard the two ends;[2] much more difficult in Babylonia, though the home area is in itself more compact; organised defence also against internal raiders, the local profiteers, whether princelets or priestly corporations; the suppression of Nile-side barons by the wearer of the "double-crown" having its counterpart in the eventual supremacy of a "Dynasty of Babylon" over the other cities; (3) *organised means* for the communication and perpetuation of ideas and experience; of precedent and observation; organised record of sequences in time, on earth or above it; organised apportionment of space, time, produce, energy and other valuables, by standards and systems of measures.

We are accustomed to attribute these great advances in the art of "living well" to the Riparian civilisations without qualification; without asking ourselves, what really is an obvious question, "If the River Valleys had been like that as long as seems probable geologically, how was it that their great civilisations only began so late and so suddenly?" For the last few years' work in Babylonia has made certain this fact of comparatively recent date and abrupt beginning; and even in Egypt, where the discovery of the predynastic culture a generation ago seemed to throw back the beginning almost indefinitely, later discovery has gone far to re-establish the contrast between this and the culture of the United Kingdom of Valley and Delta, and to fix an initial date—and even a probable cause—for the dynastic regime, of which Egyptian history is the record.

For explanation we seem to be thrown back, *first,* upon the circumstance that both lower Nile and lower Euphrates border, at their most accessible points, on the same strongly contrasted region, the northern lobe of the Arabian plateau, with its sun-dried heart, and its grassland fringe "between the desert and the sown" passing rather abruptly into parkland as it approaches its Palestinian frontage toward the Levant, and the foothill frontage of the Armenian highlands further northeast; and *secondly,* upon the recurrent outbreaks of nomad pastoral people from within this grassland, of which at least four are recorded historically: the Saracen exodus in the seventh century A. D.; the Aramæan in the second millennium B. C. (from about 1300 to 1100); the Canaanite, late in the third millennium; and the Semitic occupation of northern Babylonia considerably earlier still. The process by which societies originating in the pastoral economy of a grassland adapted and transformed themselves, after such transfusion, into the populous agricultural valley-states is still obscure; and obscurer still would be the analogous process of acclimatisation of similar intruders all along the parkland frontage, from the upper Tigris to the "good land beyond Jordan," if we had not by good fortune the autobiography of one group of them.

THEOCRATIC SOCIETIES

These great discoveries once made in the Riparian cultures and propagated, like the produce of cultivation and industry, around their valley-cradles, we find maintained and defended by political organisations of uniformly "theocratic" type. Sublunary experience of the Will-to-Power on which the whole of these essentially artificial fabrics of society rested provided a working hypothesis for the interpretation of what was still outside man's physical control—the movements of stars, seasons, in regular routine, and the paroxysms of Babylonian weather, worst enemy of the cultivator except an invasion or a bad king, "wind and storm fulfilling His Word," like the taxgatherer or the Bedouin. Manners and morals similarly are sanctioned rather than interpreted—for the ways of the Highest are "past finding out," like those of His Majesty on earth; and imperfect knowledge counsels restraint and abstinence—as ignorance earlier and grosser had bred panic fear and imposed *tabu*. Even in the Hebrew Code, the fine flower of theocratic lawgiving, commandments are negative, except the one "commandment with promise" which transcends all political order because it originated before it, "Honour thy father and thy mother," that thine own days may be long. What the Greek found wanting—when he came to know these societies of the Old East, compacted into their last and maturest superstructure, the Persian Empire—was all trace of government by consent, all inward sanction of the commandment imposed from without; and it was just this inward sanction for which later Hebrew thought was ever searching, and never wholly finding, till it had been Hellenised through and through. To Cyrus the Persian, Greeks seemed to live in an anarchy of antisocial individualism: "They meet daily in the market place, but it is to get the better of one another."[3] It needed a Greek, himself an ex-king, to explain the paradox to Xerxes in terms of the code that he knew. "For though they are free, yet are they not free in all respects; for over them there stands a master, even Observance, before whom they are in awe even more than thy people are before thee, O king." For the Greek, as for the Oriental, law was a "gift of gods"; but Greek law was countersigned, "Agreed among sensible men."[4]

THE POLITICAL LEGACY OF THE GREEKS

We turn, then, to the political ideas of the Greeks, for these, side by side with the moral ideas of the Hebrews, have been the chief formative influences which have converted the tribal communities of unromanised Europe, first into the feudally articulated empires or kingdoms of that period of transition which we rightly call the "Middle" Ages, and then into the national states of modern times.

I would even go further, and submit that it is in great part to renewed need of such standards of behaviour and of criticism, in our own period of unavoidable and rapid transition, that we may ascribe the revival of interest in these ancient attempts to solve fundamental and eternal problems; and that the forms actually taken by some current attempts to solve those problems afresh under present conditions, are in some degree—and I think in increasing measure—due to their unexhausted value as inspiration and guidance.

But while it is on its political side that Greek thought has been most obviously operative, and Hebrew thought in its moral aspect, it is essential that we should realise that the political thought of Greece stands as intimately related to a characteristic conception of individual morality as Hebrew morals are to the political philosophy of the Theocratic State.

No less essential is it to full and just appreciation of the significance of the politics and the ethics alike of both these great peoples that we should study them in relation to those historical and, in the widest sense, sociological conditions in which they respectively originated. Only vaguely, it must be admitted, can the connexion be traced as yet between these systems of ideas, and the facts and events in the midst of which we first have sight of them; but it is the purpose of these lectures to survey such progress as has been made in one of these inquiries, and to suggest some lines along which further advance seems possible.

In particular it is not unreasonable to call attention to the progress which has been made, in the last half century, toward ascertaining at all events the main outlines of those earlier stages of experience which count for so much in the making of a people, no less than in forming the character and defining the outlook of an individual. On several different sides prehistoric studies are extending the range of our acquaintance with the history both of Israel and of the Greeks. Morphological analysis of the adult peoples is being supplemented by glimpses of the processes of adolescence, and even of what may be likened to those embryological studies which have been so rich a source of information to the student of other kinds of comparative anatomy.

HEBREW FOLKMEMORY

In the study of Hebrew thought this historical aspect has never been allowed to be neglected utterly. The children of Israel preserved with unusual vividness, in their own traditional history, the memory of a nomadic phase, a period of isolation and probation, a "temptation in the wilderness"; of their intrusion, already disciplined in the strict school of pastoral society, into the "good land this side Jordan," a "land of milk and honey," "of corn, wine and oil," of "fenced cities" and sedentary agricultural communities; and of the great adventure, imposed upon their forefathers, of entering into that "good land" to enjoy it, without breach of allegiance to the God of armies, the "Lord of Hosts," who had served them so well—even as they served him faithfully—while they were on the march, and he abode among them in his Tent of Witness, the migratory "Tabernacle." How they fared in that adventure of acclimatisation, exposed to the daily seductions of those unfamiliar incompatible surroundings; how, in spite of efforts and warnings and experience of the result, they "mingled with the heathen, and learned their works"; how, more tragically still, they "went a-whoring after their own inventions," using their mere human wits to devise satisfaction for very human needs and desires; and what became of them as their national history passed through the centuries —all this we know from that unique national autobiography, that "history of their own times," which has become the first and often the only schoolbook for successors in the same supreme adventure, of the entering into a "promised land," capable in determined and competent hands of becoming "God's own country."

In retrospect, that is, the history of the "chosen people" falls into well-marked phases, which, as we shall see, are of more than special interpretation. Organised already, like other Bedouin bands, in a composite tribal confederacy, they enter the stage of their national drama by force, and occupy it tribally during a period of national incubation which lasts till the Philistine overlordship was broken, and the nation momentarily unified by the house of David. Then follows a period of political independence—intermittent (it is true) but eloquent in its repeated revolts and reconstructions, of the intensity of the national spirit; it lasts from the tenth century to the sixth, and is closed by the strict inhibition of all secular activity, by the deportation first of the Northern tribes by Assyria, then of the Southern by Nebuchadnezzar of Babylon. But within the period of exile, a philosophy of life, only vaguely and partially foreshadowed by some few "prophets" of the two kingdoms, took shape and found expression; and the new regime of toleration for local cultures, and removal of old frontiers and obsolete restrictions which was inaugurated by Cyrus and systematised under Darius, made possible at the same time an empire-wide distribution of Jewish settlements and synagogues, and therewith widespread proselytism, in the conviction that this "way of life," made known by long national experience and contemplation, was indeed for manifestation to the Gentiles as well as a guide for the "chosen people" themselves.

English Origins: A Parallel Example

It may serve to illustrate this analysis of the life history of the Hebrew people, and also the pendant picture of Greek culture which is to follow, if we apply the same criticism briefly to the English-speaking world, regarded, at all events in respect of its political ideas, as one of the more important motive forces in the "European" type of modern civilisation. With successive occupations of the British Isles by varieties of Celtic-speaking folk, with their characteristic implements and institutions, and even with the temporary occupation of large parts of the region by imperial Rome, and the incorporation of tribes and *civitates* alike in a provincial administration of quite alien origin, we have no more concern than with the Minoan culture of the Ægean bronze-age, or the Canaanite culture of Palestine before Joshua's time. Our story must begin with the forcible occupation of the lowland regions of the larger island by tribally organised immigrants of Teutonic speech and a phase of material culture recognisable as belonging to the fifth century A. D. in certain parts of central and northwestern Europe. From the fifth century to the twelfth there is progressive acclimatisation, slow assimilation of Angle, Jute, and Saxon; exposure to common dangers from Norseman and Dane, oversea, and from survivors of the Celtic population in the highlands of the west and the north; a partial

31

conquest by partially Latinised Northmen from Normandy facilitates intercourse with continental centres of material culture, and imposes a closer-knit superstructure of administration, without serious breach in popular culture or local institutions. We might compare the effects of Assyrian overlordship on eighth- and seventh-century Israel, or that of the Lydian kings on the Greek cities of western Asia Minor. Then, about the close of the twelfth century, as in Greece at the end of the eighth, the period of coalescence and national gestation ends, and an "English" people appears in political history, in literature, in the material arts; above all, in a mode of political behaviour and political thinking, and in a way of life distinct from what had preceded and what was going on elsewhere, even in the northern district of the same Teutonic-speaking half of the island. Continental cultures, from Teutonic and Latin Europe, contribute materials, techniques, and ideas, without detracting from the originality of this Englishry. And if the counterpart be demanded to the phase of inhibited effort which threw back the Greek genius on its own resources in the centuries of Persian antagonism, it may be found in the long rivalry with France, the loss of our Ionia (the continental seaboard), the dynastic rivalries of the Roses, as pitiably futile as those of Sparta and Thebes, and the resolution of the whole tangle by a new dynasty and a new outlet for enterprise, on new continental front-ages inaccessible before. Closer parallel, how-ever, at this point is the general check of European expansion and access to resources and higher aspects of thought, which was im-posed first by Islam and then by the Ottoman conquests; for in this general advance of west-ern culture England had by this time its active share, like other adolescent nation-states. For what the victories of Alexander effected for the Greeks, by throwing open the great inland regions to settlement and exploitation, the voyages of discovery did for ourselves by re-vealing at the same time new continents and new avenues to old sources of wealth and culture in the Indies. With this revelation of a larger world, opens, for both peoples, a pros-pect of what it is surely no lapse from modesty to describe as an "oecumenical mission" of settlement, acclimatisation, realisation of ca-pacities long inbred and now spontaneously at command; enhancement, in use, of a tempera-ment and outlook racial rather than national, in the sense that political severance affects its achievements only in such degree as the parti-tion of Alexander's kingdom into the successor states infringed the unity of Hellenism, and made the Greekness of Alexandria to be of another glory than that of Antioch, or Pergamum, or Rhodes, or Athens.

GREEK FOLKMEMORY

The Greeks, too, knew that as a people they had had a beginning; that, as Thucydides expressed it, there had been a time, not so very long ago, when there had been no distinction between Greek and barbarian "for the reason that there were not any Greeks yet," or, at all events, no considerable body of people who could be called by such a national name. Moreover, "in the times before Hellen son of Deucalion there was not even this designation at all." There was folkmemory of a time when "Hellen and his sons grew powerful in Phthia," tribally organised in one little district among the northern hills, and of how, "when people called them in to their aid into the other states, severally, and mainly by their intercourse with them, they came to be called Hellenes," though this name "could not, for a long while at all events, establish itself for them all." But whereas the "House of Israel" took pride in its exclusiveness—with whatever qualifications in fact, we only gradually perceive—Hellenism was justified of its proselytes;

the earliest Greeks were such, "city by city, as many as understood each other" through adoption of Hellenic speech. And through adoption of the language, came conversion to Hellenic habits, beliefs, and outlook on the rest of the world. Here it was not so much that the newcomers "mingled among the heathen and learned their works" as that the aborigines— "born of the land," as the Athenians more especially boasted themselves to be—mingled among the "sons of Hellen," and "learned the works" of these missionaries of a new way of living.

That some Hellenic communities claimed more direct and exclusive derivation from one or other of the sons of Hellen, while others besides the Athenians prided themselves on descent from "nut-eating" men from the wild woods, devoid of agriculture and the arts of life, and others, again, displayed little pride of ancestry because they merely knew that they were originally "mixed," was a matter of detail. That some of their societies had, at all events, genealogical folkmemory back to comparatively recent "founders," or to tumultuary "migrations" into the districts which became their homes, while others thought that, "Hellenised" or not, they had been there always, was no less accidental, and compatible with their actual inclusion among "the Hellenes," and consequent exemption from the reproach of "barbarism," a picturesque way of describing all peoples, civilised or not, in the material sense, who were "unintelligible" in their speech, and incomprehensible in much of their behaviour. What was essential in Hellenism was increasingly felt to be this, that Hellenes were mutually intelligible, not in speech only, but in beliefs and ideas; their doings too were comprehensible and rational to this extent at least, that they were what another Hellene, without shock to reason or sentiment, could think of himself as doing.

Main Phases of Greek History

In the lifetime of the Greek people the relations between the men who composed it and the lands which they inhabited and attempted to exploit changed no less fundamentally than those of the Hebrews or the ancestors of the English people, as the nation came into being and passed from self-discovery to manifestation among all nations within its reach. The period of formation began here about 1400 B. C.—for we may neglect, as in our own case we neglected the Celtic phases and the Roman occupation, the long ages of the Minoan civilisation whose collapse preceded, and permitted, the Hellenic regeneration—and it was hardly over in 750 B. C., though the first symptoms of new national outlook such as the general recognition of the Olympic festivals were dated by Greek historians a little earlier. It was in this "Dark Age" of disintegration of older societies, and ill-recorded habituation of heterogeneous incomers and aborigines to the common rule of life imposed austerely by the peculiar physique of Greek cradle-lands, that the social foundations were laid for the political superstructures which we know as the city-states. It was within the same "Dark Age," too, that the structure of the Greek language, or, rather, of the several well-marked groups of Greek dialects, became fixed, and the traditions and legends of the older world, and of the "age of heroes" which inaugurated the new, became canonized in epic literature; and that the national stock of accredited deities gained customary occupancy of Olympus, as their votaries became acclimatised to the valleys and gulf-heads of the peninsula, the main access to which it dominated; while the customary abodes of those deities, when they descended among men, acquired quite as canonical a shape, in Greek temple-architecture, as did the conceptions which their builders were forming of those deities themselves, and expressing in Greek sculpture and painting, and as the arts and craftsmanship with which they ministered to Greek needs in their own Greek homes.

It was a true and genuine nationality, that is, bred out in regional isolation from mongrel ancestry, and educated to inventive originality in the stern nursery of regional necessities, that began, about 750 B. C., to outgrow the utmost limits of subsistence in the lands of its origin, and to explore and exploit new regions oversea, along the coastlines which radiate from its Ægean cradle-land.

The period of colonial expansion, it is true, lasted only about two hundred years; but it was checked, not by any failure of the mother countries to produce adventurers true to type, but by the fact that almost all accessible sites for settlements of "city-state" pattern were either occupied already by such cities or were foreclosed to Greeks by rival or uncongenial peoples, no less well organised, though not by the same processes, nor with the same habits or traditions. Examples are the Phœnician cities in Syria, Punic Africa, and western Sicily, the Etruscan cities of middle Italy, between the Tiber and the Arno, and the Lycian, Pamphylian, and Cilician states along the south coast of Asia Minor. It happened also that in the very generation which was realising that colonisation on the old system was over, the whole of the continental regions eastward of the cradle-land fell under the single dominion of the first self-conscious and rationally conducted imperialists, the Achæmenid dynasty of Persia; and it needed two centuries more of intermittent danger from this external source and of almost uninterrupted controversy as to the means by which it was to be averted, before the barriers were broken and the Greeks of Alexander's generation were let loose upon a world-mission to "Hellenise" the continental East, as they had already Hellenised the Mediterranean coastlands.

This period of continental Hellenisation, commonly called the "Hellenistic Age," runs from the accession of Alexander the Great in 336 B. C. to the collapse of the Roman Empire of the West. It opens with a stroke of individual genius, the replacement of the worn-out Achæmenid house by a Greek prince, as overlord of the Persian dominions, and the admission of Greek city-state colonies to those continental regions, from which they had hitherto been excluded less by the positive ill-will of the native populations than by the inability both of Oriental governments and of the colonists

themselves to devise any terms of co-operation
which would secure two essential conditions:
freedom for each city-state to conduct its own
affairs in its own way, and freedom of communication between such city-states both
within the continent and across its coastlines.
With a Greek dynasty—or, as eventually happened, with several regional dynasties of Greek
descent—in command of the means of pacifi-
cation and defence, both conditions were realised; since every such dynasty could count on
the loyal support of the city-states in its dominions, so long as their freedom was respected
and their communications secured; and the
city-states could count on the friendly patronage of the dynasty, so long as political and
economic freedom were not abused to dis-
integrate the territorial kingdom or upset the
reigning house.

But while successful defence and efficient
administration by the dynasty were the condition and guarantee of the loyalty of the
city-states, failure and neglect as surely for-
feited allegiance; and it was the initial good
fortune that Rome entered the political system of the Hellenistic—and by this time essentially Hellenised—world as the champion of the
liberties of city-states against the abuses of
the successor-kingdoms, and of free communi-

cations by sea, and in due course by land
routes also, against obstacles of every kind,
which marked the Romans as eventual heirs
of each and every dynasty which might fall
short of the new standard of government exemplified in the *Pax Romana*.

Now, it is noteworthy that the self-conscious
formulation of the Greek view of life was not
postponed till the Greeks' oecumenical mission
had been politically and geographically realised in the period which we rightly describe as
Hellenistic, because it is essentially a period
of proselytism and propaganda—literally "making the world Greek." It is the outcome,
rather, of that intermediate period of cramp
and inhibition, which lasts from the fall of
Sardis in 546 to the victories of Alexander
rather more than two centuries later; and it
culminates in the latter of those centuries,
when the Persian incubus was all the more
oppressively felt, because the failure of the
Cimonian and Periclean project of rallying all
Greeks to follow up their initial successes
against the forces of Xerxes, was frustrated by
the refusal of certain indispensable states, not-
ably Sparta, Corinth, and Thebes, not so
much to admit that objective as desirable, as
to cooperate with the Athenians and their
allies in realising it.

Precluded from further extension, regionally, by the foreclosure of almost all foreshores of the Mediterranean Sea which were not already occupied by Greek cities; and from pacific penetration of the interior, eastward by the Persian administration; to the north and west by large movements of barbarous peoples, Thracians, Illyrians, Gauls; and in Italy by Sabellian highlanders;—as well as by fresh aggression of old rivals, Phœnicians in Cyprus, Carthaginians and Etruscans in the western seas;—Greek enterprise and initiative were diverted from geographical pioneer work and development of new countries, and restricted to intensive cultivation of what was already won, and the discovery, in the literal sense, of a *modus vivendi* in this overcrowded world. Are we not ourselves experiencing a similar period of cramp and inhibition, and discovering, under Providence, the same double necessity as was set before the Greeks by the God in Delphi, to "know ourselves" and aim at "nothing in excess"?

Thus the political ideas of the ancient Greeks are of value and interest still; and they are so for several reasons.

In the first place, they result from an unusually successful attempt to solve the problem of living, not merely in so far as to maintain life with a fair degree of security against external and internal dangers, but in the sense that the life so maintained was a good life, with an ideal of behaviour and of well-being in view, and large measure of success in attaining it. That ideal was a high one, nothing less than independence, in its two aspects of self-sufficiency and self-mastery; reasonable control over "external goods" and physical circumstances, and self-control no less guided by reason in the corporate enjoyment of the fruits of cooperative effort. That, in few words, is the Greek view of life. However imperfectly realised in detail, that notion of what men may achieve, if they will, inspired all that is most admired, and much even that is regretted, in what we know of Greek history, and explains it to us. And if ever a people wore its heart on its sleeve, and carried its soul in its eyes, for the making of a historical portrait, it was the Greek people of the city-states. By their works we know them, and in their works we read their faith.

In the second place, the problem of living well was for the Greeks no simple nor easy one. It was, indeed, unusually arduous. Their country, as we may still realise if we will learn to know it as they knew it, is of exceptional and intricate build, tolerant of human occupancy only on condition of conformity to rigid physical conditions, with resources, climate, opportunities for exploitation, all strictly defined. In Greek lands, at all events, there was "nothing in excess"; only by "knowing itself" against the background of its own cradle-land, could a Greek people hope to live well, or, indeed, to maintain life at all. The population, too, out of which the Greek people of historical times grew to national maturity, was unusually composite, and had the varied experience of a long history and a whole cycle of civilisation before it can be fairly said that there were any Greeks at all. And the historical crisis, which brought to ruin almost all that an older culture had achieved and accumulated, has been revealed, so soon as we began to discover even the outlines of it, as one of the great catastrophes of all time. Seldom, in any region, has any body of men had so completely to begin over again, with such utter devastation of habitual resources, with so radical emancipation from habitual safeguards and controls, as the founders of the city-states, among the islands and around the shores of the Greek Archipelago, in the Early Iron Age.

And, thirdly, out of that chaos, and, as we shall see, mainly owing to the intensity of the stresses and collapse of old institutions, that necessity which has been the mother of invention throughout the long history of mankind, and has seldom been so austerely cogent as then, created a mode of existence, an outlook on the world, a code of behaviour, and a type of society, wherein a more profound appreciation of the fundamental issues, a more thoroughly logical analysis of the factors in the situation, providentially found expression, uniquely lucid and coherent, and left literary monuments which have exceptional value still, and historically have had almost unparalleled influence on human efforts in the same direction. It is the unexhausted vitality, the permanent inspiration, the eternal humanity of Greek political ideas which gives them their claim to be restudied and restated in our own time.

For the study of Greek political ideas we have several sources of information. There are, in the first place, what I may describe as the Major Prophets of Hellenism, the great philosophic writers of the fourth century; and among these Plato and Aristotle, different as they are from each other, stand in a class by themselves, if only because we know what they wrote. They lived within the Greek political system, they were familiar with its institutions, they attempted to explain them, to suggest how they might be improved or replaced by something better. But Aristotle had not the opportunity nor Plato the ability —for, at all events, he made the attempt—to put their opinions into practice: consequently, the ethereal imagination of the one and the massive common sense of the other stand like an artist's perspective between us and historical realities. Did Greek democracy, for example, like a table "as the artist sees it," always support a trapezoidal top on legs of unequal length; or were there states where equality of apportionment, of contribution, of co-operation was as nearly realised as in the parallelogram-table of the carpenter? Was there no solitary city worthy of that happy compartment of the twelvefold classification of states, in which a majority, consisting of the richer, ruled in the interest of the whole, as was so near to happening in Victorian England? At the other extreme there are embodiments of political ideas in enacted laws, numerous now but isolated and incoherent, and from their usually late date, fragments rather of a Deuteronomy than a Leviticus, and very far removed from the Tables of the Law as Solon or Zaleucus knew them; still further from the "ordinances" of a settlement-

founder in the colonial age, or the period of
conquests and migrations. Between these ex-
tremes of what was and what ought to be,
there are the pleaders and pamphleteers, appealing to "customs of our fathers" which
they frequently do not quote; and the poets
of the *ancien regime* who have no use for
the "bad men" now in power, but are less
open about the reason why they are no longer
in power, or even in their own country, themselves, much as the Psalmist is usually the just
man suffering wrongfully, and only slips out a
word now and then to say what he wants
done to the other side when it is his turn to be
"in" and persecute them. There are the Minor
Prophets who have seen the "King in his
beauty" from the sidewalk; Xenophon, especially in the *Memorabilia;* Lysias, like Amos,
showing up profiteers, and then, like the gay,
disreputable Andocides, expounding the Golden
Rule *to*—rather than *before*—a democratic tribunal. There are the dramatists, read by us,
alas! "in selections for use in school" made by
Byzantine priests; a gloomy enough collection
of problem-plays, passed "for edification" by
censorship. Even the *Cyclops* is a cautionary
tale for abstainers, and the *Alcestis*—if it be,
indeed, satyric—teaches that a prince, like a
bishop, should be the "husband of one wife."

There are the historians, of whom the two
greatest are the historians of war, not of either
codes or revolutions, but linking the dramatists
with the pre-Socratic philosophers by their
rendering of things "worth record" because
they actually happened, and "worth explaining" because in these incidents of modern
time eternal truth shines through. These, like
Hebrew chroniclers, have their Xerxes, "doing
evil in the sight of the Lord all his days";
their Darius, in wisdom and splendour like
Solomon, yet gathered to his fathers still "re-
membering the Athenians"; their Cleomenes
and Pisistratus, utterly human Greeks, in their
genius as in their shortcomings, as Saul and
David are great Hebrews, marred in the
moulding. Lastly, and for our present purpose priceless, as we shall see, there are the
Homeric poems, the Pentateuch rather than
the Bible of the Greeks; idealised retrospect of
a Heroic Age so different from the settled
existence which followed, yet peopled with
characters so typically human; Achilles with
Barak, Agamemnon with Jethro, Odysseus and
Ajax with Gideon and Samson; and illustrating in its greater schemes, and in minute detail
also, the working of some of those great notions already, which we shall find to be fundamental in the Greek view of public life, yet

either assumed, or else projected backward, as the bonds of a society in which there were no "city-states" yet at all.

Now, linking all these different sources together, there is a common treasury of speech, and in particular a small eloquent vocabulary of political terms. Nearly all of them are words taken from the talk of everyday life; charged with quaint popular associations, and never wholly losing them in common speech; applied, with deepening intensity of meaning, to more precise and significant notions, and gradually brought into new unpremeditated associations with each other, as opposites or correlatives in a terminology which eventually is philosophical and abstract, though never, perhaps, so abstractly used on Greek lips as in modern attempts to explain what Greeks succeeded in saying so simply and clearly, just because their own thoughts were for the most part not only clear but simple.

This is perhaps sufficient necessary explanation of the frequent recourse, in what follows, to etymology of an old-fashioned but no less wholesome kind. We are ourselves much the slaves of our phrases, and increasingly, as it seems to me, tolerant of noisy, careless people who have neither the knowledge nor the courtesy to use correctly even the smatterings of a

great language that they have picked up.
Thucydides knew something of this trouble,
writing as he did while people were still dazed
and unsettled by the Great War of his time.
The greater sophists invented etymology itself
and grammar, in their effort to get their pupils
to say what they meant, as well as mean what
they said. The fourth-century encyclopædists
created a standard terminology for politics as
well as morals and physics, only just in time to
record what they did about the city-states,
before the new world of Alexander's conquests
confronted them with new notions and experiences to which fourth-century idioms fitted
none too well. And the result has been an
unavoidable and very subtle danger of interpreting early uses of some of these persistent
terms by their later significance; worst of all, a
tendency to read Greek words, collected at
hazard out of popular speech, as if they had
quite the same implication and suggestiveness
as the Latin words, no less popular and incidentally specialized, by which those Greek
words were laboriously, pedantically, and per-
versely translated, from the times of Polybius
and the Gracchi to those of Lucretius, Cicero,
and Seneca.

On the other hand, and for the same reason,
there will be here less explicit account than is

usual, of the theories of the principal schools of philosophy, and especially of the Platonic and Aristotelian commentary on what Aristotle at all events recognised as fundamental, namely, "things as they grow" in the social and economic substructure of public life and all explanations of it. Both these interpretations being the work neither of historians nor of men-of-affairs—least of all of men "competent to take citizen's share under any scheme of citizenship"—are as inspiring as they are because when they describe what existed they are expressions of dissent and protest. When they sketch what ought to be, they are more or less frankly innovators and sometimes revolutionary; philanthropists, not historians.

GREEK POPULAR IDEALS

It will serve perhaps to bring this general survey of our subject down to solid ground if we pause at this point at a notable summary of what less gifted thinkers were saying about Greek public life and the function of a fourth-century state, and from that standpoint on the street-level of Greek thought collect out of the philosopher's analysis of it some of its leading notions; and then trace the growth of these, if possible, down from a nonpolitical origin, and at all events up to a phase where their

51

political meaning begins to diverge from some other.

In a well-known passage of his *Treatise on Rhetoric*, Aristotle summarizes current opinions about human felicity in a series of experimental definitions, as follows:[5]

(1) *Prosperity with efficiency;* due, that is, not to chance, but to active qualities in him who enjoys it. The alternative is illustrated by the phrase of Democritus about the "phantom of chance" which is so often the "excuse for the man's own want of will."[6] And the dependence of felicity for man on the realisation by effort of something contemplated as desirable is emphasised by Aristotle himself elsewhere.[7] The significance of this element of initiative, this striving after achievement, and the provision made, and to be made, for insuring it, will engage our attention presently.

(2) *Self-sufficiency for the maintenance of life,* in the first place on the material and animal plane, for the word used is *zoë*, applicable to all things which maintain themselves and reproduce their kind. What is contemplated is freedom from impediments offered either by external nature or by other men; unrestricted living in accordance with man's capacity for animate existence. We are reminded of the exhortation of the "Unjust Argument" in the

Clouds of Aristophanes to "use your nature," or, more familiarly, to "enjoy life";[8] and we shall have to return later to examine the content of this "physical" life-according-to-nature.

(3) *The most pleasant human life compatible with safety.* Here the substitution of *bios*, the specific word for human rational self-conscious life, for the mere *zoë* of the second definition, is instructive. Few animals knowingly risk their life, though they frequently find themselves in circumstances where they lose it through causes outside their control. Man, in his conscious efforts to achieve something which seems to him desirable, knowingly runs risks, takes chances, as we say, beyond the range of adventure which instinct allows to an animal. He can and does contemplate enhancements of his felicity, which are, however, to normal individuals not worth the risk, involving (as they do) prospect of curtailment, or frustration, of whatever felicity is already attained. Unbridled power, as in Herodotus' sketch of the absolute ruler, can "shift ancestral observances," and make temporarily and precariously "safe" courses of action and forms of enjoyment which ordinary men among their fellows forego, because "ancestral observances" impose forms of retribution which it is not worth while to incur.

(4) *Abundance of possessions and aids, with ability to keep and utilise them.* What is meant is full equipment with the persons, as well as the things, needed to realise projects conceived as desirable and safely practicable. It goes very much further than the previous definitions in amplifying the range of such projects. Enterprises too risky for unaided effort are brought within reach of achievement by organised co-operation; and it is of the essence of Aristotle's "freeman" that he has the capacity not only to provide for himself but to make use of the efforts—the labour, in the economist's sense—of others. But here, too, there is the same qualification that such enterprises shall be within the margin of safety. "While the strong man armed keepeth his palace, his goods are in peace," but a stronger "taketh from him the armour in which he trusted, and divideth the spoil." And there is the necessary further qualification, that the possessor of these facilities be himself competent to make use of them. It is the same stipulation, both for efficiency and for constructive initiative, with which we began.

These definitions, then, form a series elaborating the formally adequate terms of the first by successive enhancements and expansions of its scope and content. The social, co-operative qualification, though not explicit till the fourth, is implied in the third, because the principal risk which the seeker after pleasure incurs is interference with other such pleasure-seekers, and consequently interference from them, so that the first rule of safety is due regard for the desires, efforts, and enjoyments of those others. It is more explicit, even than it appears, in the fourth definition, because here, too, the principal risk of losing one's possessions and one's equipment for the achievement of one's projects arises from the existence of other organisations like one's own, mobilised by other adventurers in the same quest of felicity. Only by observance—by taking account of human, even more than of physical, factors—it is possible to defend and conserve, as well as to use, that which is at one's disposal now.

How, then, are possessions and helpers to be maintained, defended, utilised, and enjoyed with the fullest efficiency and the smallest risk to them and their possessor; that is to say, with the greatest consideration for other possessors and their belongings? That is the problem, more fully stated and elaborated, which is to be solved by society—of which human felicity is the objective—or, in the particular Greek instance, by the *Polis*.

Now, these various definitions, or, rather, descriptions, of the "end of man" are not offered by Aristotle as his own but as phrases in current popular use; and as the same word for "felicity," which is here used for the "end of man" as an individual, is also that used by Aristotle himself for the "end" of the state, we are for once very well informed as to popular Greek notions of the fourth century, of the aim and function of society. "Felicity" depends on reasonable freedom to fend for oneself in one's own way. This in turn depends, in the first place, on initiative of a specifically human kind, far outrunning that vouchsafed by instinct to any animal, and fraught with corresponding risks. Safe exercise of initiative and, indeed, the exercise of initiative at all on a scale where the effort of others is required, depends on co-operation, and this on concurrence of the others in that which the man of "push" and initiative proposes. But this concurrence presumes confidence that the privilege accorded to initiative will not be abused; that it will be exercised "with safety" in respect both of external risks of retaliation, and of the domestic risk of forfeiting that confident co-operation on which its efficiency rests. And this confidence presumes acceptance, on both sides, of a normal way of behaviour in normal circumstances, which can be counted on in advance and expressed in general terms.

Here, then, we have a series of related notions, implicit in popular belief as to the origin, function, and purpose of society, which may serve as a text for interpreting Greek political ideas. We shall first examine the circumstances in which the Greek city-state came into being, the purpose which it historically served, and the ways in which those circumstances affected the means adopted to attain it. Then we shall trace the growth of the notions of *Authority* based on initiative, and of *Ordinance* based on custom, as provision against abuse of initiative either by Authority or by an ordinary man. Next will come the Greek notion of *Justice*, as a standard of reparation in the event of a breach of customary order. Then the notion of *Law*, as a coherent interpretation and reasoned revision of custom; and therewith the Greek solution of the problem how Law is ascertained, formulated, and kept in accord with experience both of the processes of external nature, and of normal folks' ordinary way of behaviour. And, finally, with these notions of Authority, Ordinance, Justice, and Law historically reviewed, we shall be confronted with the Greek notion of *Freedom*, and with the relation between the state and the individual, as a provision for securing and maintaining this.

LECTURE II

THE GREEK NOTION OF SOCIETY. THE *POLIS*, ITS ANTECEDENTS AND CIRCUMSTANCES

GREEK LANDS

IF the philosophy of the ancient Hebrews may be described as the fine flower of the view of life characteristic of the Ancient East, with its great river-valley cultures, its Semitic nomad-pastoral motive-power, and its "theocratic" organisation, it is no less true that the Greek view of life originates in, responds to, and is profoundly influenced by, the Mediterranean circumstances of its cradle-land. And by the Mediterranean we mean, in general terms, that "lake-region" of the Old World which includes not only the west Mediterranean Sea, enclosed and enfolded between northern and southern members of a great zone of folded mountain-structure, Pyrenees, Alps, and Apennines on the one hand, Atlas and its eastward prolongation through Tunis into Sicily on the other; not only the east Mediterranean, lying wholly south of the Mountain Zone, from Albania to Cilicia, and encroaching irregularly southward on the slightly foundered slabs of

the North African flatland; but also the "Lake
Superior" of the Black Sea, partly enclosed
between Balkan, Anatolian, and Caucasian sections of the folded mountains, but also partly
flooding the southern margin of the Eurasian
flatland north of them. In addition we must
reckon the long secluded trough of the Adri-
atic, thrust far inland between the Dalmatian
and Apennine ridges; and, finally, that amazing freak of geological accident, the Ægean
Sea, where the Mountain Zone itself has been
repeatedly and profoundly cross-fractured and
collapsed, so that mountain folds and plateaus
sink in rapid succession to form promontories
and gulfs, and then chains of islands separated
and yet interconnected by open seas. In
this midland sea within the larger Mediterranean, the peculiarities of the whole are in-
tensified to diagrammatic sharpness of
contrast; rugged and weather-sculptured ridges
of Alpine grandeur and austerity, screening
and separating deep valley- and gulf-heads of
alluvial lowland, often capable of some extension up the foothills by laborious terracing,
but usually quite strictly limited in extent
between mountain spurs and high pastures
inland, and seaward the barren beach with
perhaps a strip of pasturable fen.

The climate and vegetation of this region

are almost as peculiar as its structure. The turn of the year comes not, as with us, in the spring, but at the close of the hot dry summer, when the first rainstorms of October or November make new growth . possible, winter plowing begins, and green things grow toward a brilliant spring of flowers and fresh vegetables; followed by grain crops harvested in June or July, and then the succession of fruit crops, the produce of deep-rooted trees selected from the natural vegetation or introduced from the forested highlands near by— vine, olive, fig, myrtle, mulberry—lasting on through the dry season, till the rain supply is renewed once more. Above the limit of cultivation there is pasture for sheep and goats on the hills, for pigs in the oak and walnut forests, a little fen-land and reed-brake for horned cattle behind the seafront, and a little fishing and sponge-diving down the gulfs and round the smaller islands. In these restricted and isolated habitations there had grown up, in the second, third, and fourth thousand years before our era, the graceful, artistic, and cultured people who created the "Minoan" civilisation of the bronze age, with frequent intercourse at all periods with Egypt, but very little contact either with the continental areas of Asia Minor to the eastward or with the contemporary civilisations of the middle Danube and the South Russian grassland to the north.

Of the social arrangements of the Minoan peoples we know something from the planning of their palaces and smaller houses in Crete, in the Cycladic islands, and in their colonial settlements on the eastern frontage of mainland Greece. Of their political administration we know less, except that in its higher stages it was closely centralized round palatial courts, which were at the same time a sanctuary, a counting-house, with warehouses for produce, and an academy of artists and craftsmen, employing their skill on new materials gathered from far, and interpreting into native styles the decorative repertory of the contemporary art of Egypt.

So long as the seclusion from continental neighbours was maintained, and intercourse with Egypt and other parts of north Africa was unimpeded, the development of this Minoan culture went on without serious accident. But about 1400 B. C. begins a series of violent disturbances, partly due to estrangement of the mainland colonies from the primary centres in the island world, and eventual replacement of the Cretan by the Mycenæan tradition, violently and generally; but partly, and as time went on, mainly, by the intrusion of less civilised and more aggressive peoples, whose aggressions are so distributed as to suggest that their origin was from southeastern Europe, and probably in great part from the middle Danube. Their ravages extended to Cyprus, the coast of Syria, and the Nile Delta, and probably also far to the west. Their conquests, repeatedly devastated and made tributary to these new masters, lost much of their industrial and artistic skill and material prosperity. We begin to trace large feudally organised confederacies of territorial chieftaincies, in peninsular Greece, and extending from a centre on the Hellespont—the "Troy" and "Ilion" of the Homeric poems—along the north shore of the Ægean and the north and west shores of Asia Minor; and we have glimpses between 1330 and 1180 B. C. of quarrels and struggles between these confederacies, and between an "Achæan" seapower in the Ægean and the Hittite empire or the kings of Egypt. Finally, about 1100 B. C., yet another crisis, due to an exodus of tribally organized highlanders from the direction of Epirus and Albania, wrecked almost all that was left of the older culture, drove many of its representatives in disorder through the island-world onto the west coast of Asia Minor and parts of the Levant, and established a regime of conquerors and oppressors over a large part of the Ægeanward regions of mainland Greece, the Dorian and Æolian districts of the classical age.

THE HEROIC AGE

Of the later stages of that period of marauding adventure which was brought to a close by these Dorian and Æolian conquerors, and especially of the "Achæan" feudalism which seems to have been established about five generations before their destruction of it, we have vivid and coherent reminiscence in the Homeric poems, the earliest, and, in many respects, the most remarkable monuments of the Greek language.

This is not the occasion to discuss the difficult problems suggested by their literary form and at first sight historical content. But it would not be proper to make the large use of Homeric allusions to political matters, which is inevitable in a discussion of this kind, without indicating in advance those assumptions as to their value and meaning, which every student of them must make for himself, and confess if his use of them is to be intelligible. Briefly, then, the *Iliad* and *Odyssey* are here regarded as poems which attained their present shape rather rapidly, and perhaps within a single generation, early in that "Dark Age" which follows the "Period of Conquests" and leads on into the "Period of Colonisation." Their allusions to features in a larger geographical experience than that "Dark Age" can easily be supposed to have enjoyed, are interpreted rather as reminiscences of the Sea Raids of the thirteenth and twelfth centuries than as anachronistic allusions to the colonial movement in the eighth and seventh. The political history which they presume as familiar to those who first transmitted and enjoyed them is identified with that of the Achæan feudalism of the thirteenth and early twelfth centuries; and the political and moral standards, the administrative and judicial procedure, of that "Heroic Age" as described in the poems, may therefore be regarded as derived from the same store of copious and coherent folkmemory as the references to localities and events. That folkmemory in this instance should be so valuable a source of evidence is precisely what we should be led to expect if there had really been an age of violence and adventures of the kind which the poems portray; for this is exactly what occurred during and after the Norse colonization of Iceland, the Saxon occupation of Britain, and more generally during the migrations of the Teutonic peoples along and across the northern frontiers of the decadent empire of Rome. In those instances there is contemporary historical record of many of the more important personages, incidents, and localities, and the credibility of the popular traditions can be demonstrated. For the Heroic Age of Greece, we are only beginning to acquire from contemporary Egyptian sources, and more recently from the archives of the Hittite Empire in Asia Minor, the materials for analogous proof; and for the moment it is the inner consistency of the contents of this Homeric storehouse of reminiscences that guarantees its value as evidence for the political conditions of an age when, as Thucydides puts it, "there were not even any Greeks yet," and when we can only establish indirectly the use of the Greek language among some part at least of the population of Ægean lands.

In view, however, of the opinions maintained by a number of distinguished scholars, that the Homeric poems in the form in which we have them have been translated, so to speak, into more strictly Hellenic shape, in respect of the morality, religion, institutions, and social practices of the age they profess to describe, it seems desirable to examine carefully, before going further, the Homeric usage of some of the terms which are conspicuous in the political vocabulary of classical Greece. If these words are found to be used in the poems in their later political sense, it is obviously a strong argument in support of such a theory of remodelling or "expurgation" of pre-Hellenic and non-Hellenic features. If, on the other hand, the Homeric usage is distinct from the Hellenic, or only agrees with it in respect of Hellenic survivals from a pre-Hellenic state of things, then the position is reversed: we may at all events be assured that in regard to these aspects of the civilisation which they describe, the poems have not undergone any serious revision; and we gain thereby fresh confidence that their allusions to such matters rest upon continuous, coherent, and vivid folkmemory of a period antecedent to that which experienced and, indeed, conditioned the formation of the Greek political system.

THE *POLIS* IN THE HEROIC AGE

The Greek city-state, says Aristotle, came into being "to maintain life"; or, as he expresses it in another passage, "for security's sake."[1] How literally true this was, perhaps Aristotle realised, for his knowledge of early Greek history was wide; but neither he nor any ancient writer has left us any description of the reign of terror out of which the creation of their city-states rescued the Greek people, and in rescuing created it.

The folkmemory which is transmitted in the Homeric poems comes nearest to giving us a hint of the significance of that creation; for though the word *polis,* and its derivative *politai,* is in common use, it never means a "city-state" of the Hellenic type; nor is the word *politai* ever used for the citizens of such a corporation. Neither word, that is, had acquired as yet its *political* meaning.

The Homeric *polis* is a geographical and a military expression: it is a fortified place. Its epithets are "precipitous," "well built," "well walled," "with broad ways," "with fair habitations," "set about with towers."[2] It can be "seen from afar," as when Zeus from the mountaintop "looks upon the *polis* of the Trojans and the ships of the Achaeans."[3]

The establishment of a *polis* is thus described:[4] "He drew a wall about the *polis* and built houses, and made dwellings of the gods, and distributed ploughlands;" providing thus for purely material needs, for defence, for residences for men and gods, and for orderly foodsupply. There is even a verb formed from the noun, to describe these proceedings:[5] "In a plain it had been fortified [*pepolisto*], a fortress [*polis*] of articulate [intelligible, and therefore civilised] men." It is "holy" as other places and persons are "holy," because they are guarded and maintained by some divine power.[6] If that power fails, it is the "summit" or "head" of the *polis* which is ruined and "let down," as a tree or a great rock falls;[7] it is "taken" and "held" by the enemy, who have camped "round about" it.[8] During the struggle men go "into the *polis* and wall."[9] and come out from it. It is coupled with, but distinguished from, another word, *asty*, which, as we shall see, is applied as strictly to the city as a place of residence, as *polis* is to its function as a fortress.[10] "Consider now, how thou mayest save *polis* and *asty*"—citadel, that is, and lower town: and the champion of its cause is described as the "buttress of the *polis*."[11] When it falls, "they kill the men, and fire devastates the *polis*."[12] The derivative word *ptoliethron* similarly "contains" the property of its defenders. The enemy, for example, debates whether "to sack it utterly or to divide up everything, all the goods that the fair *ptoliethron* might contain within it."[13]

Sometimes a *polis* belongs to an individual, either its founder or its actual ruler; in Lemnos, for example, is "the *polis* of Thoas";[14]

and on the other hand an individual may be identified by the *polis* to which he belongs locally, as he is identified in respect of descent by the names of his ancestors: a stranger, for instance, is asked, "Where are your *polis*, and your parents?"[15]

Similarly its *politai* in Homer are the defenders of this fortress, neither more nor less. The enemy is said to "capture steep Ilion and kill the *politai*," its garrison.[16] At Hector's death "so Priam spake weeping and thereat the *politai* wailed."[17] In Phæacia there was a conduit "at the lofty palace, whence the *politai* took water," and another in Ithaca, "near the *asty*"; it was provison for the resident garrison, not for the country side.[18] Once only the word *polis* is used for the defending force in a sortie, "the whole *polis* of Trojans advanced confidently."[19]

For the inhabitants in military array—for the field army, that is—there was another word altogether, *laos* (or in the plural *laoi*), denoting the same individuals as the *politai*, but in another of their functions. Precautions are taken "lest a band [of the enemy] enter the *polis* while the *laoi* are away,"[20] besieging another *polis*, for example: or in Sarpedon's reproach to Hector;[21] "Thou sayest thou wilt hold the *polis* without *laoi* and allies, alone with thy brothers and brothers-in-law." So, too, among the scenes on the shield of Achilles:[22] "about the other city lay two armies of *laoi*," who, being merely human forces, were represented on a smaller scale than the two deities who led them "beautiful and large in their armour, as gods should be, conspicuous on either hand, and the *laoi* were smaller below them." They are preceded by "two vedettes of *laoi*, alert to espy sheep and oxen with curved horns." The *laoi*, then, were separate companies or troops in the military organisation.

To this other word, *laos*, alone does any political or, rather, civil significance seem to be attached as yet, for, in the "trial scene" on the same shield,[23] "*laoi* were in the place of assembly, in multitude," and as the two litigants approach the court "*laoi* cheered on both of them, supporting them on either hand; and heralds then were trying to restrain the *laos*,"[24] which is used here in the singular for the plural *laoi* which composed it, in a way which suggests that the plural *laoi* are organic subdivisions—tribes, clans, or what-not—to which each individual belonged primarily, while these subdivisions collectively constituted a body politic, corporately concerned in the proper settlement of any dispute between members of it.

The contrast between the words *polis* and *asty* reappears in their compounds. From the one we have "destroyer" or "sacker" of fortresses; from the other, "pacifier" and "lord" of a people in its homes.[25] And, to anticipate for a moment the later usages of these words, even in classical times when *polis* was used without further qualification by an Athenian, it meant the Acropolis on its fortress-rock,[26] while *asty* denotes the "town" as opposed to the country districts, as an Englishman speaks of "going to town," meaning London; *astos* describes the townsman,[27] as resident proprietor with his *ius agri possidendi* (to use the Roman equivalent for the Greek term), and *asteios* his refined manners or his cockney wit, in contrast to the boorishness of the *agroikos*, who merely "had his home in the fields."[28] Similarly, a court open to freeholders only was *dikasterion astikon*; and the correlative of *astos* in this aspect is, rather, the "resident alien," *metoikos*, than the "foreigner," *xenos*.[29] It is now easy to see how words like *polis* and *politai* acquired their later meaning; but it is significant that it was from the common bond of mutual defence and the maintenance of a common camp of refuge, in an age of violence, that the Greek city-state and its citizens took their eventual nomenclature.

Other terms describing the community in its various aspects and functions throw a little more light on early stages of society in Greece. Mere "multitude" is expressed by *plethos*, as by its Latin equivalent *plebs*, *plebes*, by the *pleme* of the southern Slav peoples, and by the descriptive *homados* which is a "collection" or fortuitous "crowd," contrasted expressly in the Iliad with the organised *laos*.[30] If the latter, as some have supposed, and as its cognate *leïton* suggests more clearly, is connected with the verb for "ravage,"[31] it has a close parallel in the Latin *populus* with its verb *populari*, which retains the same sense. But it may be doubted whether closer analogy is not offered by the Teutonic *leute* (old-high-German *liut*, with a Gothic verb *liudan*, to "grow") and old-Bulgarian *ljudo*, "people."

THE WORD *DEMOS*

Homeric uses of *demos*, which has so prominent a place in the later political vocabulary, are as significant as those of *polis* itself, as to the comparatively recent emergence of the political regime of the Greek people. Though the word itself has been compared philologically with the Iranian *dam*, "following," in Homer, it is always used in a territorial sense, either for the habitable area, as where the Bœotians are "holding a very fat *demos*," with an epithet appropriate to cultivable soil; or a man lives "in the fat *demós* of Lycia."[32] So, too, when a good and a bad man are described respectively as a "joy" and a "disaster to the *polis* and all the *demos*,"[33] the contrast is between fortress and open countryside; and in this sense the ship of Odysseus came to the "*demos* and *polis* of Cimmerian men"; and Odysseus himself "wanders to a *demos* and *polis* of men of other speech."[34]

It is in general accord with this original meaning that in Attica later, and also in some other districts where the population lived sparsely over the countryside, smaller economic groups, village settlements or townships, are severally called a *demos* and their inhabitants "*demes*-men" (*demotai*), as well as *kômê*, which is akin to Gothic *haims*, Lithuanian *kemas*, *kaimas*, Prussian *caymis*, and old-Islandic *thing-heimr*, a "crowd" attending the *thing* or mass meeting. We may infer that *kômê* had originally much the same sense as the cognate word *kômos*, a crowd gathered for a festival or for recreation. Collectively, therefore, the whole countryside population was *demos* in its economic and statistical—indeed, in the demographic sense.

THE NOTION OF SOCIETY

A notable survival of this earlier sense of *demos* is the distinction observed in Athenian public documents between *polis* and *demos*. In all resolutions dealing with their own internal affairs the Athenians describe themselves as the "demos"; decrees begin, "It seemed good to the 'council and *demos* . . . ,'" and conclude with the hope "that it may be for the best with the *demos*."[35] But treaties with other states are either between their people and the "Athenians" simply,[36] or between them and the *polis* of the Athenians,[37] the motive here being security rather than internal adjustment. In Sparta similarly the whole state, in its relations with other states, consists of *Lakedaimonioi*, "inhabitants of Lacedæmon" concerned with the integrity and welfare of that region, whether serfs themselves or free; whereas the *Spartiatai*, "men of Sparta," the patch of "sownground" along the upper reaches of the Eurotas River, never occur in treaties, for this word applies only to the members of the governing body, which decided all questions of internal order within the territory of Lacedæmon or Laconia itself.[38] The same meaning of *demos* is illustrated by its early compounds, and especially by its use in proper names. Thus we have *demos*-elders, who are over fighting age, but still good public speakers, and sit on the fortress wall to watch the battle.[39] Agamemnon is abused by Achilles as a king who "devours the *demos*, since he is master of nobodies"; he has, that is, no resources of his own, but "lives on the countryside."[40] A chief with his following "blows in" on his way to the wars, to the place of a friend's friend. His host says that he entertained the leader in his own house "and to the rest of his companions, who came with him, I gave meal from the *demos*, and collected dark wine and oxen to sacrifice, to their hearts' content."[41] Here the rank and file were quartered on the resources of the district, the local prince organising the contributions of his people.[42] Later, but still in early phraseology, the poet Stesichorus described a public entertainment as a "*demos*-gift of graces."[43] Proper names such as Demosthenes, "the people's strength," Demoleon, "lion of the people," Demophon, "voice of the people," Demodocus, "receiving the people," reflect the later political usage; but Demouchus can hardly be other than "holding (owning) the township" or "district."[44]

Finally, a man of exceptional skill—seer, physician, crier, carpenter—is a "*demos*-workman," *demiourgos*, for his craft is at the service of all his neighbours, not only for his family or kindred,[45] and in the *Hymn to Hermes* the dawn is metaphorically such a "public servant," because, like the "wakener" in some old English towns, it calls the countryside to its work.[46] These "public servants" ranked for maintenance wherever they happened to be, like the war retinue of a friendly chief; and in their own countryside we may infer that they were maintained by the inhabitants collectively, as you may still be shown in some English villages the "Smithfield" or the "Hayward's Piece" which was formerly cultivated by the rest on behalf of such men, whose special job preoccupied their time.

THE MASS-MEETING IN HOMERIC COMMUNITIES

Homeric descriptions of the mass-meeting, *agora*, illustrate the simplicity of the terms used to describe these social relations; a simplicity which we shall find to be characteristic of the Greek political vocabulary throughout, and eloquent of its popular origin. For this word *agora* is simply the verbal substantive of a stem meaning "to collect" or "get together," as when Meleager is described "getting together hunting men from many a *polis*."[47] Especially it is used of collecting people for war or business.[48] Lack of such an *agora* was one of the marks of savagery in the Cyclops-folk,[49] for it "brought decision" by expression of the general "will." On the other hand, even in camp before Troy, Odysseus' contingent had a regular meeting place, and it is described as an *agora*.[50] Altars of the gods stood in it, and some spot or contrivance called *themis*, to which we shall have to return later. To do business in such an *agora*, and especially to address a mass meeting, is *agoreuein*, an equally simple expression and quite colourless in origin; and such a speaker is *agoretes*.[51] Speech "in *agora*" was free and privileged, even if it challenged the views of a superior.[52] There is clearly here a measure of political organisation and political sense, but it is described very simply, and there is one instance only when men gather in an *agora* without regular summons by a member of some privileged family. This, however, was on an exceptional occasion, when the news of the murder of the Suitors came by mere rumour, personified and described as "going in all directions through the *polis*"; and it is in a passage which was recognised in antiquity as probably a later addition to the poem.[53]

Group terms based on difference of language do not appear in Greek; there is nothing analogous to the Latin use of *nomen*[54] or old-Slavonic *jezeku*, "tongue." This is the more

notable, seeing that differences of language
were matters of common experience in the
Heroic Age,[55] and were even associated with
different peoples within a single region such
as Crete, where there were "men many, count-
less, and ninety *poleis*, and the language is
mixed, one of some, another of others, and
therein are Achæans, and high-hearted Eteo-
cretans, and Kydonians, and Dorians threefold,
and godlike Pelasgians."[56] Even *ethnos*, which
becomes later a term of mild contempt for
un-Hellenic peoples, with no organisation
higher than that of the clan, like the Roman
use of *gentiles* for "foreigners," has no such
implication. Its derivation is obscure, perhaps related to *ethos*, "custom," perhaps to
hesmos, "swarm," but more probably to old-
Prussian *amsis, amzias,* "lifetime" and so "generation of men." In a striking passage of the
Iliad we find within eleven lines *ethnos* used
of birds, of a swarm of flies, and of the contingents of Agamemnon's army.[57]

On the other hand, the words used, in classical times, for the groups, members of which
are members of the city-state which those
groups constitute, are almost always descriptive of kinships: (1) *genos*, like the Latin *gens*
and *natio* (*gnatio*), Sanskrit *jana*, old-Slavonic
narodu[58] (2) *phratria*, "brotherhood," equiv-

alent to south-Slavonic *bratstvo;*[59] (3) *patra,* "paternity," and probably also (4) the Homeric *phylon* (more commonly *phyle* in later Greek), which is used also for a "swarm" of flies, for the whole "sex" of women or goddesses,[60] both in the *Iliad* and by classical authors; and also specifically for "offspring" of a man or woman,[61] wholly in accordance with its root meaning "grow," "come into being," representing a primitive Indo-European root, *bheu.* In later Greek it is usually a larger group, of which the *phratria* is a division, standing thus as the south-Slavonic *pleme* to the *bratstvo.* Thus Nestor advises Agamemnon to marshal his army in kinship groups, "divide the men by *phratry,* by *phylon,* that *phratry* may defend *phratry,* and tribe, tribe," and demonstrate to the general "which of the leaders, and which of the clans [*laoi*] is bad and which is good, for they will fight each by themselves."[62]

We arrive thus, from examination of the mere vocabulary, at a picture of a state of society in which each habitable territory has sedentary inhabitants of its own, consisting of kinship groups, larger or smaller, which for corporate action in peace or war are *laoi.* These *laoi* are only brought into relation with each other by two means: one is the "mass meeting," *agora,* of their fighting strength of adult males, in which disputes between members of different *laoi* are adjusted by a panel or bench of elders, *gerontes*, and speech is free and privileged; whereas, outside an *agora*, the protests, or incitements to discord, of individuals are liable to repression by force, as when Thersites speaks evil of the paramount chief, and is publicly beaten by Odysseus,[63] with general approval. The other is the initiative authority of the "divine-born" leaders, which must engage our attention later.

This picture of Homeric communities is, however, very different from that of the city-state in Hellenic times. Even Thucydides' description of an early Hellenic phase in which there were still "hereditary kingships on terms of specified privileges" is very far from describing the baronies of the Achæan feudalism; the "divine-born" kings of the Heroic Age ruled by divine right and their own good swords; they were "shepherds of the people," but they lived on their flocks. They could cheerfully "sack a town or so, of those who live round and are mastered by oneself,"[64] to make room for friends of their own, as Menelaus offered to do for Odysseus if Telemachus could find him. Survivals indeed there were, both in Sparta and other conquest-states, in Samos and some other settlements of the migration period, and even in a few colonies of comparatively late foundation, as at Cyrene, where the family of the leader of the original settlers ruled for seven generations, and had its privileges eventually curtailed in the way Thucydides describes. But the relation in which the constituent kinship-groups stood to the community as a whole, in its political aspect, is different; and seeing that we have now been able to fix fairly accurately a period in which there was still no such *polis*, in the Hellenic sense, we may turn to the geographical distribution of the *polis*-regime in classical times with some hope of ascertaining, at all events approximately, the region within which such communities came into existence, within the comparatively short limits of time to which we have now been able to confine our inquiry.

THE GEOGRAPHICAL DISTRIBUTION OF THE GREEK CITY-STATES

In the period when Greek history begins to be recognisable as a continuous and coherent narrative, about the middle of the eighth century B. C., Greek city-states were being founded already in considerable numbers outside the cradle-lands of the archipelago; and the fact that there was already recognised a formal procedure for establishing a "home-

away-from-home"—to use the graphic Greek
name *apoikia* for these foundations—shows
that it is not in these outland regions, nor in
this comparatively late period, that the origin
of the city-state is to be found. Even within
the Ægean itself, too, considerable stretches of
coast line have only establishments of this
secondary colonial kind; for example, the
northern coast, from the frontiers of Thessaly,
north of Mount Olympus, to the Hellespont,
was for the most part colonized late, piece-
meal, and in face of opposition in all the
eastern half of it from the native Thracian
tribes. Only in the Chalcidic peninsula were
there cities old enough to have no very accurate dates for their establishment; and even
here, the Chalcidic cities knew quite well, as,
indeed, their name implies, that they were for
the most part colonies of Chalcis in Eubœa.

Nor was the whole area over which Greek
dialects were spoken occupied by political
communities of the city-state type. Throughout the mountainous and forest-clad districts
which lie between the watershed of the Greek
peninsula and its western coast society was
tribal still in the fifth century.[65] The Æto-
lians, for example, "were living in unwalled
villages and these far apart" when they were
invaded by an Athenian force in the year 426,

and had no regional government, though they rallied their lightly armed forces swiftly and handled them with vigour and skill, in mountain warfare, against regular troops. The Acarnanians, further west, had a fortress at Olpæ "on a strong hill by the sea, which they had fortified once upon a time and used as a common court of justice";[66] another of their settlements, Stratous, is described as a *polis*, and was walled; but they had no field-army, and relied on guerilla tactics.[67] How unlike the normal city-state regime were the societies of this whole region, is illustrated by the fact that here alone, of Greek-speaking districts, were there established colonies from another Greek city; for in the seventh century Corinth had founded here a chain of regular *apoikiai*, from Œniadæ on the coast of Ætolia to Ambracia north of the gulf of that name.

Even in Phocis, among the foothills of Parnassus and Helicon, though several small communities are described as *poleis*, there was no city of the Phocians; only a Phocian meeting-place, *Phokikon*, like that of the Acarnanians, but apparently unfortified, like the Althing of Iceland in the Saga-period.

Arcadia, in the Peloponnesian highlands, is not much better. Independent *poleis* it had, but on a minute scale, and embarrassed by tribal or regional groupings, as in Parrhasia. Only in the larger eastern plain are there two rival *poleis*, Tegea, capable of holding its own in early times and never insignificant, and Mantinea, founded later and experimentally by five self-conscious, politically sophisticated "villages," and resolved into those villages, in the fourth generation only, by a similar political manœuvre. On the Argive border, to the northeast, Orchomenus, Phlius, Cleonæ, and Nemea, mark a transition from Arcadian immaturity to conquest-states of quite different structure; Orchomenus including at least six distinct communities, three of which formed a kind of inner ring, or *tripolis*, perhaps the aboriginal group.

For on the eastern slopes of the watershed the structure of the country is different. The ranges veer apart, intercross, and inclose considerable lowland areas. Among these, Thessaly, the most northerly, is large enough to support a ranching regime, of great antiquity, though the ranch-owners change; and the last conquerors, in the twelfth century, held the plain in large baronies, and exploited the labour of former occupants in large villages, and of the tribally organised folk of the foot-hills and highlands, Perrhæbians, Magnetes, Dolopes, and the like. Here the conquerors were completely dominant, though race-feud smoulders; and as the conquerors lived on their ranches, there was little place for town-life or a town population. The perennial shortage of citizens in the precarious *polis* of Larisa was a byword. In the more rolling country toward that flooded duplicate of Thessaly, the Gulf of Volo, Pagasæ, Iolcus, Pheræ, and Phthiotid Achæa ranked as *poleis* but were infested by "dynasts," by the rule of force, that is, of the rancher-baron with the largest troop of retainers. So far north as this, it should be noted, the Minoan culture had only begun to spread at the moment of its collapse. There had, indeed, been very little earlier civilisation at all, and the flat-topped mounds which mark the pre-Minoan hamlets perished almost simultaneously with their initiation into Ægean culture.

South of Thessaly lie old tribal territories whose contingents are marshalled territorially in the Homeric Catalogue, whereas Thessaly paraded feudally by baronies. There was little Minoan heritage, but also discontinuous and imperfect conquest; *poleis* are few and minute, as in Phocis; and there are glimpses in historic times of mass-meetings suggestive of tribal structure.

In the larger districts which compose Bœotia, there is again conquest, and occupation of the plains by the conqueror; there is race-feud as in Thessaly, but doubly expressed, in the rigid minority governments normal in all these communities, and in an antipathy between central plain and marginal foothills, of which the feuds between Thebes and its neighbours Platæa and Thespiæ are the best known examples. But there are well-established *poleis* in Bœotia, and Thebes at all events had a Minoan past, of some distinction. In point of ancient fame, however, and real political importance in the far past, Orchomenos, an important secondary centre of the earlier "Minyan" culture, quite outranged "Cadmeian" Thebes.

Similarly, in the southern conquest-area, Elis in northwestern Peloponnese had been flooded with miscellaneous immigrants from the tribal districts north of the gulf, and only created a precarious imitative *polis* in the fifth century. From Dorian Megara—which never found a name of its own, but remained merely "the houses" throughout—to Argos, there were uniformly conquest-states with minority government and more or less acute race-feud, tempered at Corinth, though not in its rival Ægina, by commercial prosperity, and in all cities of this "Isthmus region" by compromises which admitted at least a section of the conquered to political privilege, more or less qualified, within the *polis* of the conquerors. In Laconia alone the garrison-state of Sparta risked no such compromise, only gradation of social status from unprivileged but free and comparatively tractable "neighbours" to the far larger serf-population of "captives," or "fen-folk"; opinions differing even in antiquity as to the meaning of the Helots' name. In Messenia we have only folk-memory of a foundered conquest-state, and actual servitude to later Spartan conquerors. The Dorian colonies of Crete, on the other hand, repeat the conquest-structure of their founders, most closely, as would be expected, in those which were established by Sparta. In Carpathos, however, and perhaps in Rhodes, the older population maintained its tribal structure independent of the Dorian settlements.

Clearly, it is not in the conquest-ridden districts of the eastern side of the peninsula that we are to look for type-specimens or original phases of the political *polis*. Between tribal vestiges, and scarcely veiled army organisation of conquerors, themselves "sprung from Pindus," the highlands along the watershed, or beyond it to the northwest, and tribally brigaded when they descended thence, there was as little need as there was chance for the creation of the kind of community in which "freedom among equals and similars" could be matured.

Only one consideration need detain us here. As between Thessaly and Bœotia, in the northern conquest area, and between the Isthmus-states and Laconia in the southern, greater capacity for accommodation among alien and hostile elements seems to be correlated with more prolonged and intimate habituation to the Minoan culture, of which the centres of origin were in Crete and the Cycladic island-world, and the principal mainland expansions in Argolis, around the Saronic Gulf, and along the sheltered Eubœan channels as far as the Pagasæan fore-court of Thessaly. Of the political structure of Minoan communities we know too little yet to be able to draw conclusions as to the significance of these coincidences; but we have evidence enough of their capacity for organised exploitation and for industrial and commercial enterprises to presume a fairly high level of intelligent teamwork among their inhabitants. If the rulers of Cnossus and Mycenæ were despots, it was in many ways an enlightened despotism, and compatible with a vigour and originality of handling on the part of craftsmen and traders which is in marked contrast with the scrupulous conventionalism of Egyptian and Mesopotamian life, in almost every phase and aspect.

Before examining the Hellenic societies of the island world and the coastal settlements on the mainland of Asia Minor—the latter at all events established only in the latest stages of the conquest-period—we have still to deal with what may be provisionally described as the strongholds of the old population. Of these there are three—Achæa, Eubœa, and Attica—all lying in intimate marginal relation with the two conquest areas. Ægina was probably at one time a fourth, an alternative citadel and camp of refuge in the heart of the Saronic Gulf for dispossessed folk from the Isthmus region; but in spite of its seagirt position, Ægina fell early before Dorian aggressors from Epidaurus, and must count thereafter as an Isthmus-state, with minority rule, as in Corinth, but with inveterate internal feud which ruined it early in the fifth century and led to its extinction as a free state. Of the other three strongholds, Achæa avoided conquest by Dorians, partly through the strong frontier defences and internal obstacles provided by its physical features, partly because it seems to have been able somehow to maintain (perhaps by sea-borne resources) the large accession of desperate refugees from the Minoanised districts of Argolis. And here, from the neighbours of Sicyon on the east to Patræ, where this northern "riviera" widens into the conquest-harried lowland of Elis, we find numerous minute but well-characterized *poleis*, communities with strong local loyalties, and local independence, but an unusual unanimity of outlook and interests, and, moreover, a loosely federal superstructure (probably a heritage from the time of their early perils), which later rose to political and almost national importance, in conflict with Macedon and with the rival league of Ætolian villages across the Gulf, and eventually in alternate alliance and altercation with Rome; so that it is by the Achæan name that we know Rome's provincial administration of Greece. Achæa, too, in early days when overpopulation began, after the war drain on its man-power slackened, seems to have been among the first districts of Hellas to organise relief-settlements oversea, reviving for this purpose old Minoan memories of the larger-featured regions of the far west; so that a large part of the south coast of Italy becomes a "Greater Hellas" in the hands of Achæan and other gulf-land colonists.

Eubœa is as well defended by its twin gulf-like channels, as Achæa by the snowpeaks of its Arcadian border, against military shocks; its lowlands, though less numerous, are larger; its natural resources ampler. The strong bridge-head position of Chalcis, in Macedonian hands one of the "fetters of Greece," secured the only point of real danger, provided that the islanders held the gulfs, as their copious timber-supplies and Minoan heritage of sea-lore quali-fied them to do. That so commodious a region should receive large accessions of refugee-folk from all the northern conquest-areas, might safely be assumed, even if it were not illus-trated by the family history of the Gephyræan tribe, which belonged to the neighbourhood of Tanagra, escaped in the twelfth century to Eretria in Eubœa, and only later moved on into Attica, where it is found incorporated late in the sixth century. Just as Achæans uti-lised the westward avenue of the Corinthian Gulf to decant their surplus population into colonial homes, so Chalcis drafted its emi-grants northward by its own gulf-avenue to the Chalcidic peninsula, and Eretria mainly by the southward channel into the island world, though it had its colonies on the gulf west of Chalcidice as well.

Now, in historic times both Chalcis and

Eretria, and with them other smaller and historically obscurer cities of Euboea, are *poleis* in the full sense of the word; of mixed origin, yet undisturbed by race-feud or differentiation of status among their corporators. In Hellenic times they are in some sense "Ionian," and in this "Ionian" capacity they participated, like the inhabitants of Attica, in the ceremonies and privileges of the venerable Pylian League, the constitution of which carries back its origin far into preconquest times. Now, in the Homeric poems, describing events long before the traditional date for the colonization of Ionia, there are Ionians hereabouts, for they are brigaded with the men of Bœotia, Locris, and Phthia up the northern channel. Yet the Chalcis, Eretria, Histiæa, and so forth, of Homer are not Ionian cities, but belong to the Abantes, a people of whom there were memories (perhaps even traces) in classical Eubœa,[68] and numerous descendants in the "Ionian" colonies on the coast of Asia Minor.

Precisely how Chalcis or Eretria became "Ionian" it is not easy to say; but the fact of this change of ethnic character implies a profound reconstitution between their Homeric and their classical phases. Since there were also in the Ionian cities of Asia "Minyans from Orchomenus mixed up, and Cadmeians

93

and Dryopes and sundry kinds of Phocians and Molossians" from far Epirus, as well as Arcadians and Dorians—of whom more later—it seems probable that this transformation of these Euboic towns into Hellenic *poleis* is itself an incident of the general expulsion of large elements of the mainland population during the period of conquests. In Eubœa, then, as in Achæa, we have the double coincidence of intermixture of peoples, and of the enforced inclusion of refugees from Minoanised areas, among the ingredients of the mixture, in a district which not only contains thereafter Hellenic *poleis* as its normal type of community, but *metropoleis* which are among the earliest and most prolific of the mother-cities of colonial *poleis* further afield.

THE SPECIAL CASE OF ATTICA

Attica, the third refugee-stronghold of Old Greece, is more instructive still, since we know more of its early history, and can analyse our local information in the light of that from Achæan and Euboic sources.

Considered as a geographical region, Attica includes more than was ever united politically in the Athenian State of historic times. For the main watershed range of the Greek Peninsula, the general trend of which, as far south

94

THE NOTION OF SOCIETY

as Parnassus and Helicon, is from northwest to southeast, swerves eastward beyond this point, so that the axis of that section which is represented by Cithæron and Parnes runs due east, forming an abrupt barrier south of the Bœotian lowlands, from the Corinthian to the south-Eubœan gulf. Parallel with this range, the steep gable-ridge of Geraneia, precipitous eastward over its Saronic shore and projecting boldly at its west end into the Corinthian gulf, cuts off even more completely from the Isthmus-region the western or "Megarean" section of what in early times seems to have been known as *Akté*, "the promontory," or, more familiarly, Attica. Against both the northern and the southern conquerors these natural barriers seem to have been held long enough to enable the "promontory" to serve first as mere refuge for the dispossessed on either hand; then, since its own natural resources were not large—a considerable part of its area being not only mountainous but marble-built, and therefore unusually barren even for Greek mountains—as a swarming-ground for new settlements in the island-world which looms up on the horizon of its flanking seas. We hear, indeed, of one great Bœotian raid, but it was repelled; of a Dorian raid as far as the central plain where Athens stands, but this too was temporary; and the westernmost region already mentioned was permanently alienated by Dorian occupation, though the name of its eventual capital, *ta Megara*, "the houses," or "huts," shows how precarious even this conquest was at first.[69]

The political history of the Attic promontory was throughout as peculiar as its structure. Unusually copious folkmemory pictured its half-dozen distinct lowlands supporting numerous "peoples" separately organised economically, and at one time as many as a dozen independent chieftaincies, politically a prey to a late phase of the old Cretan seapower, which we can trace on several sites exploiting their resources, as it did those of the Argive promontory, and many parts of central Greece. Then, about the middle of the thirteenth century, came insurrection, reprisals, and a general revolt, under the leadership of Theseus, prince of Athens, whose unification of the "promontory" peoples, though perhaps intermittent in respect of the plain of Eleusis, and certainly undone in respect of Megara to the westward, laid the foundations of an unusually large and uniquely coherent territorial regime, the United States of Attica, with a federal capital and common meeting-place defended by the natural fortress which Athenians of all periods knew familiarly as the *polis*, and by its local guardian, the armed goddess Pallas Athene, whose double name may well commemorate an identification of *Our* Lady of Athens with *Their* Lady of Pallene, a leading township of the "midland" plain, "Mesogæa," on the other side of Mount Hymettus. The quite subordinate part played by the people of the "promontory" in the days of Achæan feudalism, within which the exploits of Theseus fall, is the counterpart of this nationalist rejection of the overlordship of Achæan Cnossus; and the traditions of dynastic rivalries within the new Attic state suggest that old loyalties died hard. But the story of the "coming of Ion the war-lord" into Attica in the lifetime of Theseus is a glimpse of an earlier occasion when this region became a defensible rallying ground for dispossessed people from the southern area of Achæan domination, and of a notable facility with which it absorbed and domiciled aliens; anticipating, and enhancing, its eventual rôle as central asylum for such remnants of the *ancien régime*.

In Attica, then, even more clearly than in Eubœa, we find the physical circumstances, and more than one traditional occasion, of a regrouping of previously self-contained peoples, which was a "political" reconstruction, in the strict sense of that word; in that an over-mastering emergency, perhaps also an individual of genius, "made them acquainted with each other" and superimposed on tribal and regional loyalties a conscious deliberate adherence to an executive and administrative organisation, which superseded for the general good the several administrations of the confederate groups, insofar as their activities impaired its paramount authority; while admitting the continued exercise of local and tribal functions, and, indeed, guaranteeing their conservation by the massed forces which the loyal co-operation of each community placed at its sole disposal. As Thucydides says of Theseus, "Abolishing in the other strongholds [*poleis*] their council halls and executives, he embodied them all in the stronghold we have now, assigning one council hall and one president's office, and compelled them to avail themselves of this single stronghold while conducting their several affairs just as before; which, since they all now contributed to its maintenance, became powerful and was transmitted by Theseus to those who followed," adding that "before this time what is now the citadel [*acropolis*] together with its southward slope was the stronghold [*polis*]" which he had previously mentioned, and thereby defining the sense in which that almost untranslatable word is to be understood in this context.[70]

Tradition was no less explicit, that it was in the light of this quite exceptional series of experiences, that the mobs of refugees which poured into Attica from north and from south were rallied and reorganised into those colonising expeditions which passed out of the promontory-region into the island-world and on to the central districts of the west coast of Asia Minor. Many of these retained folk-memory of their Attic origin, and a considerable number observed annual festivals which were the counterpart of Athenian cults.

Distressful and violent as was this crisis of transmigration through Attica, Thucydides makes his account of it subsidiary to his explanation of the deep-seated aboriginal adherence of the Athenians of his own time to their unfortified country towns, scattered homesteads, and local sanctuaries, which to them were still what the fortified stronghold (*polis*) was to the Greeks of all other districts, their immemorial home, incidentally demonstrating the coexistence of political with communal loyalty in this uniquely constituted state. How unique it was—how completely in the following centuries political loyalty had atrophied all other—is illustrated by the pendant picture of the fate of those Ionian colonies themselves at the next clash of cultures, the Persian conquest of their Asiatic hinterland, when Thales, like Theseus of old, advised "that there should be founded one council hall—to be in Teos because this was central for Ionia—and that the other cities, though inhabited as before, should be regarded as if they were townships"—*demes*, like the mediatised townships of Attica—a project, as Herodotus grimly notes, "which had its advantages even before Ionia was ruined" but which found no more support than the alternative plan of evacuation.[71]

Both north and south of the region thus occupied by "Ionian" colonies, similar city-states were established during the same migration period, both on the mainland of Asia Minor and in the coastal islands. The northern colonies, speaking "Æolic" dialects akin to those of the conquest area of northern Greece, traditionally traced their descent from that region, and, in addition, some of them claimed continuity with rather earlier settlements consequent on the "Trojan War," the traditional date for which was early in the twelfth century; two generations, that is, before the conquest, but also two generations after the

100

establishment of the Pelopid and Æacid dynasties of the "Achæan" regime. But in their historic shape these "Æolian" colonies present much the same structure and follow the same political development as their Ionian neighbours, and, as some of the latter included "Æolian" families, they may be regarded as standing in much the same relation to motherlands around the Pagasæan Gulf and the north-Eubœan channel as the Ionian to the south-Eubœan and Saronic areas.

The southern, "Doric"-speaking colonies originated traditionally from Argolis during the same migration-period. A few of them broke new ground on the mainland in a region already assailed, like the northern Æolic coast, by "Achæan" aggressors, as we learn from Hittite archives. The majority occupy islands inshore and also the scattered archipelago of the Sporades and eastern and central Crete. All these "Dorian" areas had been already settled in Late Minoan times—Ialysus in Rhodes as early as the early fourteenth century, but the majority not before the thirteenth, though they formed populous baronies under Achæan dynasties in the twelfth. But their tribal organisation in historic times, so far as it is known, was based on that of the southern conquest-area of their traditional origin; and it is probably safe to regard them as due to deliberate provision, on the part of the compromise-states in that area, for irreconcilable or superfluous elements from both the conquered and the conquerors. This is still more clearly seen in the Laconian colonies in the islands Melos and Thera, and in the west of Crete, all organised late and deliberately by the Spartan conquerors when they extended their rule over the lower valley in the ninth century, as depositories for recalcitrant natives, rather than for any natural increase among themselves. What is instructive here is the traditional formality of their establishment, a historical link between the more tumultuary settlements of the migration period and the *apoikia*, or "home away from home," which in the eighth century was already the recognised remedy both for overpopulation and for incompatibility of tempers within established city-states, whatever their own origin might be.

The Origin of the *Polis*

From this geographical survey of the distribution of Greek city-states and historical retrospect of its causes the conclusion seems to emerge:

(1) That this new type of community and form of government did actually originate in

the exceptional circumstances of a sudden, violent, and universal dissolution of the public order inherited from the Minoan civilisation.

(2) That the cause of this collapse was the conquest of almost all the mainland districts, which had been the recipients of that civilisation from its insular originators, by new comers who had been previously organised in tribal societies but whose tribal structure had itself been severely strained and modified in the course of their irruption.

(3) That in the northwest, and southwest—for example, in Ætolia and Elis—where the newcomers most completely overwhelmed the older order and where also such older order as there had been was itself least affected by Minoan exploitation and settlements, tribal societies with small, scattered, and primarily economic groupings remained characteristic and ubiquitous far down into historic times.

(4) That in some parts of the conquered area—Thessaly, Laconia, and probably Messenia—where the Minoan heritage was insignificant, the cultural gulf between conquerors and conquered was never closed, and a rule of force was either perpetuated into classical times, as in Sparta and Thessaly, or exterminated early, as in Messenia.

(5) That, on the other hand, in districts

which had been more thoroughly Minoanized, such as Argolis and the Isthmus-region, and to a less degree in southern Bœotia, various compromises were effected, and city-states came into existence in which both the conquerors and the conquered were corporators, though never with complete acquiescence in the political equivalence of all constituent groups, which remained tribally organised and cherished inter-tribal animosities which complicated those economic readjustments which befell all city-states alike, as soon as the restoration of more normal conditions of maintenance allowed population to grow toward the margin of productivity.

(6) That it is only in the last refuges and rallying-grounds of the older populations, and in districts repeopled by mixed streams of emigrants hastily and provisionally reorganised in one or other reservoir of that kind, that there is any close approximation to the typical city-state, as analysed and idealised by the political thinkers of the fifth and fourth centuries, the period of Greek self-consciousness and self-expression; and, finally,

(7) That in Attica, where we might have expected to find most completely realised the coalescence of the dislocated remnants of older communities, the form actually assumed by the

THE NOTION OF SOCIETY

Polis Athenaiôn was itself rendered abnormal by the persistence, right through the period of transmigration, into classical times, of a political structure, essentially federal, and due to historical causes antecedent to the period of conquest and disturbance; so that here the political unity, which became exceptionally close-knit, in spite of the extent and diversity and complexity of the region itself and its inhabitants, was nevertheless compatible with remarkable survivals of a communal and economic regime which is in essentials that of the Minoan culture which the conquerors annihilated elsewhere.

It hardly needs to be observed, that our knowledge of the internal organisation of the Greek city-states is far too fragmentary to allow of any proof, by simple enumeration of those which conformed to this generalisation. We cannot wholly bridge the gulf between the tribally organised populations of this region in the Heroic Age, and the close-knit political corporations which make up the Greek world at the moment when we begin to perceive it emerging from the "Dark Age" of its infancy. But enough is now known of the structure of some of these *poleis*, sufficiently widely distributed over the region which we have found reason to regard as the cradle-land of this type of society, to justify the conclusion that in principle the *polis* originated in tribal society, and represents a rearrangement of tribal units in a new political relation to each other. Moreover, we have already seen, when we were examining those parts of the Greek-speaking region where the *polis*-system is least typically and most precariously represented, that its place is filled by communities which were still of essentially tribal structure. The same state of things existed also in those parts of western Asia Minor, of which we know something, far on into classical times, with regional and tribal communities, organised in what are described as "systems of townships" with only the most elementary provision for any kind of concerted action. It is certainly, therefore, not from this side, any more than from the Greek interior, that political inspiration came; and, as we have seen, the circumstances of the age of migrations were themselves exactly such as to enforce rather than inspire, in the first instance, that toleration of unrelated neighbours and partners which alone made possible the joint efforts which were necessary if life was to be maintained at all, still more if it was to be in any sense a life worth living.

Thus the *polis* originated in tribal society,

or, at all events, in its most original and typical variety, among individuals bred up in tribal societies and habituated to tribal life. But in the fully formed *polis* tribal organisation and institutions play but a subordinate part; in the life of its members, public, or, as we may now call them, *political* functions occupy a much larger place than private duties and stand on a far higher plane of importance. In this respect there is strong contrast with the political development of early Italian communities, and even with that "most Hellenic city," Rome, where the functions of an organised private life within the limits of hereditary *gentes* remained elaborate and vigorous. For the Roman, good patriot as he was, there existed a *res privata* of real significance alongside the *res publica* of which we hear so much. In a Greek city-state the correlative to *polites* is *idiotes*, and it is but little exaggeration to say that if a man's conduct and discourse ceased to be *politic* it became *idiotic*—self-centred, unregardful of his neighbour's need, inconsequent in itself, as is the course of a rudderless ship, and without consequence, therefore, in his neighbour's eyes.

From the first, and from the necessities of the case, tribal and all such sectional associations, and the bonds which constituted them, suffered a double encroachment, corresponding with a double trend of positive political evolution. The *polis*, in virtue of its *suprema lex*, the maintenance of the lives of all its members, challenged the prerogatives of less inclusive groups and overrode the citizen's obligation to any one of them. In criminal law it substituted trial for blood-feud, associated the members of a man's *phratry*, his political next-of-kin, with his blood relatives, as the prosecutors, the "pursuers"[72] of his murderer, and ultimately substituted public functionaries for the corporate "pursuit" by any such posse of individuals. In civil law, and especially in regard to the tenure of land within its territory, it intervened repeatedly and drastically, to remedy abuses arising from the corporate exploitation of entailed estate, and from the dissolution of partnership between cooperators and estate, as families died out or their representatives drifted into other occupations than agriculture. In administration it was continually finding fresh spheres for corporative and public intervention, supervising, revising, exploiting the energies and activities of its members, irrespective of their traditional duties in any other kind of association.

On the other hand, and concurrently with these encroachments of the *polis* on hereditary

aim. But the *polis* is not itself engaged in a "foodquest," any more than it is responsible for the expenditure of the resources of its members, so long as these activities do not impair the *political* function of the *polis* itself. "Economic" science is, in fact, at this point first expressly distinguished from "political"; the maintenance of lives, from the maintenance of life; and the attainment of well-being in this or that minor association in accordance with its presumed aim—the sustenance of this or that family on the produce of this or that parcel of land, for example—from the "political" aim of securing to each and all such association freedom and opportunity to maintain and enjoy itself in its own normal way, with only the same implicit provision that its doings are compatible with analogous doings of other like associations. It is indeed precisely because Aristotle is content to leave so large a part of the citizen's activities to his own discretion that he lays so much stress on the "political" necessity of providing for the training of the individuals who are to assume this responsibility in their turn.

THE CITY, THE CLAN, AND THE INDIVIDUAL

From the twofold encroachment, then, of the *polis* and those economically emancipated individuals who ultimately compose it, upon the previous autonomy of the tribal or family group, emerge certain fundamental conditions and functions of citizenship common to all citizens, whatever the peculiarities or antecedents of the hereditary or economic groups in which they are corporators.

There were occasional exceptions whose rarity is itself instructive as evidence of the general uniformity of observance. At Athens the Gephyræan clan, to which belonged the murderers of the tyrant Hipparchus, was known to be of foreign northern origin, and "the Athenians admitted them to be citizens of their own body while prescribing their exclusion from a number of things not worth mention;"[74] but there were compensations, a certain reciprocity in this kind of *tabu*, for "they have chapels built in Athens, with which the rest of the Athenians have nothing to do, other rites apart from the other temples, and in particular a chapel of Achæan Demeter and secret ceremonies." For ordinary Athenians, as we know, Demeter was Our Lady of Eleusis: this Achæan Demeter is presumably she whose high-place was the conventicle of that north country "League of the Gate," the Pylian Amphictyony, which has its name from the Pass of Thermopylæ, as the pass itself has from the warm springs where the presence of the Earth Mother was manifest.

Another Athenian example, of which unfortunately we know less in detail, is the family of Isagoras, the political opponent of Cleisthenes, of whom Herodotus (always curious about the foreign antecedents of great Athenian houses) has only this to say, that "his kindred sacrifices to a Zeus who is a Carian;" normal Athenians by that time worshipping the Olympian Zeus, and the Carians having old-time reputation for deeds of violence on the high seas, and a "Lord of Hosts" of their own at Labranda, where his sanctuary still partly stands, emblazoned with his spear and shield.[75] Imagine, for a counterpart, an English family of crusading prestige, of whom you might learn in confidential whispers that "Would you believe it, at family prayers they use the name of Allah?"

While tolerating thus occasional idiosyncrasies among its constituent groups, the *polis* did, on the other hand, reserve the right to interfere in the most intimate affairs of any family which should exercise its "private rights" in ways which threatened the free exercise of similar rights by other constituents, or endangered the security of them all. For instance, the family, and the *genos* com-

115

posed of blood-related families, existed, like the
polis itself, "to maintain life," and was competent to give or withhold the right to live, to
each "little stranger" who appeared, in course
of nature, in its midst. With the details of this
recruitment of the membership of a Greek
family the *polis* had in general absolutely no
concern. It was to no public "registrar of
births" that an Athenian father presented the
newly arrived infant for acceptance, but to his
own ancestors, obsolete but by no means
negligible corporators—sleeping partners, as it
were—in a perpetual association of which he,
the house-father, was the executive partner and
actual trustee. It is for them, as he carries the
child three times round the house-fire,[76] to confirm or revise his private judgment as to the
needfulness of this candidate for membership.
Only if he has first approved its candidature,
and they have concurred in it, has the newcomer any right to live; and there is evidence
enough that the risk of exceeding the precarious margin of subsistence was terribly
realised in Greek households at all periods.[77]
But if the child was accepted, it was in ordinary circumstances no concern of the *polis;*
admission to public rights, of an adolescent
member of an economic unit, was a separate
and much later affair, and this decision rested

with that *political* constituency within the *polis* in which the family of the young man was itself enrolled; in Athens the township, or *deme*, elsewhere the "brotherhood," "father-hood," "thousand," "block-house," or other picturesque survival from days when the *polis* was hardly yet more than a fortress or an armed camp of pioneer-settlers, rallied to "maintain life."[78]

But in exceptional circumstances the *polis* could and did interfere to revise the verdict of an economic group on political grounds. At Sparta, soft-hearted fathers were prevented, by public inspection of their offspring, from conceding the "right to live" to children for whom there was no reasonable expectation of maintenance on the family farm, or from whom there was no prospect of normal public utility as fighting men, in view of their physical condition. At Thebes, in later times, the political control operated the other way, to prevent niggardly or self-indulgent fathers from rejecting recruits whom the *polis* was likely to need later on, and for whom on public grounds it was desirable to make room in that family, in view of the risks of war or disease.[79] And in view of Sparta's standing need of men there is no reason to suppose that the public inspection of infants did not operate in this direction too; though our information comes as an attempt to explain the fine physique of the Spartan soldiery, and consequently lays exclusive stress on the state's right to eliminate weaklings. Certainly, the fact that among Spartan kings Agesilaus was lame from infancy and Cleomenes otherwise abnormal, shows that in special circumstances allowances were made.

We have seen that Synœcism, in the sense already described,[80] involved what we must recognise as a definitely political act, the deliberate choice of a mode of life and a mode of government. It presumed the resignation of inherited privileges and prejudices, the acceptance of restrictions on habitual or newly acquired freedom, the putting of heads together as "like and equal" copartners, for large common ends; the necessary end of mutual maintenance and defence, at a moment when to act separately was to perish; and the ideal end of saving from the wreckage of the past what was most worth saving, the heritage of beliefs and habits which had made that old order worth fighting for to the last.

It is hardly necessary to insist that in such circumstances and in Greek lands, with their rugged, austere landscape and strictly limited oases of habitable ground, "self-sufficiency of maintenance," in the words of the popular definition,[81] for an expatriated mob, was a question of organised labour, intensively and intelligently applied. Only those who have seen a Greek community in some such crisis realise either the amount of physical energy which is sunk and immobilized in the mere construction of terrace-walls to concentrate and conserve the soil before the first crop can be sown elsewhere than on the valley bottoms;[82] or the labour, even here, of clearing the tough scrub-land vegetation and haling together the strewn boulders into cairns and party walls, as you may see done in moraine-strewn districts of New England. Under the circumstances, the physical energy was there and the good will; what was needed for well-being was efficiency, which comes from foresight and initiative.[83] The workers must be led, organised, distributed; they must know what they are doing, and they must know each other.

In such a predicament Aristotle's phrase rings like an echo of some Founder's Day hymn: "He who first made them acquainted with each other was author of the greatest benefits."[84] Literally, the word means to "place together"; in modern Greek it survives to describe the "introductions" which make

you acquainted with the right people in the
districts where you travel. What was needed
was a "good mixer," "well met" with all and
sundry, instinctively and spontaneously making them feel at home: in official Greek of the
colonizing period, when the same elementary
work was to be done over again, he is described simply so: *oikistes*,[85] "he who made
them to be at home."

Secondly, there was the need for initiative,
for an executive over and above the "natural"
authority of elders and heads of families over
their several households and kindred-groups.

Thirdly, but not wholly distinct from this,
there was the need for a common rule of life,
expressing rights and duties as between persons and groups unconnected by any natural
tie of lifelong association; and for the maintenance and current day-to-day revision and
adjustment of this customary behaviour, some
means of habitual conciliation of conflicting
claims.[86]

Thus from its very origin the *polis* in its
new political sense was a makeshift in a supreme emergency: it came into being literally
"to maintain life"; but from the beginning also
it was an experiment in adjustment, in construction of a new way of living, out of the
discrepant, anomalous survivals from the old,

and out of the daily spontaneous struggle of each of its members to make his own life worth living under the sole condition that it remain compatible with the better-being of the rest; and it never ceases to have this ideal aspect. Its essential function is to make life worth living, and for this reason efforts, early and late, to realise this function more abundantly, stand in the closest relation of thought and of historical fact with all other efforts to make life more worth living in respect of nature's gifts.

LECTURE III

THE GREEK NOTIONS OF ORDINANCE (*THEMIS*) AND INITIATIVE (*ARKHÉ*)

FROM the history of the word *polis* itself we have at all events a glimpse of a phase in the constitutional, or, rather, institutional, experience of Ægean communities, when their external relations were such as to require organised material defences against aggression—an age of frequent turmoil and general insecurity. This is something very different from the long vista of Minoan insulated advancement, illustrated by the open Cretan villages excavated at Palaikastro and Gournia, and the rural chateau at Hagia-Triada. And in the pictures of Achæan society in the Homeric poems the marked distinction between Achæan princes and barons, with their retinues of "companions"[1] (*hetairoi*) and "attendants" (*therapontes*) owing personal service to these hereditary "leaders" (*basileis*) and "masters" (*anaktes*) on the one hand, and the tribally constituted "clans" or "kindreds" (*phyla*), subdivided into "brotherhoods" (*phretrai*), whose regional contingents serve, grudgingly and perforce, to promote the projects or avenge the grievances of their overlords, is sufficient explanation of this precarious state of things.

Both the Trojan league of Priam's allies and the feudal array of Agamemnon and his followers are represented as dynastic regimes of quite recent origin. Troy was founded by Priam's grandfather, Dardanus, and fortified by his father, Laomedon; the Pelopid dynasty by the grandfather of Agamemnon and Menelaus; the Æacid kingdom in the Spercheius valley and its neighbourhood, by the grandfather of Achilles. And these founders are themselves "divine-born"; there was little or no human memory of their antecedents beyond the point when they established themselves in place of older dynasties, whose heiresses they married, whose palaces they occupied, and whose territories they ruled by right of possession, as a shepherd his flocks. They are at best "shepherds of the people," and their title, *anax*, "master," is used to denote also the relationship between a man and his horse or his dog.

Some measure of concurrence, however, is presumed, even in a dynastic regimen of this kind. The paramount chieftain in an emergency lays his project before a mass meeting of the whole fighting forces, if only to test their morale;[2] and within the camping ground of the separate baronial contingent of Odysseus, there was (as we have seen, p. 78) a "gathering place," *agorá*, with altars of the gods, serving for public worship therefore, but also for mass meetings of other kinds;[3] for it also was (or at least it included) something which is described as *themis;* and it is the absence of such *agorai* and *themistes* (in the plural) among the barbarous "round-eyed" folk, to which the Cyclops encountered by Odysseus belonged, which characterized them as outlandish and impracticable.[4] In this instance the word *agorai* has the epithet "bringing decision"; that is to say, in such mass meetings agreement was reached on matters of common concern. In the same context the Cyclops is described as "a man girt about with great strength, fierce, not well knowing either *dikai* or *themistes*."[5] As both words are used here in the plural we may regard the *themis* which was in the *agorá* of Odysseus' camp before Troy as collectively used for all such individual *themistes*, or for the place and equipment whereby they were attained. Provisionally translating *themistes* by "ordinances" in accordance with later Greek usage, we see their immediate relation with the *dikai* with which they are coupled here; for *diké* in later Greek, as in Homeric, denotes both justice in the abstract—as *themis* is "ordinance" in the abstract—and also enunciations of justice in particular matters. Since *dikai* are linked with *themistes* in the one phrase, as *agorai*, "bringing decision," are in the other, we may infer that such enunciations of justice and expressions of a general will were among the occasions which brought men together into such mass meetings in customary meeting places.

What were these *themistes?* How were they obtained? And what is the connexion between *themis* and either *diké*, in its judicial sense, or *boulé*, "decision," or "will," in the psychological sense, which a mass meeting in an *agorá* "brings"?

The word *themis* derives from a stem (*the-*) signifying to "set firm."[6] Cognate words have the meaning "put," "steadfast," "seat," "rule," "proposition" (in logic), "foundation," used also for "eye socket" and the "articulation" of the jaw. A verbal equivalent of *themis* is used for putting a ship on her course. In classical Greek *themis*, like the kindred word *thesmos*, means "ordinance," or, in general, that which is in accord with such ordinance or rule: "They say it is *themis* to do so-and-so," writes Plato,[7] using the substantive almost as an adverb; and this popular usage is also Homeric.

Here are examples of things which were
themis in Homeric society: to entertain strangers (and to refuse them their due is "not
themis"); to make trial of the morale of an
army;[8] to testify on oath in a matter of which
there could be no independent evidence, for
example, the chastity of a woman, or the
absence of intention to play foul in a race[9]; or
to contest the rash words even of a superior—
"As is *themis*, my lord, in open meeting [*agorá*];
so be thou not wroth;" freedom of speech
being the right of every member of such a
gathering.[10] It was even *themis* to intrude
upon a chief in war time, in his hut, at all
hours, for advice. So, Achilles has to ask
Priam to come outside for privacy, "lest any
of the Achæans come upon us here, bringing
something to be decided; for they sit ever at
my side making up their minds, as is *themis*";
that is to say, as it is a right and proper thing
to do, and allowance has to be made for it.[11]

On the other hand, it was "not *themis*" for a
mourner to bathe before the funeral was over;[12]
for a man to withstand a god in battle;[13] or to
lay low in fight a divinely wrought helmet;[14]
these all being things which simply "are not
done," as we say; or, if you attempt them, it
is at your proper peril. They are, in fact,
tabu. But this inhibition might be suspended

by divine command, as happened when the
divine helmet of Achilles was worn by Patro-
clus, and even then "Zeus gave it to Hector to
wear upon *his* head, but to him destruction
was nigh," the outrage recoiling on the per-
petrator.

Another instance of such suspension of an
ordinance is notable, because it was to be
effected, if at all, by *themistes*. The question
is how a man of princely family shall be put
out of the way; one conspirator suggests murder, "but fearsome is it to kill the seed of
kings. Nevertheless, let us ask the will-and-
pleasure of the gods," for which, as we shall
see, there were accepted means. "If the
themistes of great Zeus approve, I will kill
him myself, and I will bid all the rest [to do
so]: but if the gods warn us off, my bidding is
to refrain."[15] For sufficient reason, that is,
Zeus might suspend the *tabu* on murder; and
the expressions of such divine will and ordinance are *themistes*.

But how are *themistes* revealed to men? The
procedure is clear enough in Homeric society.
Mutiny is rebuked thus, and authority vindicated, by Odysseus: "Let there be one ruler,
one king, to whom the Son of Cronos, of
crooked counsel, has given a staff [*skeptron*]
and *themistes*, that he may be king over

them."[16]   We are clearly among archaic beliefs here; and the function of this "staff," or
sceptre, in the transmission of *themistes* must
engage our attention at this point.   Literally,
a *skeptron* is merely a staff, for support, or for
beating people; the cognate verb is used in
both senses; the stem is an old one, for it appears in the Latin *scipio*, "staff," familiar
from its adoption as a family name by a
branch of the great Cornelian clan in Rome.
In Homer, the *skeptron* is a symbol of rank,
carried by chiefs, and transmitted from father
to son.   But it was more than this; it was
itself an object of power, a vehicle of inspiration.[17]   Achilles, wroth with his overlord, who
has wronged him, sanctions his revolt by an
oath, which is an appeal to his *skeptron*.   "Out
I will speak, and will swear a great oath hereto.
Yea, by this staff, which never shall put forth
leaves and twigs, since once it has left its
stock on the mountains, nor shall it grow
green again; but now again sons of Achæans
bear it in their hands, wielders of justice
[*dikaspoloi*], they who win *themistes* from Zeus:
that shall be my great oath to thee."   Thus
he utters his threat, and "cast on the ground
his staff studded with golden nails, and himself sat down," throwing off his allegiance by
the token of the dead hand-fashioned wood.

"May *that* return to life and bear leaves"—such is the implication of his curse—"if ever I serve thee more." We are reminded of Aaron's "rod that budded" in the presence of the king of Egypt, on a similar occasion of protest against tyrannical behaviour.

But lifeless as it was, there was power of another order in such a staff. Helen, comparing her bluff, outspoken husband with the brainy, temperamental Odysseus, describes how when in council the latter "sprang to his feet, he would stand and look downward, fixing his eyes on the ground, brandishing his staff neither backward nor forward"—as we see Minoan braves wielding it on the steatite vase from Hagia Triada[18]—"but would clutch it stiffly, looking like a witless fellow; you would say he was one distraught and merely without sense; but then when he let loose his great voice from his breast, with words whirling like winter snowflakes, then no man alive could dispute with Odysseus." It is in the power of his *skeptron*, too, that the willing subjects of the barony offered by Agamemnon, to reconcile Achilles, are to do his will; "they shall give him his due with gifts as a god, and beneath his staff shall perform his *themistes* which do them good."[19] Inherited from animistic notions like these is the authority conferred by the mace on the Speaker of the House of Commons: only a king who had lost all sense of the majesty of his "faithful commons" could risk and lose all when he bade, "Take away that bauble." So, too, when Agamemnon's violence prevailed over reason and free speech, Achilles "cast his staff on the ground," for the mystic bond of loyalty had snapped.

In the power of the *skeptron*, then, "that they hold in their hands," the sons of the Achæans, when they do justice, "extract *themistes* from Zeus."[20] The phrase translated "extract" denotes effort; the verb is rare in classical Greek, used, however, for shaping bricks, drawing a bow,[21] and removing an obstruction;[22] in Homer it is common, for all kinds of dragging or pulling;[23] in the middle voice, as in this passage, it means to "draw to oneself"—as when Priam is to recover the body of Hector by golden ransom[24] —and it has sometimes the derivative sense of "taking under one's protection," as when Agamemnon left his minstrel at home to look after his wife;[25] and even of "concealing" in the mind;[26] but this clearly does not concern us here, though it has misled some commentators. Especially is the word used for eliciting the thoughts, wishes,[27] intentions, and decisions of the gods,[28] and in one passage for literally "dragging" Zeus himself down from heaven to earth.[29]

That *themis* is the "voice of the gods" is stated explicitly in a passage which (though it is not in the main narrative, but in a simile, and may therefore reflect the notions of the poet's own day rather than of the heroic age which he purports to describe) is in any case notable as contemplating the possibility of errors in transmission, and of perversion of the divine message.[30] Storm, in this simile, is sent by Zeus "when in wrath he deals hardly with men, who by violence in an *agorá* discern *themistes* askew, and out they drive *diké*, not regarding the voice of the gods."

Taking these lines in conjunction with previous passages, we can now trace the whole procedure. First, the gods, or Zeus, at their altar in the place of meeting, utter a voice. Next, men qualified by birth and possession of a rod of power, observe the voice, and painfully elicit its meaning. But they may discern it amiss, and utter "crooked *themistes*" in support of acts of violence. This drives out justice (the nature of which, in the word *diké*, we already know from its association with *themistes* in the description of the Cyclops, who had neither),[31] and, as this results from disregarding the divine voice, Zeus is angry, and the storm of his wrath assails those men. The history of this word *dikê* will occupy us more in detail in Lecture IV.

In a rather later context the ritual of discovering the divine voice is described in detail, but with superadded features alien to the pure anthropomorphism of Homer, and due to the contamination of it with local and naturalistic beliefs. The priests of Apollo at Delphi in the Homeric Hymn are men "who perform sacred rites to their lord, and announce *themistes* of Phœbus Apollo with golden sword, whatsoever he may say, offering help out of a laurel from down in the dells of Parnassus."[32] So, too, in the same hymn, Apollo promises his newly founded priesthood that "to all these will I utter *themistes*, my unerring will-and-pleasure, offering help in my rich dwelling-place," namely, his "place of inquiry," as its name "Pytho" denotes.[33] Here we have in the word translated "offering help" the essential part played by the god, as in that translated "discerning" in the previous passage we had the function of the human observer; and the two words taken together characterize the whole procedure as a transaction worthy alike of Greek religion and Greek political instinct. All that a god can do is to make known the truth: he can utter a voice, reveal the matter as it really is.

But he can only "offer help." Man may be deaf or stupid, and mistake what is offered; he may conceal or misstate it, for violent and selfish ends; or he may discern the truth, among all else, using that *critical* faculty which has derived its very name from this word for "distinguishing" or "discerning." For this is, as we say, the *crisis*, the act of discernment distinguishing between alternative issues, and adopting one or other of them; and man is free so to decide: to encounter a god in battle, or pass by on the other side; to honour a stranger, or fail to give him his due. Man's will, that is, is free: the divine wisdom is there at his service, if he will learn it, carefully and painfully; if not, on his head be it! *Gegen die Dummheit streben die Götter selbst umsonst.*

Similarly, the *themistes* of a human ruler are his interpretation of the real course of events to his subjects. If they are intelligent and well-meaning subjects, they will give him his due as a god, acknowledge his wisdom, and "beneath his staff perform his ordinances which do them good."[34] And in this sense, even the Cyclops-folk could be said to "utter *themistes* each for his own children and wives."[35]

Examples of the content of these ordinances we have already seen; the close relation which *themistes* bear to *dikai* is further illustrated by

the description of Minos, seen by Odysseus in
the Lower World "holding a golden *skeptron*,
giving *themistes* to the dead, seated he, but
they all around were asking their lord for
dikai, sitting or standing, throughout the wide-
portalled House of Hades."[36] Another instructive episode in the Odyssey is where the swine-
herd apologizes to Odysseus, whom he has not
yet recognised, for the frugality of his entertainment. "Stranger, it is not *themis* for me,
even if a worse man than thou were to come,
to withhold from a stranger his due. For
from Zeus are all strangers and beggars. But
what I am offering is both scanty and my very
own. For that is the *dikê* of serfs, who are
ever in fear when lords who are young bear
rule;"[37] and he illustrates his point by praising
the generosity of his former lord, who would
not have required so strict an account of his
stewardship as young Telemachus does. Consequently, his entertainment of the stranger
will not be at his master's expense at all, but
out of his own allowance or savings. Here
the general principle that all strangers are
entitled to hospitality—a principle which a
master must respect as excuse for a servant's
gift at his expense—is a *themis*, while the
practical limitation on a servant's hospitality,
because he has to economize when "the young

master is so particular," is a *dikê*, a statement
of the way things actually happen. To the
significance of this distinction we shall have to
return later.

The personification of abstract ideas or
mental processes is not common in Homer,[38]
but in three passages we have a personal Themis, whose attributes and functions are instructive. Telemachus, protesting against the
behaviour of the suitors, appeals to their own
self-respect, to public opinion of their doings,
and to the wrath of the gods, "lest astonied
they make ill deeds to recoil," so shocking, in
the literal sense, is this outrage. Then he
calls to witness "Zeus of Olympus, and Themis
who dissolves assemblies [*agorai*] of men, and
orders their sitting."[39] Themis, then, is that
power which makes people come together when
there is something that has to be set straight
in their dealing with each other, and dismisses
them when decision has been reached and
normal behaviour restored. As Miss Harrison
expresses it, using a Latin equivalent; "she is
fas, the social imperative . . . , the social fact
is trembling on the very verge of godhead."[40]

Among the gods in their Olympian home,
Themis has the same work to do. "Zeus bade

Themis call the gods to meeting [*agorá*] from the top of glen-scored Olympus: and thereon she went all ways, bidding them come to the house of Zeus," for there were decisions to be taken by them all, the "voice of the gods" to be expressed.[41] Most graphic of all, after an unusually brisk quarrel between Zeus and his wife,[42] Hera flings herself "quick as a man's thought," among the other gods feasting on Olympus, "and they, at sight of her, all sprang up, and hailed her with their cups. And she," still very angry, "let be the rest, but accepted the cup from fair-cheeked Themis, for she first came running to meet her, and speaking winged words addressed her: 'Hera, why art thou come, and lookest like one distraught? Surely Cronos' Son, thy husband, hath scared thee sore!' To whom answered then the Lady |Hera: 'Question me not of this, Goddess Themis. Thou too knowest what his temper is, overweening and harsh. But do thou start the gods on the fairly-served banquet in the hall; thus thou shalt hear, and all immortals with thee, what ill deeds Zeus is decreeing; nor, I promise thee, shall all alike have joy at heart, either men or gods, even if there be any one now who feasts with easy mind.'" Themis here is the first to detect something gone awry and to react to it; she wants to know, so as to put it right. Outraged as she is, Hera cannot but respond, and for her the first thing is to conserve what is left of decency and order. "Don't keep the others from their dinner, my dear; best fed is soonest mended." Themis, that is, stands for the normal order, and for repair of it after infringement. And outraged order is repaired in open meeting by free speech, common counsel, and agreement in a common will, that "will of heaven," and "voice of the gods" which men too may elicit, if they will, in their own *agorá*, wherein *themis* is, and the altars of the gods.

Another function of the personal Themis has already begun to emerge, in the command of Zeus and the request of Hera. Themis not only embodies and recuperates the normal order, but sees to its observance. It is she who, at meeting time or dinner time alike, calls the gods together for the matter in hand, "as is *themis*," to borrow the phrase already current in Homeric speech, and proverbial in Hellenic. And the word used by Hera, "start" or "set going," is one which has a long and momentous history, as we have soon to see.

THEMIS SUMMARIZED

We may now summarize the Homeric conception of *themis* as follows:

(1) A *themis* formulates a normal mode of behaviour, and supplies guidance in repairing a breach in normal behaviour. It happens that all those Homeric *themistes* whose content we know, are about man's doings, but among the gods, too, a personified Themis gives guidance in ordering their lives.

(2) A *themis*, as elicited by duly qualified men, transmits the voice, the counsel, the will-and-pleasure of a god, or the gods. It is not a capricious command, nor in any sense a *privilegium* or special dispensation to fit a single occasion. It enunciates a general rule, "offering help" to man, which he accepts or neglects at his own free will. It expresses divine wisdom, deliberation, and counsel, not divine whim or power.

(3) A *themis* is made known to men in various ways:

(a) By transmission from the gods to men qualified and authorized to elicit it Such a man (i) holds a *skeptron* which is hereditary and itself a vehicle of power; (ii) performs ritual acts, and thereby puts himself into communion with the gods, or a god; (iii) convokes (like the divine Themis herself) open meetings of his fellows, which "bring decision" in the same way as a meeting of gods in Olympus, deliberatively. Such men may forfeit their privilege of communion through misconduct: on men whose *themistes* are crooked the wrath of God falls disastrously, "making ill deeds recoil."

(*b*) By statement and argument in such an *agorá*, wherein it is *themis* that free speech is privileged, even when it disputes the will or deed of a superior: it is *themis* also that in certain cases a man's statement upon oath must be accepted as decisive.

(4) Many *themistes* are popularly current, and accepted as valid, from of old: and such observances as hospitality to strangers are in this sense *themis*. In later Greek such accepted precepts are *thesmoi*, and were collected and preserved as guides of conduct.

(5) Having elicited *themistes*, men of experiences are enabled to enunciate *dikai*, which are consequential formulations of normal behaviour governing a particular case. In the sense that *themis* represents the Latin *fas*, these *dikai* may provisionally be compared to the *formulæ* of Roman legal procedure.

THE NOTION OF AUTHORITY: *ARKHÉ*

When Hera bade Themis on Olympus "start the gods at dinner," she made use of a word which has a momentous history in Greek political thought; for when Aristotle reaches his eventual definition of citizenship,[43] it is neither more nor less than this—"the capacity among free men, in either aspect, of starting and being started," using the same verb to express, on the one side, the exercise of initiative, on the other, the voluntary response to such initiative, and acceptance of it.

This verb, to "start," or "make to begin," is used commonly, in this literal sense, in Homer: both absolutely, "Son of Atreus, do thou make a start;"[44] "Let him make a start, and I will indeed do as he says,"[45] and in several grammatical constructions which illustrate its essential meaning. It is followed by an infinitive of the action initiated:—"start to carry the corpses";[46] by a genitive of the thing begun:—"he started [him] on the way," "he started a panic," "to start disastrous war"; or of a body of persons habitually "started" thus;[47] by a dative of the person caused to participate in the action—"I got the men going;" "Let each man give the signal to those whom he starts."[48] These usages are freely combined, dative of the person with infinitive of the act, or with genitive of the thing begun, as when Themis "started the gods at dinner,"[49] or one man "started another on his way,"[50] or very commonly "started them on speeches."[51] There is a cognate word for a "starter,"[52] and for exercising the starter's function, with similar dative of the persons started; and such a "starter" is characterized as "bringing decision," like the open meeting for free speech and deliberation with a view to act. And there is a verbal substantive, *argmata*, for [53] "initiatory offerings" sacrificed to the gods at the beginning of a religious rite.

Another such word used only in titles is *orchamos*,[54] the verbal form of which means to "set in violent motion," and specifically to "make to dance" in regular figures and rhythm; and the substantive *orchos* is used for a row of trees, following, as it were, their leader, down the *orchard*, as we call it.

The same verb in the middle voice is not so common in Homer as in later Greek, but its occurrences are instructive. It means "to set oneself doing," and so, simply to begin; with the thing begun as direct object, and those affected by it, in the dative: "for them the old man first of all set himself to weave a plan;"[55] or, in the genitive: "of them canny Telemachus took the lead in speech."[56] Two special uses should be noted. At a sacrificial feast the president is described "taking the lead in respect of all the joints," his duty being to see that the food was properly distributed:[57] and the blind minstrel Demodocus, when the lyre was placed in his hands, "being moved began with [a] god, and showed forth song";[58] what he set himself to do was to experience the inspiration—and out came his voice singing.

THE SUBSTANTIVE *ARKHÉ*

With these usages of the verb clearly established, we turn to the substantive, *arkhé*, which in classical Greek has meanings so different as a philosophical "principle," a "cause" (in relation to its effect), a public "office," a "foundation," a "beginning" generally, and also the "end" of a rope. In Homer it already has the general meaning of the "beginning" of anything and is so used almost adverbially in the *Odyssey*,[59] though not in the *Iliad*. But apart from this it means not merely the first point in time, in any matter, but also the originating fact or circumstance, the efficient cause. Thus we find the "beginning of evil," "of trouble,"[60] "of the quarrel". Penelope propounds the famous bow "for contests and a cause of slaughter";[61] the bow, that is, will lead to, and cause, massacre, as iron "itself draws a man on"; and in the recital, afterward, of the event, we see how this worked upon Odysseus: "some god was helping him."[62]

This same bow, like a royal sceptre, was an object of power. It had belonged to Eurytus, whose son Iphitus gave it to Odysseus, "and to him Odysseus gave a sharp sword and a strong spear, a cause of guest-right, creating kinship; nor did they even know each other at table;" before that could happen, Iphitus died.[63] But, though the two men never met, this mystical bond united them, and that was the doing of the bow, and of the presents given in exchange; as in the ballad of Irish courtship, " 'twas the little pigs as did it," when the lady consented. Other objects of the same kind are the necklace of Protesilaus, the cloak of Heracles, the world-wide series of love tokens and keepsakes, the shell-bracelets of the Trobriand Islanders, irresistible "beginnings of intercourse" in this causal sense, for it is when they are about that the thing first happens.

Such *arkhé* could be attributed to a person. Menelaus, proposing a truce with a view to the restitution of Helen by the Trojans,[64] says he thinks that "Argives and Trojans are already discerned of one another"—they have come to know one another better after ten years of war; they have, in fact, fought the matter out and are ready to be friends—"since ye have suffered much evil on account of my grudge and the *arkhé* of Alexander," that is, of Paris, who was the cause of the trouble. Alexander's spontaneous interference with the normal course of events, that is, was a *primum mobile*. As the old professor said, excusing his absence from a college feast, "Man arranges but God disarranges." And how does Menelaus propose to counter this disturbing factor? "But bring the *might* of Priam, that he may slay the oath-victims himself, since his sons are overweening and faithless"—quite literally, they "are overgrown," beyond the normal course and process of things. They are "too big for their boots"; they have "swelled heads." "For always, the wits of younger men are [easily] roused, but where an old man is concerned, he looks before and behind, that it may be for the best on either hand." Men like Alexander, that is, are possessed by a force, an impulse to do something all of their own, not to say "self-pleasing," as Æschylus and Herodotus call it.[65] And force such as this can be constrained only by superior force, guided by greater knowledge, wider comprehension "on either hand."

We are here in a fairly primitive system of ideas. The bow of Iphitus, and Odysseus' sword and spear, had that in them which made the two men understand each other—though "at table they never knew one another"—and were in this sense *arkhé*, initiative, of friendship as between blood-kinsmen. Alexander's *arkhé* initiated the trouble over fair Helen; the "might" of King Priam could initiate the new

144

state of peace between Argives and Trojans, who had now come to discern one another after ten years of war. In this connexion we should perhaps note that *polemos*, the Greek word for "war," signifies "violent shaking" and mix up, like its cognate verb *pelemizein*;[66] and *eiréne*, meaning "peace," appears to contain a metaphor from continuity, as of a chain of beads, or flowing speech, or orderly assembly.[67]

In Homer, then, *arkhé* is not primarily an office, or status; like its verb, it signifies simply "initiative," that personal quality of spontaneous "drive," "push," "vim" (to borrow modern words forceful enough to characterize it), which "gets things done"; manifested especially as a cause of activity in others. Thus a Homeric king is a *basileus*, one who "makes the people to march," as an early Roman magistrate was *praetor* (*præitor*), one who "goes in front" of the others. Quite accurately, too, later Greek writers described as *monarchos*— that is, "of sole initiative," or, as we say, "monarch"—the functions of the Roman *dictator*, who is literally "he who says" what everyone else is to do.

That such "initiative" resides in a person qualified by birth and antecedents is clear; that it could be conferred on a man who had it not is not contemplated in Homeric society, where princes are of "divine-born" family. But that it could be enhanced, where it existed, seems probable from the habitual transmission, in such a family, of an object of power, the *skeptron*, which has been discussed already (p. 128). We have now to supplement the direct evidence of Homeric passages with some parallel examples from other sources.

The stem from which *arkhé* is formed is represented in Sanskrit by *arh-*, giving a verb *arhami*, "I am able," "I have it in me to do," like *valeo* in Latin, which has a similar extension of its root-sense of "physical strength." An adjective, *arhas*, has the same force as *dignus* in Latin or *valens* in *equivalens;* or the Greek *axios*, used both for personal dignity and for economic value. The substantive *argham*, like *pretium* and *valor* in Latin, and the Greek *timê*, has the same double sense. And it should be noted here that this Greek word *timê* stands in the same relation with *arhké*, as we shall presently see that *nemesis* stands to *aidôs*. A man's personal initiative, of which he himself is conscious and of which others become aware by his manifestations of "push," is *arkhé; timê*, which provisionally we may translate *worth* rather than *honour*, is the recognition of this quality by the others. In the barony offered to Achilles, for example, his subjects "will *value* him like a god," and express that

value, crudely enough, in the presents they
bring; less crudely, too, in the accomplishment
of his *themistes* "which do them good."[68] It
is in this sense that *"arkhé* reveals a man," in a
Greek proverb which we first find in a fourth-
century context;[69] and a man is "dear to all
and valued"[70] when his deeds keep pace with
his words—a sense which is exactly preserved
in the modern usage of the adjective *timios*.

ARKHÉ AND IMPERIUM

In early Rome the spontaneous initiative of
an executive official was described by a word
which had almost as momentous a history as
arkhé itself, in its political aspect, and might
have had a similar career as a philosophical
term if it had not been for a literary disaster,
of which note must be taken presently. To
"get things ready," in Latin, is *parare;*
"to get them ready against" an occasion fore-
seen, is *imperare.* So, we read of *imperata pensa,*
tasks assigned;[71] of an *exemplar imperatæ
schemæ,*[72] a copy of a projected plan. So, too,
a farmer *imperat arvis,* when he is forearmed
against accidents of season and pest;[73] in barbarian Germany *sola terræ seges imperatur;*
provision is made for one crop only off the
land;[74] *iungere equos Titan velocibus imperat
Horis,* the Sun-god "orders his car" to be

ready at the proper time;[75] more literally still, like the middle voice of the Greek verb, *imper-avi egomet mihi omni assentari*, "I have prepared myself to concur in it all."[76] The cognate verbal substantive for this kind of foresight and initiative is *imperium*. Here is an early example of its use from Plautus—*si quid opus est, impera; imperium exsequar*—"If anything is wanted, tell me beforehand; I will follow your instructions."[77] Virgil couples it with *præcepta*, "things anticipated," in accordance with his characteristic re-phrasing of an identical thought—*et Iovis imperium et cari præcepta parentis.*[78]

But, whereas in Homeric Greece and among its "divine-born" kings we found no trace of conferment of this initiative grace, the more composite and artificial Roman state, with a far more crudely animistic background to its culture, took, at all events, precautions against the lack of it. Of King Numa it was traditional that *ipse de suo imperio curiatam legem tulit;*[79] and an older authority describes the transference of it to a new dynasty: *Tarquinio dedit imperium simul et sola regni,*[80] authority to initiate, and territory over which to exercise it, the latter anticipating one aspect of what in later times is the necessary correlative of every regular *imperium*, namely, a *provincia* within which it is to be exercised. The ceremony of conferring *imperium*, thus ascribed to Numa, remained in observance throughout Republican times, and it was possible to delay the enjoyment of his rightful initiative by a regularly elected official, by the simple device of postponing the ritual act of consecration, as one might imagine a constitutional king debarred from exercise of the royal prerogative until he had been crowned. More significant still is the Roman ceremony of *salutatio*, whereby on the occasion of some particularly successful exercise of personal initiative in a well-ordered victory the assembled troops reasserted their leader's possession of *imperium*, formally saluted him as *imperator*, and were held to have in some mystical—we might even say "magical" —way enhanced the efficiency of the *imperium* he already had, as Achilles' subjects were to "acknowledge his value as a god" by the gifts they should bring. All such enhancements by rehearsal of a person's gift of initiative are in Greek described as *timai*—acknowledgments by others of the *arkhé* inherent in him. The magical value of such iteration is very clearly conceived among all unsophisticated people, as when the people of Ephesus repaired the insulted majesty of their goddess, "all with one voice about the space of two hours crying out,

'Great is Diana of the Ephesians.' "[81] Nor is the practice extinct in modern politics; as the Bellman said, in the *Hunting of the Snark*, "What I tell you three times is true."

ARKHÉ AND MANA

In view of the peculiar significance attained by the conception of *arkhé* at a later stage of Greek thought, it may be found instructive to study at this point a term which has in some respects a similar import in the philosophy of its users. The word *mana* is used among Melanesian peoples to denote "a force altogether distinct from physical power, which acts in all kinds of ways for good and evil, and which it is of the greatest advantage to possess or control"; "a power or influence, not physical and in a way supernatural; but it shows itself in physical force, or in any kind of power of excellence which a man possesses . . . ;" "that is what works to effect everything which is beyond the ordinary power of man, outside the common processes of nature." . . . "When one has got it, he can use it and direct it, but its force may break forth at some new point; the presence of it is ascertained by proof." . . . "This power, though impersonal, is always connected with some person who directs it; all spirits have it, ghosts generally, some men."[82] In Polynesian languages the same word means "super-natural power, divine authority, having qualities which ordinary persons and things do not possess."[83] It is applied, for instance, to a wooden sword "that has done deeds so wonderful as to possess a sanctity and power of its own"; to a "magic staff given to a man by his grandfather"; and in a more "secular" sense to chiefs and other persons "gifted" with persuasion or other forms of personal skill. This conception of *mana* has been generally regarded by students of these matters as a type specimen of a widespread notion, of which the *orenda* of the Iroquois and the *wakonda* of the Omaha people are examples, sufficiently well known through careful and sympathetic observation to deserve mention here.[84] Such conceptions have been usually approached from the point of view in which they throw light upon magic, religion, or those anticipations of philosophy which profess to explain the general structure of things and the course of events; and the attempt has been made to interpret some of the conceptions, and still more some of the phrases, of early Greek philosophy, in terms of these widespread and very archaic notions.[85] Without hazarding an opinion as to the success of these attempts, it is, however, perhaps worth while to illustrate by such comparison some of the associations which seem to cling to the conception of *arkhé* in its "secular" and political manifestations, if only to form a clearer idea of the extent to which Greek phraseology seems to have cleared itself of some of the more positive implications of them, and advanced to the simpler and more rational view of what authority is.

In the Omaha tribe "chiefs were respected not only because of their authority, but as having been favoured by the unseen powers who had granted them help and strengthened their ability to be steadfast in purpose during the years wherein they struggled to perform the acts required to enter the rank of chief. Because of this relation to the unseen powers a chief had to be deliberate in speech and in movement, for all his words and acts were more or less connected with the welfare of the people, and by the authority invested in his office the chief was allied to the all ruling and mysterious *Wakonda*." Discounting, in the Homeric conception of the "divine-born kings," that anthropomorphic presentation of the "unseen powers who had granted them help," which is characteristic of Olympian religion, and converted *themis* itself into a "fair-cheeked" mistress-of-the-ceremonies in the dining hall and council chamber of the gods, we recognize in the "struggle to perform the acts required," the same notion of personal effort which is conserved in the Homeric phrase "extorting the ordinances of Zeus;" in the chief's belief that "all his words and acts were more or less connected with the welfare of his people" the same conception as that which pictured the Homeric chieftain as "shepherd of the clans" uttering precepts "which do them good"; and in the explanation that "by the authority invested in his office the chief was allied to the all-ruling and mysterious *Wakonda*," a counterpart of Minos, the infant prodigy, "ruling at five years old," who was the "confidant of great Zeus," and continued after death to "sit holding a golden sceptre, giving *themistes* to the dead." But in proportion as the perfected humanity of the Homeric gods, and complete humanization even of abstractions like the Olympian *themis* and *dikê* condensed into vivid material shapes the "unseen and mysterious *Wakonda*" circumambient in Omaha belief, it became possible for Homeric speech to express the procedure by which the divine wisdom and purpose was made available for the "welfare of the people" through the personal initiative of its "lords," in verbal substantives from the vocabulary of everyday life: "laying down" and "establishing" custom, "indicating" courses of action, exercising "push" or initiative, "making the people to go" either "straight" and "doing them good" or, in less happy instances, simply "askew."

This actuality and concreteness of presentation, indeed, goes far to explain the circumstance that in our Homeric documents we miss all description of such devices to insure or enhance the initiative of "leading" men, as we were led to perceive in the ceremonial of the *lex curiata* and the *salutatio* by which the less completely humanized beliefs of early Romans conferred *imperium* or supplemented it by "sympathetic" rites of recognition, and thereby supplied their lack of those "divine-born" families in which initiative authority was transmitted in Homeric society.

Not far outside the limits of Homeric tradition on this matter stands the Hesiodic portrait of the *basileus* as public servant, at a stage in the political development of Central Greece which there is every reason to believe to have been historical, when the "divine-born" families of the Heroic Age were already giving place to the headmen of the kinship groups which constituted the communities of the conquest area, in that Early Iron Age which followed; though "divine-born" individuals were still to be met among these coequal princes.[86]

154

THE NOTION OF ORDINANCE

"Whomsoever the Muses, the daughters of Zeus, value"—the word is the same as is applied to the recognition of Achilles' authority by his subjects—"and behold him begotten of Zeus-nurtured kings, upon his tongue they pour sweet dew, and forth from his mouth flow gentle words.[87] Upon him all the clans gaze as he distinguishes among *themistes* with straightforward rulings. This man, by the sureness of his public speech, can abate skilfully in a moment even a mighty contention. For to this end are kings possessors of wisdom, that they may effect redress to clansmen who suffer wrong, in the place of meeting, quietly persuading with gentle words. As he walks to and fro in the city they seek his favour, as they would a god's, with gentle self-respect, and he is eminent among them as they gather round. Such is the holy gift of the Muses to mankind."

We can hardly mistake in all this the counterpart of one of those Omaha chiefs who "had to be deliberate in speech and in movement; for all his words and acts were more or less connected with the welfare of the people," as he "struggled to perform the acts required to enter the rank of chief." Those chiefs too "were respected . . . as having been favoured by the unseen powers, who had granted them help and strengthened their ability to be stead-fast during the years." So, indeed, Hesiod goes on, widening his conception of initiative beyond the political. "For from the Muses and far-shooting Apollo come men on earth who are singers and harpers, and from Zeus come kings; and he is blessed whom the Muses love, and sweet is the voice that flows from his mouth;" and the poet goes on to describe the consolations of verse, and song on high themes, to men in trouble, especially songs about the gods, and the "fame of former men."

THE WORD *ARKHÉ* IN CLASSICAL GREEK

In view of the selection of the word *arkhé* by Aristotle to denote inclusively the function of the citizen in the city-state, it is necessary to trace in some detail the history of this word, and its cognates between its Homeric and its fourth-century usages. Among the poets, as we should expect, the active verb retains its meaning, "to start" a hymn, for example, a calamity, a course of wrongdoing,[88] a ritual act, or a political covenant sanctioned by such acts; and in the New Testament the "ruler of the feast" is literally the "starter" of it, like Themis in Olympus. In the middle voice, too, it is used as in Homer; "to begin from Zeus,"[89] as Demodocus "began with the god" as inspiration seized him. Similarly, Athenians, returning to their ravaged city, "started themselves a-building";[90] and the soul of a dying man "starts itself to depart."[91] In the political sense, Herodotus speaks of the mob "initiating," when it takes control of the state.

But we have also new usage now, transitional in Herodotus' vivid sketch of the rise of Deioces to power,[92] but already mature in other passages of the same writer, the only pre-Socratic thinker (let us never forget) whose works are preserved in full. Deioces, like any candidate for Omaha chieftaincy, begins by deliberately doing chieflike acts, for the welfare of this people "as if courting initiative." We are reminded of the less fortunate Cylon, who, like another Samson, "grew his hair long for a tyranny."[93] Deioces, too, like Theras, "when he tasted initiative"—not *office*, as we say, but the freedom to start things in his own way—which he had been only "courting" before, "compelled the Medes to make for themselves one single fortress,"[94] and the result was *imperium et sola regni*, as Ennius says of Tarquin,[95] for "he concentrated the Median nation only, and *ruled over it*," the same word now being used in its full political significance. It is in this sense that the overlordship of Croesus is an *arkhé;*[96] and an Athenian admiral after the death of a colleague had "the whole *arkhé* over the ships."[97]

It is now clear that in compounds the prefix *arkhé* (as in our words "architect" and "archbishop") describes not merely the first or chief man of a company or organisation, but the initiatory function of him who "starts" the others to work, and originates the design which they are to complete. And this appeal to Greek practical life confirms the view that what is essential in the notion of *arkhé* is just this initiatory "push" or "drive" with which the gifted man imposes his will-and-pleasure on the rest. This meaning is even clearer in poetical phrases such as "lord of the sea," "lord of the thunder," "lord of light," or "life;" and in names of the "leader" of a crowd of other people, robbers, worshippers, feasters.[98] The familiar "architect" in Greek is oftener "master workman" than "designer," as with us.[99]

Finally, both noun and verb are used of the *sola regni* over which such *imperium* is exercised, as when Brasidas "comes to Arnissa, first point of the *arkhé* [dominion] of Perdiccas,"[100] or impersonally—"as far as this mountain it is ruled by Persia."[101] But the primitive meaning of "starting" recurs in unexpected phrases: geographically, of the peninsular territory of the Cnidians, turned [trending] toward the sea

. . . and being started from the Bybassian isthmus;"[102] or morphologically, when a man pulls at the beginning of the cord where we should give him the "end" of it.[103]

These reminiscences of the primary meaning pass gradually over into the secondary senses in which the substantive *arkhé* is used in classical Greek. But it is difficult to be sure that the secondary senses are not really nearer to the primary than has been sometimes supposed. In particular the circumstance that *arkhé* is a verbal substantive, standing in the same relation to its verb as *logos*, "word," to *legein*, "to say," or *tykhe*, "chance," to *tykhein*, "to chance to meet," is significant in itself, and still more so when it is found that this is common in the vocabulary of Greek political thought.

Achievement *Telos* as Correlative of Initiative *Arkhé*

A good example is the term which in the philosophical vocabulary is the direct correlative of *arkhé*, but in its commonest political usages either becomes a synonym of it, or else goes off into special meanings which at first sight have no connexion with it. This word is *telos*, commonly translated "end," as *arkhé* may often be translated "beginning." Like *arkhé*, it has a cognate verb, *tellein*, "to make to be," which is found later uncompounded, though in the Homeric poems only its compounds, *ana-tellein*, *epitellein*, occur. There is also a derivative verb, *telein*, meaning simply "to bring to a *telos*," "to complete." At first sight *telos* in Homer means simply "end" or "conclusion;" "*telos* of war," for example, or "of speaking."[104] But phrases like "*telos* of death,"[105] and still more, "*telos* of marriage"[106] imply more; they signify that which makes the event decisive and complete; not the ceremony, but the consummation, of a marriage. Similarly, "in our hands is the *telos* of war, that of speeches in our decision" shows *telos* with a verbal and dynamic sense, not merely substantival and static. Still more clearly in this:—"when at last the joyous hours brought forth the *telos* of our hiring, then Laomedon, outrageous man, wrested from us all our hire"[107]—the *telos* is the completion of the work for which they were hired, their pay completing the transaction, as death may be said to complete a life, or the decision a debate, or victory the violent efforts which achieve it. In the passage about Laomedon we have also the verb: "we came from Zeus and laboured for a year at an agreed hire; and he showed us our work and *set it us to do*," and of this the *telos* of their hiring, above quoted, was the completion. In the common phrase, "the *telos* of speaking," we now see that the word has the same force; it is not merely the ending or cessation of talk, but the decision to which the discussion has now led; as life leads to death, or labour to pay. Says one speaker, "you will speak lies, nor will you put a *telos* to your speaking"[108]—not that the lies would never end, but that they could have no result; and, again, "not even Achilles will put a *telos* upon all his words," crowning speech with persuasion. So, too,.."obey, as I shall put the *telos* of speech in thy heart," namely, consequent action. When Hephæstus is interrupted at his work,[109] he had put the wheels on his tripods, "and they had thus much *telos*, but the ornate ears had not yet been put on; them he was fitting, and hammering links." He was, that is, at this stage of realizing his design.

But what of the passage in the *Lay of Dolon*, where a messenger is to "go to the holy *telos* of watchmen and *set them to do*" an order (where the same word is used as of Laomedon above, setting labourers to work); and again, "quickly they went and reached a *telos* of Thracian men"?[110] The whole lay is queer, loosely knit with the rest of the *Iliad*, and suspected to be of later composition; but it is none the less epic in diction; and here *telos* is clearly the squad of persons to whom orders are given, tasks are set; their action is the response to, and correlative of, the initiative of their commander which those orders convey. This use of *telos* persists in classical Greek, for a flock of birds, a territorial contingent, a squadron of cavalry, chariots or ships.[111]

Homeric usages of the cognate verb confirm this general sense of *telos;* quite explicit is the meaning of performance, in such phrases as to "fulfil burial";[112] "speak what thou thinkest; my heart bids me *fulfil,*"[113] "if I am able to fulfil and if it has reached fulfilment,"[114] in the sense that *telos* is attained, in any matter, under two conditions; first, the ability of the agent— and this we have already seen depends on his *arkhé*, the quality of "push" or initiative—and, secondly, the concurrence of the "unseen powers," as an Omaha would say, in this event, The chief's will, in quite modern parlance, must be in accord with the divine will.

Thus *arkhé* and *telos*, while alike matter of human will and push, are alike from Zeus. The subjects of Achilles, so often quoted already, "*fulfil* beneath his sceptre his ordinances;" and in his quarrel with Agamemnon and its tragic sequel "the decision of Zeus was being fulfilled."[115] Thus, too, seen from outside, "*arkhé* reveals a man" because fulfilment, *telos*, reveals him; as Menelaus says as he slays the boastful Othryoneus, "Thee would I praise above all men, if, indeed, thou wilt *fulfil* all that thou didst promise."[116] It is, indeed, exactly in this sense that Solon advises Crœsus to "look to the *end* of every matter, whither it will arrive."[117]

TELOS AND *PROVINCIA*

It is in precisely this sense that in classical Greek "those in *arkhé*," public officials, are also "those in *telos*"; and that *telos* means the function of such men, as Euripides speaks of the "sleepless functions of the eyes."[118] In this aspect *telos*, like *arkhé*, has its precise counterpart in Roman terminology, in the *provincia* which is the correlative of all *imperium* that is not expressly unlimited, *infinitum*. This is a more picturesque but hardly more homely word than *telos*, for it is literally the "leash" or "tether," within which a man invested with *imperium* is free to exercise initiative; beyond its radius he may bark but cannot bite. For entry on such function formal phrases are *provinciam inire, in provinciam cum imperio proficisci*;[119] and for resigning it *provinciam deponere*, or *tradere*; but, popularly, one could say in assigning military commands, *Sicinio Volsci, Aquilio Hernici provincia evenit*,[120] or of an assassin "he demanded this function, to kill me in my bed"[121]—as Æschylus speaks of "those to whom this *telos* has been assigned."[12]

That *telos* in later Greek should have been used for various kinds of "performances" is, therefore, only what we should expect. Of these, two are significant as illustrations of its history. In respect of the state the ordinary citizen, too, has to "do his bit," in military service—as the Thracians served in a *telos* in the *Lay of Dolon*—and by contribution to its resources; consequently, "to settle *telos*" is to pay one's taxes; and a person exempt from this or other public duties is *ateles*—"without *telos*." And, further, among these public duties, the service of the gods ranks high, and *telos* means any religious ceremony; the participant in such rites is *teletes*, "performer," and by a curious accident the Roman equivalent for the most intimate kinds of *telos* is *initia*—"entering upon" a new plane of experience in what a Greek no less properly called a "place of performance:" for at Eleusis the name of the Hall of the Mysteries was the *Telesterion*.

ARKHÉ AND *TELOS* TRANSLATED BY *PRINCIPIUM* AND *FINIS* IN LATIN PHILOSOPHY

Into the use made in Greek philosophy of the words we have been discussing here it would be improper to digress at this point. Our consideration of their Roman equivalents, in the sphere of their political and administrative senses, would, however, hardly be complete without reference to the disaster which befell philosophy generally when Latin writers began to popularize the conceptions of Greek philosophy, and invented a vernacular terminology for them. Had Cicero persisted in his translation of *arkhai* by *initia*,[123] or followed up his own happy phrases about *causa* as implying initiative as well as priority in time;[124]—still more, had his political experience led him to translate *arkhé* by *imperium*—the course of speculation might have run smoother, and reached conclusions (if not different) more comprehensible than they have, in fact, been, with the rendering *principium*, which lays stress on priority and superiority rather than on initiative and causality. In a world where the origins and limitations of *imperium* were being forgotten except by antiquarians, and where the *causa causans* of most things that mattered was a *princeps*, the choice was as irrevocable as it was fatal; and it was not the only accident of this kind. What more incongruous juxtaposition could have been conceived than that of *finis* with *telos*, translating "performance" by "boundary," and correlating *principium* with *finis,* "commencement" with "extremity"? What more lamentable failure of scholarship than that, if the title of Cicero's own treatise, *De Finibus Bonorum et Malorum,* be retranslated into Greek,[125] it becomes impossible to recognize whether it is a treatise on the principles of taxation, or on good and bad public servants? And in no case could the Greek words refer to the "Latter Ends of Good and Bad Men," which is what Cicero actually meant.

LECTURE IV

THE GREEK NOTION OF JUSTICE: *DIKÊ*.

THROUGH the two main trends of political development which we have been following—encroachment of the state on the tribal corporations, of whose members it is now felt to consist, irrespective of their lesser loyalties; and encroachment on the solidarity of the family and clan, on the part of individuals intolerant of communal restrictions or embarked on a way of life which removed or at least alienated them from the rest of their hereditary group—ancient and traditional forms of authority have been traced falling into disrepute and disuse. A new conception of what authority meant appears in the Hesiodic description of the "man whom the Muses love;" for while "from Zeus come kings," (belated, in many places obsolete, tribute to the "divine-born" dynasties of adventurers in the Heroic Age), there is now another source of inspiration—the Muses and Apollo. In Hesiodic theology they, too, are Zeus-born; but their relations with men are not quite those of Zeus. From the Muses and Apollo come "singers and harpers," and these, like the seer, the physician, and the armourer, in Homeric society, are "public servants;" they have a public function and responsibility to perform as it may be required—to comfort those that mourn, to dissipate ill thoughts and cares. But beyond these the Muses enhance the native ability of the "Zeus-nurtured" king. It is to them that he owes the *savoir faire*, the *mot juste*, the gracious presence, the quiet influence, which brings the others crowding round him—like the dead round Minos in Hades—"in gentle self-respect;" already, that is, in a mood to follow his lead, whatever that may be.

Now, the procedure of the "man whom the Muses love" is for the most part described in quite general terms; it is rather the spirit in which he acts, than what he does. This elicits that "gentle self-respect" in the others and enhances his initiative by their willing concurrence. But in one point Hesiod is precise, even technical, in his phrases: "The clansmen all see him distinguishing among *themistes* with straightforward rulings." It is not, indeed, quite clear whether he distinguishes or discerns *themistes* as such, perceiving what is the will and pleasure of Zeus directly, like a Homeric chief, or distinguishes, among

168

themistes already extant, that one which is applicable to the matter in hand. But the context of the *Theogonia* is, on the whole, quite as clearly subsequent to the period of conquest and resettlement, as that of the Homeric poems is projected back into the Heroic Age which preceded it. And though *themistes* are still part of the political outfit of Hesiodic society, what chiefly preoccupies the poet now is another aspect of social order and prerequisite for well-being; what are described here as *dikai*, and their collective substance which is *dikê*.

DIKÊ IN HOMER

There were *dikai*, it is true, in Homeric society, and we have already had to anticipate, in general terms, the establishment of their exact quality. *Dikê*, like *arkhé*, is a verbal substantive, of which the stem means to "show" or "point out"; in Latin the corresponding root yielded words for to "say," and to "point out," for the autocratic *dictator* with his plenary *imperium*; for the "finger," *digitus*, with which you point; and there is trace in the legal phrase, *dicis causa*, "for form's sake," of an exact counterpart of the Greek *dikê*, alongside of the Latinized *dica*, which is a late loan-word, identical with it. Primarily, then, and in common speech, *dikê* is the "way a thing happens," as

you would show another fellow how to do it,
or recognize it when it occurs.[1] For example,
it is the *dikê* of old men, a "way they have," to
bathe, eat, and sleep warm, to "do themselves
well."[2] And it is the *"dikê* of divine kings" not
to say or do anything out-of-order in public.[3]
So, too, Telemachus set out to inquire about
his lost father from Nestor, "since he knows
all about the *ways* and thought of others;" he
will know, that is, what Odysseus is likely to
have done with himself.[4]   And, as we shall see,
this popular sense persists in classical Greek.

But, by the side of this, there is well-established Homeric usage of *dikê* for pronounce-
ments as to the "way things happen" under
normal circumstances, which have the force of
a legal ruling on any occasion when things have
not gone so, but the normal order of events has
been disturbed. This was one of the remedial
processes of civilisation which, like *themistes*,
the Cyclops-folk did not know.[5] In Hades,
it was for *dikai* that the dead asked Minos;[6]
and "with *dikai* and his own strength,"[7] Sarpedon "drew toward him" Lycia for gover-
nance.   In the trial scene on the Shield of
Achilles two talents lie there before the bench
of elders "to give to him who along with these
speaks a *dikê* most straightly;"[8] who offers, that
is, the clearest ruling on the point of custom

which govern the matter in question. So far, a *dikê* is a ruling of a judge or other wise man on a dispute between other parties. It may be a "straight" ruling, like the arbitrament of a man of age and experience, such as Priam, who "looks both before and after, so that it may be quite for the best on either hand;"[9] or "crooked" and "awry," given "with violence," so that *dikê* collectively is driven out, because the "voice of the gods" is ignored. *Dikê* collectively may be "driven out," when men "with violence discern crooked *themistes*, not regarding the voice of the gods."[10]

But *dikê* is also, in one passage, clearly the statement of the aggrieved person: where Antilochus protests that he has been overlooked in the prize giving after the funeral games, and "rising up, answered Achilles with a *dikê*," that is with a statement of what should have happened and did not.[11] In one other passage *dikê* may have either sense. Odysseus is urging Agamemnon not to fail on the side of generosity in appeasing Achilles: "and then let him be contented with a rich feast among the huts, that you may leave nothing lacking of the *dikê*,"[12] Is this *dikê* the "award" of compensation, to which Agamemnon has agreed, and has now to give effect, or is it the "claim" of Achilles which that award was to satisfy?

171

Probably the former, because Odysseus goes on to say that if this is done, Agamemnon "will then be more observant of *dikê* than another, for it is no cause for cavil that a king should give a man full contentment when he was the first to behave harshly." Moreover, at no point in the quarrel has Achilles stated a claim for compensation; that was the pity of it, that he thought Agamemnon past forgiveness.

Those "sons of Achæans" who carry a sceptre, and "extort *themistes* from Zeus," are wielders of justice, *dikai*," as we have seen.[13] Such a one is Telemachus in Ithaca, since "he dines at equal feasts, which it is proper for a man conversant with *dikai* to attend; for all invite him."[14] And persons great and small may have the quality of a *dikê;* they behave orderly and normally, not "wildly" like the Cyclops-folk and others who were not *dikaioi*,[15] which provisionally we may render "just," though rather in the French sense of *juste* than in our own more legal and moral shade of meaning. This was what was wrong with the suitors of Penelope, "because they are not willing to woo in accordance with *dikê*," the way decent people do their courting, "nor to go to their own place, but squander the property at their ease, over-roughly, nor spare it at all." Elsewhere men who are not *dikaioi* are also "not intelligent;"[16] on the other hand, Athena "rejoiced in a man *dikaios* and of a good spirit." This kind of "justice" is also "fair" and admirable; for it does not "confound" or "bring to harm."[17] Speech which is "just" is contrasted with words of "opposing violence" and the kind of "harsh" dealing with which Odysseus gently reproaches Agamemnon, and is exempt from such rejoinder. Summarily, the qualities of a *dikaios* are intelligence, clear-headedness, good will, absence of violence, harshness and bad temper. All civilized people are *dikaioi* more or less, and in the Hymn to Aphrodite wild nature and "shady groves" are contrasted with the "cities of men who are *dikaioi*," who know how to behave. It is instructive that even in these early passages the *dikaios* is intelligent as well as good-tempered and mannerly.[18]

But this quality had its degrees. Agamemnon, if he behaved generously, would be "more *dikaios* than another;" Cheiron, who taught the young Achilles, was "most *dikaios* of the Centaurs;"[19] and on the northern edge of the world are "gracious horse-milkers, milk-eaters, without livelihood, most *dikaioi* of mankind."[20] Later, in a Homeric hymn, the war god is "master of the men of opposing violence, leader of folk most *dikaioi*,"[21] as well as fellow-helpers of Themis.

173

For the act of arbitrating in a dispute and giving a ruling, there is an active verb, *dikazein*, used either of an individual or a body of men: "let him decide, for Trojans and Danaans, as is fit;"[22] "decide ye between the two of us;"[23] "sons of the Trojans decided, and Pallas Athene."[24] In the "Trial-scene" on the shield the litigants were rushing into court, and the elders "began to give their ruling in turn."[25] In the middle voice the same verb describes the doings of the litigant: "them I defeated, stating my case by the ships," in the passage quoted above, where the Trojan and Athena decided it. So a chief is described "discussing many quarrels of youths stating their claims;"[26] and so, too, the dead "asked *for themselves* rulings from their lord," exactly paraphrasing the more formal word.[27]

The Notion of *DIKÊ* after Homer

We have now to trace the notion of *dikê* outside the Homeric poems. In the first place, as has been noted already briefly, the Homeric and most elementary meaning, of "the way a thing happens," persists into classical times, and not among the poets only, nor only of human behaviour, nor of living things. "Mine be it to befriend a friend; but my enemy, seeing he is my enemy, I will pursue, *the way of* a wolf."[28]   A furious man "roars *the way of* invincible water dashing down a mountain."[29] A philosopher may say "it remains, then, I think, to be filled through my hearing from alien sources, *the way of* a waterpot."[30]

The adjective *dikaios* is used, like the Old-English "kindly,"—meaning "according to kind"—of cultivable land, of thoroughbred horses which "breed true," and of well-behaved horses whose actions are "normal," in a metaphor about mutinous men.[31]   It is important to note that this usage is not confined to ordinary speech nor to poetry, but is employed also by a "physical" philosopher, Empedocles, who speaks of the "*dikê* of smoke," meaning the way smoke behaves.[32]

Secondly, and again as in Homer, *dikê* is man's formulation of the "way things happen" normally, whether such formula be true or false, "straight" or "crooked." Bad kings can, so to speak, "do justice" which is injustice really. So Hesiod warns them: "bearing this in mind, kings, devourers of gifts, make straight your *dikai* and altogether put out of mind crooked *dikai*,"[33] and elsewhere he describes how *dikê*, personified, is mishandled by such "gift-devouring" men, who "distinguish *themistes* with crooked *dikai*," and "drive her out" and do not distribute her "straight," contrasting them with those who "give straight *dikai* to strangers and dwellers in the *demos* alike, and do not turn aside from the way of *dikê;*" men "whose *polis* grows green and the clans blossom in it, and their wives bear children like to their sires."[34] It is characteristic of the parallelism between man's behaviour and the "way things happen" in nature, which has been noticed at the outset, that you could not be really well-bred, unless you were thoroughbred too.

WELL-BRED AND THOROUGHBRED IN EARLY GREECE

This is a consideration which it is essential to keep in mind, in estimating the claims made by the spokesman of the *ancien régime* in Greek city-states during the seventh and sixth centuries, when the political exclusiveness of the original corporators—the kinship-groups which had sunk their differences to bring the defensive *polis* into being—was being challenged by adventurers and newcomers, as opportunities for intercourse grew. In such a country as the cradle-land of the Greeks each oasis of fertile land, intensely cultivated in small freeholds by the lineal descendants of its first Greek-speaking occupants, was nearly enough "self-sufficient," in the sense idealized

176

later by the philosophers, to provide almost
perfect conditions for inbreeding, and the establishment, in the biological sense, of a homogeneous and recognizable breed of men. Just
because these original occupants were for the
most part not closely related by blood—yet
almost all belonged to a not very wide range of
varieties similarly established during the long
age of Minoan insulation—there was ample provision against overclose inbreeding of the kind
which has led to enfeeblement of the stock in
many of the Pacific island-groups. But just
because Ægean *synœcism* involved deliberate
acceptance of such accidental neighbours as
social co-partners, the traditional exclusiveness
of such kinship-groups was relaxed to the
extent that intermarriage between such confederate clans was almost universally sanctioned; and consequently that risk of overclose
inbreeding was avoided, and such enfeeblement, at all events, greatly postponed. Paral-
lels sufficiently close to be instructive as illustrations are the varieties of physical type still
recognisable in the Greek islands, after a similar
period of segregation in mediæval and even in
subsequent times; in many of the more insulated districts of Italy; in the well-marked
local breeds of Welshmen; and to some degree
in the physique of the men of Devon, Hamp-

shire, Berkshire, the Vale of York, and other geographical regions of Saxon England; and among the older families of New England and the seaboard States of the Southeast. It is, indeed, from comparative study of such examples of what may provisionally be described as regional selection, that an estimate may be formed of the conditions, and more especially of the limits of time requisite for the establishment of such human "strains" or "breeds;" and the conclusion seems to be justified that the period of about four centuries, from 1100 to 700 B.C., between the last fresh injection of new blood into this Ægean stud-farm and the beginning of the period of renewed intercourse on a considerable scale, was long enough to have established such varieties, each fairly homogeneous, and most of them sufficiently well characterized to make almost any sort of stranger a fairly conspicuous object.

Direct evidence as to physical peculiarities, of course, eludes us almost wholly. Even the varieties of "Greek beauty" as recorded in sculpture, vase-painting, and coin-types during the "great age" of Hellenic art probably represent the conceptions of individual artists rather than the peculiarities of regional or political groups. But the collateral evidence of the varieties of dialect, and perhaps also the local peculiarities of widespread cults, are direct evidence that such differentiation occurred, and enable us to reconstitute—again with the help of analogies such as the distribution of dialects and schools of decorative art among the modern Greek islands—the main outlines of a picture of the city-state regime, as the expression, not of one, but of many collateral and infinitely graduated solutions of the problem of "living well" under Ægean conditions, and of providing that primary prerequisite of such intimate co-ordination of behaviour as this regime required, namely, adequate supply of citizens who were in no ordinary sense "equals and similars" in their reaction to most of the incidents of life, in the way which the philosophers postulated. If there was not at any period a "political animal" of standard behaviour and performance—as nineteenth-century economists postulated an "economic man" with standard habits of consumption, production, and self-seeking aims—there certainly were in the Greek world well-marked "Athenian," "Bœotian," "Chian," "Lesbian," "Rhodian," "Cretan" types of men, all recognisable, and some of them, like the wretched Lerians, ludicrously conspicuous among their contemporaries.

Hesiod's anticipation of such a state of things

179

is therefore instructive illustration of what a
Greek meant, both by "equality" in the political
sense, and by "aristocracy" in the sense of
government by the men who were the "fine
fellows" in the community, the "fair-as-well-
as-good" in a quite literal sense. And equally
instructive is what at first sight seems most
fantastic in the Platonic reconstruction of a
city of "just men made perfect," namely, that,
after more than two centuries of indiscriminate
interbreeding, it seemed hopeless to expect that
any political reconstruction would be permanent, or, indeed, practicable, unless accompa-
nied by thoroughgoing selection of the best-
surviving strains from among the mongrel
population, and systematic mating of these
until a thoroughbred stock should be re-established. Equality and similarity, that is, could
be established permanently only by equaliza-
tion with the best, and assimilation to an
ideal type.

DIKÊ IN RELATION TO THEMIS

A fresh point is gained from the same passage
of Hesiod as to the relation between *dikai* and
themistes. The latter, being the "voice of the
gods," represent the order of the world as the
gods conceive it and would have it to be—
"and behold, it is very good;" they are, there-

fore, general statements, like those formulated
by physicists and lawyers. But it is not
always clear which of the divine "voices"—
of which there are many, after long experience
of many kings,—is most applicable to a particular case. Here the human interpreter of *themistes,* through ignorance or guile, may fail to
"discern" and apply, in his *dikê,* the *formula* (as
a Roman *prætor* called it) which should govern
his settlement of the matter. In this event
his *dikê* is "askew," it does not fit the facts,
though it may be consistent with a *themis;* and
consequently it is permissible to speak of
"crooked *themistes,*" as we have already seen,
in the sense that *this* ruling does not fit *that*
case.[35] The same conception of a "straight"
dikê recurs in the appeal of the chorus to
Athena in the *Eumenides:* "but examine the case
and discern a straight *dikê.*" For Athena
replies by the question, "Should, then, the
outcome [*telos*] of the accusation be mine?"
the ruling which decides the case being the
consummation of the complaint which initiated it.[36]

Ideally, then, in Hesiod, as in Homer, a
dikê is a true demonstration of the "way
things happen," resulting from honest, intelligent application of a *themis,* truly discerned
and rightly selected, to the facts of the case.

"And now lend thine ear to *dikê* and put violence utterly out of thy thoughts. For this rule [*nomos*] the Son of Cronos arranged for men:[37] to fish and wild beasts and winged fowl, to eat one another, since there is no *dikê* in them; but to men he gave *dikê*, which is by far most excellent."[38] Here *dikê* is that quality of all true *dikai*, namely, that they accord with the real order of things. It is in this sense that Hesiod speaks of Hekatê, "whom Zeus honoured [valued] above all, and gave her fair gifts, to have assignment," that is, to decide what happens and when, "in earth and the barren sea; and she has also her portion of honour"—recognition of her initiative, as we have already seen[39] "from the starry sky, and her worth is acknowledged above all among immortal gods." For it is this goddess who "even still further, since Zeus also knows her worth, greatly assists whom she will, and does him good, and in place-of-meeting she makes eminent whom she will [40] among the clans, and in *dikê* she sits beside kings who have self-respect." For, being herself the author of all "assignment" and fitness among things, the king who has her for his assessor cannot err in his discernment of the "way things really happen."

For Hesiod, too, as in Homer, *dikê* is contrasted with violence; the "way" of normal unconstrained procedure, with the "crooked" course resulting from forcible interference with it. Force, violent enough to upset the foundations of society, is compared to the reversal of the courses of rivers. "Upward flow the streams of holy rivers, and *dikê* and all things are bent upon themselves."[41] This is "crooked" conduct indeed, for in the "holy" rivers is the presence of a great power of nature; a modern poet might describe them as "living waters."

DIKÊ Personified in Hesiod

In the description of Hekatê personification has taken another course, and *dikê* remains abstract; but elsewhere Hesiod follows Homeric precedent, and makes her a goddess with a pedigree.[42] Her father is Zeus, for *dikê* issues from his will-and-pleasure. Her mother, as we might anticipate, is the personified Themis; for every *dikê* originates in, and proceeds from, a *themis*. Her sisters are Eunomia, "order;" Eirenê, "peace," or uniform sequence of events; and the three Moirai, "destinies," who have, in commission as it were, much the same functions as Hekatê in the previous passage, and, like her, are assigned the "greatest worth" by Zeus. The first three, including *Dikê*, are

alike *Horai*, "watchers," for they watch and
observe, as their name implies,[43] the sequence
of nature's behaviour, the normal doings of
men, and the conformity of both to customary
procedure, while Eirenê, as we have already
seen, simply *is* the state of things when normal
procedure is undisturbed by the "shakings" of
war (p. 145.)

How *Dikê*, thus personified, upheld the
normal order, is illustrated by the saying of
Heraclitus, that "the sun will not overstep
his limits ["measures"]; otherwise the Erinyes,
allies of *Dikê*, will find him out."[44] Here grim
phantoms from the folklore of an older world
are "allied" in the mythological as well as the
administrative sense, with the verbal substantive *dikê*, which expresses the outcome of early
Hellenic reasoning. And for an inverse personification like that of Hesiod's Hekatê there
is another saying of Heraclitus,[45] about "cir-
cuits," that is to say, the paths of the wandering
"planets," of which the sun is "overseer and
inspector, to limit and umpire"—good sporting
slang this, from the race-course—"and point
out again and again, and show them repeatedly
changes and *horai* which carry everyone."
Here it is the sun that is personified, and his
assistants, or "allies," are the "observations"
which assign to each "wanderer" his intricate

184

course, as do the course-stewards in a relia-
bility trial or a cross-country steeplechase.
This conception of *Dikê* as "accuracy" personified helps to explain another Heraclitean saying,[46] that "bad men are of opposite *dikê* to men
of truth:" their "way," that is, is not the
"way of truth;" they follow after lying. And
we may note here that "truth" itself, for a
Greek, was literally "not leaving out of mind"
some part of the facts which must be kept in
view if the real state of things is to be perceived
and stated.[47]

Naturally, personification once effected, and
constructive speculation employing "more poetical terms," as was remembered of Anaximander in the sixth century—most of all, when
cosmological notions from Babylonia, perhaps
even from India, were brought back by trav-
ellers in Persian times—an extensive superstructure of myth and allegory was created,
without, however, adding very much to the
range of political or scientific thought, and
nothing at all to its lucidity. In the well-
known summary of Pythagorean doctrine by
Iamblichus,[48] for example, it is not the identification of *Themis*, *Dikê*, and *Nomos* (replacing
Hesiod's *Eunomia*) as having "the same
commission" on Olympus, in the Underworld,
and "up and down among *poleis*" respectively,

that is of value, but the conviction, transmitted only as a motive and reason for this guess, "so that the man who does not do" with *dikê* "what he has been set to do, is shown to be simultaneously wronging the whole order of things" (*cosmos*); that is, he is out of gear with God and nature as well as with his fellow men.[49] It is open to doubt how far these allegories influenced or even interested the ordinary citizen at any period of Greek thought; and also whether they may safely be assumed to be very much earlier than the late writings through which we made their acquaintance.[50]

DIKÊ IN FIFTH CENTURY WRITERS

More relevant to the secular history of *dikê* are the frequent occurrences of the word in Herodotus and the Tragedians. Following directly on the proceedings of the dead in Hades who "were asking *dikai* from their lord" is the common Herodotean phrase for demanding satisfaction for injury, as when the king of Colchis, after the elopement of Medea with Jason, sends to Greece "to demand *dikai* of the capture and to demand his daughter back."[51] The Greeks reply that the Orientals have not "given *dikai*" for the previous capture of Io. Here *dikai* signify the satisfaction required to restore things to their normal course.

Elsewhere, the complainant is said to "take" or "accept" *dikai*, when he accepts the compensation offered:[52] from the point of view of the offender it is said that from him *dikai* "occur" or "come into being." The assessor is said to "put upon" the offender a *dikê*, either at his own discretion, or with deference to the wishes of the complainant,[53] and the offender may "undertake to give *dikai*" as "chosen" by the complainant. In the case of Evenius "they began to ask him what *dikê* he would choose, if the men of Apollonia were willing to undertake to give *dikai* for what they had done," and Evenius replied, referring to certain estates, "that if he became possessed of them, he would for the future be without grudge, and that this *dikê*, if it occurred, would suffice for him."[54] Such *dikai*, further, are described as "fulfilled" and "brought to a *telos*."[55]

To assess and impose a *dikê* is *dikazein*, as in Homeric Greek.[56] This may be done either "according to what is upright" or "straight"— using the quite everyday word *orthos*, applicable to material objects,[57] or it may be an "unjust judgment." Herodotus uses *dikazein* also once for the utterance of an oracle through its priests—"when the men of Telmessus *ordained* that Sardis would be impregnable" on a given condition. And there is now a new substantive, *dikastes*, first transmitted in the *Choephoræ* of Æschylus, for one who pronounces *dikai*.[58]

Here it is to be noted that there exists by this time a whole vocabulary of words for things and acts which are not "according to *dikê*." Thus it is at this stage in the story that we first encounter another verb, *dikaioun*, derived from the adjective *dikaios*, and used by Herodotus, according to Suidas, in two meanings, "to punish" and "to consider consonant with *dikê*." In two passages of Herodotus, certainly, the word refers to punishment, for in one an Oriental monarch, "if he found anyone acting insolently, sent for him and *justified* him according to the desert of his wrongdoing."[59] Here the word is used exactly as, in Scottish legal phrase, a criminal is "justified" when he is "executed;" what is "executed," in any event, being the ruling of the judge, not the offender. In the other passage, also descriptive of Oriental tyranny, a forbidden festival was abandoned, and the priests were "justified," that is, paid the uttermost penalty.[60] A third is ambiguous, as befits the oracle of the "rolling stone;" "It shall fall upon men who rule alone, and shall justify Corinth."[61] But as Corinth had been the victim as well as the scene of misgovernment, Suidas' doubt about the meaning is reasonable, for elsewhere the word is used in the other sense, as when Crœsus says to Cyrus, "Since the gods gave me to thee for a slave, I *think it proper*, if I observe anything further, to make it known to thee;" and of the Persians it is said that on their birthday they "*think it proper* to spread a more plentiful table than on other days;" this is, in fact, their *diké*, the way birthdays are kept in Persia.[62] And this is the commoner usage, as when Mardonius, against the advice of Artabazus, urged Xerxes to attack the Greek force where he found it, "according to Persian custom; and he thus *justifying* his opinion, no one objected, and he prevailed, for he, and not Artabazus, had command of the army from the king."[63] Pindar, however, has the word in something like the positive sense; when he speaks of "custom [or law] *justifying* extreme violence,"[64] though with closer adherence to the primitive meaning of "setting straight." Æschylus, too, in a very difficult passage [65] describes the wicked man "kicking the great altar of *Diké* to oblivion, and wretched Reason [persuasion] suffers violence; . . . but, like bad bronze, with rubbing and blows it shows black spots, when *justified*, since the child is pursuing a winged bird . . .;" that is, under treatment intended to make it behave like good bronze, it betrays its worthlessness; it has professed something beyond its real normal behaviour; the child finds that he cannot fly, and disaster follows.

It is this primitive aspect which explains the association of the personified *Dikê* with the "gods below" in the famous lines of Sophocles, where Antigonê answers Creon's question why she ventured to disobey what he calls "these laws," *nomoi*, actually his own edict: "it was not Zeus who proclaimed these, nor *Dikê*, fellow lodger with the gods below, who set these 'laws' among men, nor did I think thy proclamations have so much force that, being a man, thou couldst overrun the god's unwritten and unshaken customs."[66] But neither in Sophocles nor in the characterisations of *Dikê* in Æschylus, is her function strictly or primarily punitive.[67] In the *Suppliants* it is not she but "another Zeus"[68] who judges offences among the dead with what are described as "last *dikai;*" though clearly wherever these *dikai* were, personified *Dikê* was "fellow lodger"; and in the *Choephoroe* "The swift turn of *dikê* oversees some men in daylight, . . . and some eternal night holds."[69] She guides no less the good ruler who "chooses *dikê* as his ally" and "discerns reverence to the gods"; she is still the source of orderliness rather than the avenger of disorder.

190

THE NOTION OF JUSTICE

DIKÊ REPLACING *NEMESIS*

But there is nevertheless a difference between
the quality of *dikê* in the Heroic Age and in the
Hellenic. The Homeric king being "Zeus-
born" is qualified to ascertain the divine will
and apply it to the particular case. There
might be a bad king, here and there, but between prestige and family pride and a large
measure of personal, if not inherited, ability,
the system worked; the strong man "keeping
his palace till a stronger than he should come
upon him," as eventually befell. In Hesiod
it is another picture: most "kings" are bad;
they are "devourers of gifts"; they fear not
God nor regard man; their dispensation of
"justice" is unjust. Here and there the old
blood throws up a man "whom the Muses
love," but this is rare enough to be idealized.
It is the aftermath of the conquest period, an
"iron age" following the "heroic"; for Hesiod
is describing conditions in the conquest area
of central Greece. And what he desiderates
and demands is not a return to "heroic" conditions, but the observance, by those now in
power, of an already abstract and even person-
fied *dikê*, in performing their actual functions.
Nor for him is there hope of improvement; as
time goes on "not even a man of his oath and
of *dikê* and of goodness shall find favour, but,

rather, in a doer of evil and insolence will they see worth: *dikê* shall be in the strong hand and self-respect shall not be at all, . . . and then shall *Aidôs* and *Nemesis* leave mankind and go to Olympus."

In a much later stage, and with a different perspective of the prehistoric past, in which the cataclysms were of nature's making, not man's, Plato reverses this process, and describes the arrival of *Aidôs* among men. "They strove indeed to congregate and maintain themselves, by founding *poleis*: consequently, when they were congregated, they began to wrong one another"—quite literally "to behave without *dikê*," and therefore irregularly—"seeing they had not the art of living in a *polis;* so that they dispersed again and were being destroyed. Zeus then, fearing for our race, lest it perish, sends Hermes bringing to men *Aidôs* and *Dikê*, to be orderers of *poleis* and bonds of friendship drawing men together."[70] But here the consort of *Aidôs* is not *Nemesis* but *Dikê;* and this is significant. The vague popular feeling that this or that is "not done" is replaced by the positive and more precise notion that there *is* a right way, as well as many wrong ways, of doing everything; and that among men of self-respect, respect for the other fellow takes the rational course of ascertaining what he habitually does and how he does it, and then taking account of that: this is what makes society orderly, and draws people nearer together. Now, in this Platonic phrase, we are not far from the Aristotelian view of society as having originated by coalescence of natural groups originally distinct and unconnected;[71] and of the overcoming of this mutual unacquaintance, as the greatest step toward civilized life: "for he who first introduced them to each other was the author of the greatest blessings."[72]

THE FUNCTION OF DIKÊ IN THE NASCENT POLIS

Now, it is at this precise point—so wholly inconsistent with the general position which Aristotle is concerned to defend, that the *polis* came into existence "in the way of growth" or "naturally," not by any convention or formal agreement—that his conception of the crucial point in the formation of city-states as he knew them anticipates the discovery, in comparatively recent times, of the completeness of the disintegration of the previous social order, and the historical causes of this. In the "refugee-states," as we may conveniently call them, all sorts of men, from different districts, of different tribes and systems of tribes, speaking different dialects, worshipping different gods, observing

different customs and prohibitions, found themselves accidentally and violently forced into
close neighbourhood, in refugee-areas, and in
hastily extemporized flotillas of pilgrim-fathers
seeking new homes, and encountering there
other such social wreckage; or encountered,
themselves only recently established, by later
arrivals.

Some sort of accidental sorting together of
old neighbours, or fellow worshippers, we may
assume to have been happening from the first,
as has been happening since the catastrophe
of 1922 in every refugee-area of modern Greece,
and as happens in the cafés of the Greek
quarter in an American city;[73] and the tribe-
names of some of the older Ionian cities are
eloquent memorials of this process.

But to "congregate" thus, on the basis of
similar antecedents or customs, was unavoid-
ably also to segregate men of different habits,
to revive old feuds, or at best to accentuate
contrasts between the most coherent and
strongly characterised elements in the mixed
multitude. And there are glimpses, in the
folkmemory of more than one Greek city, of
quarrels and secessions resulting from that
tragic "lack of *dikê*"; absence, that is, of the
needful agreement as to what "was done,"
and what "not done," between men each of

whom was only trying to observe the "way of doing things" habitual to himself in happier days. Every new country necessarily passes through this phase of experience; and that is why this ancient adventure of the refugee colonisation is one of those historical occasions which cannot lose their value, however difficult it may be to reconstruct it in more than very fragmentary detail.

When we were dealing with the genesis of authority, of initiative in dealing with emergencies of general concern, we saw the "divine-born" hereditary chieftaincies giving place to the personal eminence of gifted individuals, irrespective of their antecedents; to prestige based on achievements; to the conception of *arkhé* as a gift of the gods to the "man whom the Muses love;" to the honours, almost divine, paid by the rest to the man who "made them to be at home;" and in due course to the philosopher's conception of the "man who first made them acquainted with each other," as the "author of the greatest blessings."

And on the side of law it was the same as in administration. In homogeneous societies, such as those ruled by the Homeric kings, the supreme reinforcement of the self-respect of the individual, chief or commoner, was the general opinion that this or that misconduct

"would not do," just because it "was not done";
and in an age of adventure, such as that which
produced the Achæan and the Trojan confederacies, there was no less agreement, based on
experience and argument, as to the limits of
self-seeking; an unwritten code of gentlemanly
conduct, of that chivalry which is the product
of precisely those circumstances of concurrent
enterprise which have created all the "Heroic
Ages" which history records.

But in refugee society each man, or at best
each still-coherent group of people, whatever
the bond which still kept them together, had
its own "way of doing things," its own customs
of maintenance and intercourse, of land tenure,
marriage, worship, and herewith as many occasions on which to find that the new neighbours'
customs in the same affairs of life were different,
and even abhorrent. And there were now usually no "divine-born" kings—or, at best, very
few of them, like the Codrid emigrants from
Attica—with recognized competence to elicit
themistes from gods universally revered. The
themistes consequently recede from view, and
the personified *Themis* becomes a memory of
ancient days. She had been the child and
successor of "Earth, first source of revelation,"
and in her turn she gives place to her own child,
who is *Dikê*, that "way of doing things," which

is now the consort and external sanction of
Aidôs, as *Nemesis*, the public resentment
of other repositories of "initiative," had been
before. And this "way of doing things," though
the gift of Zeus, and an essential part of the
natural endowment and birthright of humanity,
is now nevertheless, in its content and meaning,
a discovery made by man; or, rather, a sequence
of particular discoveries made by a succession
of men, accumulated in human memory and
interpreted by reason and experience.

Thus there might be, and had been, "crooked
dikai," which were revealed as perversions of the
real "way" of behaviour by sad experience
that they did not tally either with each other,
or with those "unforgetting" *dikai*, in which
nothing was left out of account that was relevant to the matter. But it was only in communities where either there had never been
complete interfusion of alien elements, as in
the "conquest states" which produced the
cynical satire of Hesiod and of Theognis; or
where subsequent events and altered circumstances drew men apart and created differences
of status and behaviour which prevented them
from "knowing one another," as in the Lesbos
of Alcæus or the Paros of Archilochus, that
there was risk of such prevalence of "crooked"
failure or neglect to "discern *dikai*," as threat-

ened to drive *Aidôs* and its old safeguard *Nemesis* back to Olympus.

We are now in a position to reconstruct the stages by which the legal procedure of a Greek city-state in classical times came into being. The first stage is presented to us in examples attributed to the Heroic Age, in the Homeric poems; and if it be objected that the poems in their present form cannot be shown to go back to the age which they describe, and, therefore, are not trustworthy witness to its customs, it will, I think, at all events, be conceded that the procedure described belongs to a stage of social development at which (1) society was still tribal; (2) the clans of which it consisted were still so loosely connected that the "avenger of blood" still claimed his option of refusing *wergeld*, and taking life for life; (3) civil cases were still perhaps decided by the spoken *dikê* of a "divine-born" king; but (4) the sole court of appeal in a criminal case was an assembly of elder men sitting in open *agorá*, apparently without any kind of president.

THE "TRIAL SCENE" ON THE HOMERIC SHIELD OF ACHILLES.

The first stage, then, is presented to us in examples attributed in the Homeric poems to the Heroic Age. In these justice is administered in two ways, applicable to two distinct kinds of case. Civil actions, to use modern terminology, in which loss or injury has been inflicted by one person on another, of a kind which permits of reparation, are brought by the complainant to the "divine-born" king, who examines the facts and utters a *dikê*, the fulfilment of which sets matters straight between the parties.

Criminal actions, on the other hand, involving violation of the corporate existence of one tribal group, through the destruction of one of its members by a member of another such group within the same community, are settled not by any restitution in kind, (for that, in the case supposed, is impossible); but by the more or less voluntary acceptance of a compensation substituted for the primitive practice of retribution in kind, which (it is seen) would merely add another deed of violence to that already done, and, in fact, settle nothing, besides robbing the community of two good fighting men instead of one. The procedure in this kind of action is different; and whatever its precise form, it is something apart from the civil jurisdiction of the "divine-born" king. It has been variously interpreted, even in quite modern times, and by competent students of early law, but without complete mastery of the evidence. In what follows it can only be claimed that certain mistakes have been detected and avoided; no claim is made that the picture is even now accurate at all points.

The passage is the familiar "Trial Scene" on the Shield of Achilles (*Iliad*, XVII, 497–508), and its statements are as follows, line by line:

(497) *clans were in place-of-meeting assembled:* they are *laoi*, the adult male population of the community, grouped by kindreds, as they would be arrayed in war, or for any other public business in their *agorá* (p. 71). It is what in early Rome was called *comitia curiata;* a "coming-together" of *curiæ* or kinship groups. *And*
(498) *there a strife had arisen, and two men were*
(499) *striving about bloodprice of a man who had died (or been killed).*[74] The occasion of dispute is in the past, but strife still goes on; it has not been settled yet, at the moment depicted by the artist of the Shield. The meaning of *poiné*, "wergeld," or "price of blood," is well attested, in other Homeric passages,[75] and also the facts (*a*) that for a death in battle no *poiné* was paid,[76] (*b*) that *poiné* included ransom paid for a living person, in killing whom his captor would have been within his rights; it consequently originated as a

ransom for the life of the murderer, which was forfeit under the primitive practice of life-for-life retribution. The "two men" are clearly the murderer and the avenger-of-blood, not their advocates, as has been suggested through a misinterpretation of 508 which is discussed in its place.

(499) *the one asserted that he paid it all*, namely, the accustomed price-of-blood; not that he *had* paid it, but that payment was there, tendered for acceptance. From another passage we learn that, if such payment was accepted by all concerned, the murderer could stay in the country without offence to others or risk to himself;[77] but there was the chance that he had not in his assoilment included everyone concerned,[78] and in such a predicament he might find it safer to go away.[79] Therefore, for greater security, he is described as—

(500a.) *asserting it to the countryside*, to the whole crowd of onlookers[80] from the district, irrespective of status or coherence, or interest in the business; it is public notice, required by custom, so as to reach everyone concerned.

(500b.) *but he* (the other man) *denied that he*

took any of it; not "that he *had* not taken" anything already, nor (as was formerly explained) that he had not had the opportunity of taking anything,[81] through refusal of the accused man to offer it; but that (in vulgar phrase) he "was not taking any;" he was asserting, that is, his right to have blood-for-blood.

(501) *and both were hurrying, to get a settlement at (the hands of) a man-who-knows.* The word for "settlement," *peirar,* is literally, like *telos,* the "ending" of any matter, after which nothing further can happen. It is also used, like *arkhé,* for the end of a rope, or for a rope used to confine or terminate the activity of any thing. The "man-who-knows" (*istor*) recurs in the narrative of a disputed race,[82] where Agamemnon is to act as umpire: it consequently denotes here either the whole body of elders who are described in 503 below or (more probably) the man, whoever he might be, who eventually uttered the *mot juste* which was accepted as putting the matter in the right light, so that both parties accepted his formulation. When the word recurs in post-Homeric and in classical Greek it is always in its literal sense.[83]

202

(502) *And clans-folk cheered on both, on either hand to help them.* These are the kinsmen of the two principals, concurring in their respective contentions, and prepared to support them at need: they are not the whole crowd, but coherent sections of it, each with its own *locus standi* in the case. We are reminded (1) of the Helvetian trial when Orgetorix came to the place of meeting, like a Scottish chieftain, with so large an armed following of clansmen that the court was overawed and dissolved;[84] (2) of the Icelandic litigant's habitual care to induce influential neighbours to "ride with him to the assembly."[85]

(503a.) *and heralds were restraining the people*, the singular *laos* being used, as we have already seen (p. 71), as a collective expression for the whole assembly in its organic business-transaction capacity; it is the human content of an *agorá*. That is why it is controlled by "heralds," *kerykes*, who elsewhere in Homer only attend on individual chiefs; we may presume that these "heralds" were the several *kerykes* of the "old men" who appear next in the picture.

(503b.) *and the old men sat on dressed stones in*

*a sacred ring, and they were holding in
their hands staves of loud-voiced heralds.*
These elders are presumed as familiar
figures; the place of their session is also
familiar, and very briefly described; it
amplifies in structural detail the sketch
of the *agorá* in the camp of Odysseus
(p. 124), and raises the question whether
the *themis* in that meeting place was
an extemporized "drumhead" counterpart of this ring of masonry in a city-at-
peace. It is not clear why these elders
should hold heralds' staves unless the
poet intends to distinguish them from
"divine-born kings" who had inherited
staves of their own. From the absence
of any mention of a president, and from
the order of their sitting, it would seem
reasonable to infer that this is a "round-
table" conference between heads of co-
equal kindred-groups. But in that case,
who or what is the *istor*, the "man-who-
knows"? Either the word is used collectively for "that-which-knows," as the
Icelandic *thing* is the assembly which
deliberates and bargains; or must we
picture a presidential "man who knows,"
and regard the "old men" as his assessors?
But it is difficult to explain how such a

president should take no active part in
the proceedings; and there can, in fact,
be little doubt that the conference here
is between co-equals, and represents an
alternative procedure to that of the
"*dikê*-handling" chieftain, in civil cases.
Athenian criminal procedure offers a close
analogy, as we shall see below (p. 231?).

(506) *To them they were speeding and in turn
they were giving their "dikai."* At this
point, after the description of the court,
the narrative is resumed from 501a.
The litigants, followed by their supporters, are depicted arriving before the
circle of elders, and by a facile artistic
convention the elders are simultaneously
arguing the case: on the Shield itself the
gestures of their staves would be sufficient to indicate this.[86] That it is the
elders, not the litigants, who are now
described as "giving *dikai*" is certain,
for the active verb is never used elsewhere
except of the man who is examining the
case.[87] Of the litigant's action, the
middle verb is used—"to get a *dikê* given
for oneself."[88]

(507) *and there lay then in the midst of them
two talents of gold, to give to him who, together with them, should utter a "dikê"*

most straightly. The "two talents" cannot be the "blood-price," as some have
supposed, because elsewhere [89] half-a-
talent was worth less than an ox; a whole
talent consequently much less than two
oxen; yet a female slave was worth four
oxen, and a free man, therefore, very
much more than two talents. But if
the two talents were a reward for the
ruling eventually accepted as "most
straight" (or, rather, "most straightening," contributing most to "put things
straight"), to whom were they to be
paid? Not to any member of the court
of elders, for they were present officially,
and it was a term of abuse to call a "king"
a "devourer of gifts," or a "consumer of
the *demos:*"[90] he was a public servant,
and had his proper maintenance; the
chieftain of a clan, similarly, was there
as spokesman of his kindred, whose
interest it was that public order should
be vindicated. Other passages, in which
the same phrase, "together with" others,
occurs, all denote an addition to the
group or class described;[91] there is no
difference, such as has been suggested,
between the usages of the *Iliad* and the
Odyssey. The alternative seems una-

voidable (and is wholly congruous with
what we know of other procedures in
tribal societies), that in an *agorá* there
was freedom of speech for all persons
qualified to be present, and that for the
voluntary and effective help of such an
amicus curiæ there was a customary fee
of moderate amount, defined in advance,
and awarded by the fact that the elders
agreed to adopt his *formula* as "more
straightening" than their unaided wisdom. As Mr. Zimmern has seen,[92] this
fee "is the lineal ancestor of the much-
abused fees which were paid to the large
popular juries in fifth-century Athens";
but if his explanation, that "it is not
given to all the justices on the bench,
but only to the 'straightest speaker,' "
means the "straightest speaker" among
the justices themselves, he would seem
to have missed the significance of his
own words. For the later "guildhall
fees," *prytaneia*, were paid to popular
courts, the function of which was to give
utterance to that public common sense
which in the Homeric picture is inherent in any member of an *agorá*; not
to courts such as that of *Areopagus* and
its judicial committees, on which de-

volved the functions of this early conference of elders, representing the common interest of their respective clans. Summarizing now the procedure described in this Homeric picture, there is no dispute as to the facts of the case; the murder is admitted, the murderer is known and within reach, the blood-price has been offered; the only question is, whether the avenger-of-blood *must* accept it, or *might* claim his freedom to take life-for-life? This is a point not of custom, for both customs evidently existed as alternatives, but of discussion, as in ancient Iceland, and choice of the preferable alternative; in the general interest of all incorporated clans, and of the discovery of some *dikê*, some way of describing the situation, which will reconcile conflicting claims, and bring appeasement and acceptance of the restored order by all concerned. Such a *dikê* is precisely what in Roman law is called a *formula;* in such a case as is at issue, on the Shield Scene, it might run as follows: *Si quis hominem interfecerit parentibusque poenam ultro duit, qui parens poenam accipere noluerit, sacer estod*: "If anyone has killed a man, and voluntarily offered blood price to his kindred, if that kinsman is not willing to accept blood-price, let him be *tabu*"—excommunicated from converse with fellow men whose "way of doing things" is acceptance. Insofar as the *dikê* in this case is a "child of *themis*," the parental *themis* is conceived to be, that "for blood spilt restitution follows." That is the "voice of the gods," their will-and-pleasure; but the manner of restitution is a matter for human discussion and adjustment, and is effected by a *dikê*, by "finding a way" of doing that which will be indeed "restitution" of the state of things which the murderer violated.

Exactly in the same way, in the procedure of the Cretan city of Gortyna, if in any case brought to court an accepted way of behaviour already exists, the function of the court is simply "let the giver-of-*dikai* pronounce his *dikê*,"—*formulam det*. If, however, either the facts are not clearly stated, or there is no accepted principle of behaviour applicable to the case, procedure goes further: the "giver of *dikai*" has to be put under an obligation, "fenced in" against evil contrivance and human error. This oath, *horkos*, is a cognate of *herkos*, a "fence," and of our *exorcism*, which puts evil things and persons "outside the fence." Similarly, the Roman *obligatio* is a "tethering" of the man so that he cannot stray and run risks; a reinforcement of that internal restraint on conduct for which the Roman word is *religio*. With his own common

sense thus fortified he will hear truly the voice
of the gods, and what he now utters is a *themis*,
which, like the Athenian *thesmoi*, which we
shall encounter next, becomes part of the
public store of such utterances, the case-law
of the city-state.

In the next recognizable stage of advancement, which is already well within the political
history of the Hellenic *polis*, namely, the procedure of the Athenians before the first publication of a written code,[93] "the magistrates
(*arkhontes*, literally,' 'those who are initiating,"
or "have *arkhé*") were "competent also to
discern *dikai* which were self-fulfilled, and not,
as nowadays, to make (only) preliminary discernment." Their initiative, that is to say,
carried the matter right through to achievement, without intervention from any quarter;
if there were ambiguities on the facts, or alternatives in law, it was theirs to distinguish them
and choose that *formula* which was "most
straightening" under the circumstances. This
is in exact accord with the procedure conserved
(till the fifth century, probably) at Gortyna;
and it was the risk of mistaken, corrupt, and
in either event "crooked" *dikai* from such irresponsible "initiators" that led to the long
series of innovations which are the history of
Attic legal procedure.

THE NOTION OF JUSTICE

Quite new provision for "straight," coherent,
"unforgetful" *dikai* was made when the newly
popularized art of writing was applied to the
conservation of them for future use. Writing
in Greek lands does not seem ever to have
wholly become obsolete; though the rarity of
its use on other than perishable materials,
after the collapse of the Minoan regime, makes
it difficult to follow the change from the old
syllabaries to those alphabetic systems which
are common to all Mediterranean cultures in
the Early Iron Age, from the Phœnician cities
on the Syrian coast to the Iberian peoples of a
large part of Spain. In Attica its use ante-
dates all other symptoms of reviving intercourse with less harassed lands oversea, in
arts or industries; and the earliest Attic example
of it is at all events for a semi-public purpose,
the designation of a painted jug as the prize in
a dancing match—"Whosoever now of all
dancers makes sport most delicately, this let
him receive."[94] The vase cannot well be later
than the seventh century, and (but for this
inscription) the style of its fabric and deco-
ration would assign it to the eighth or ninth.
In the seventh century, at all events, we may
be sure that there were people who could write;

and it is in accord with this evidence, that Athenian tradition placed about the middle of that century the first appointment of officials called *thesmothetai*, "setters-down of *thesmoi*." In later times they had the general management of the judicial system, and also the custody of official copies of all public enactments and (more important still) the duty of annually reviewing them, reporting on anomalies and imperfections, and drafting the legislation necessary to make things work smoothly.[95] None of these, however, can well have been their original function, because when they were first appointed there was no judicial system except the unfettered initiative of those magistrates who tried cases;—we shall have to enquire presently who these were. There was no legislation in the strict sense of the word, and consequently no occasion for amending acts.[96] What, then, were the *thesmoi*, which they were originally constituted to "set down"?

The word *thesmos* is rare. It occurs only once in Homer, and in the quite general sense of a regular mode of behaviour; it is conduct in accordance with what is *themis*, as a *logismos* or "reckoning" is a calculation in accordance with *logos*, "reason" or "common sense," which consequently "explains itself." When Odysseus and Penelope were reunited after long absence "joyously then they reached the *thesmos* of their bed of long ago."[97] The Homeric hymns have the word once, "to remain in the harmless *thesmoi* of peace," again meaning a way of behaviour.[98] Solon in the early sixth century says that he "wrote *thesmoi* for the bad and the good alike, adapting to each a straight *dikê*;"[99] and a few lines earlier in the same poem, describing his economic reforms, he says that "these things I did by force, yoking together violence and *dikê*, and went through [with them] as I promised." His achievement, therefore, was a series of *thesmoi*, forcibly substituted for those then observed, but making it possible (as those older ones did not) to "adapt a straight *dikê*" to each individual's case.[100] This was good contemporary practice, for only a few years before Draco had entitled with the same word *thesmos* each of the ordinances which he found in observance. Æschylus makes the Furies describe their own "facile and effective" function as "solemn warners of disasters, and hard for men to dissuade," and ask, "What mortal does not respect and fear this, hearing from me a *thesmos*, fate-decreed from the gods, given effectually? In me is [this] prerogative from old time, nor do I lack acknowledgment."[101] They are charged, that is, by heaven to lay this "doom" or "ordinance" on men, precisely as a Homeric king reveals the "voice of the gods." In the same play Athena says she will ordain as "a *thesmos* for all time" the procedure of the Athenian murder trial with sworn "givers of *dikai*;" the Furies greet this announcement as a "landslide of new *ordinances*;" but later Apollo confirms Athena's phrase, adding that it "is in accord with *dikê*." For Sophocles, "desire sits by in the initiatives of great *thesmoi*," describing the "ordinance" of marriage which ordains the "way" of the satisfaction of it, quite in the Homeric sense:[102] and a few lines after this, "now I myself too am carried outside *thesmoi*, at sight of this, and can no longer restrain fountains of tears." All normal observances, that is, great or small—from matrimony to manners—are *thesmoi*. Similarly, Herodotus, describing the high court of justice in Persia, says that "the royal justices give *dikai* to the Persians and act as interpreters of their ancestral *thesmoi*, and everything is referred to them."[103] Of their occasional dilemmas he gives an absurd instance. "To the enquiry of Cambyses," who was eccentric and wanted to marry his sister, "they replied what was at the same time in accord with *dikê* and without risk [to themselves], saying that they found no law which enjoins that a brother should marry a sister, but that they

214

had discovered another, permitting the king of Persia to do what he liked." Good law, and sound policy too, for Cambyses had a short way with "royal judges."[104]

Thus the formal utterances of a public official on matters of procedure or behaviour were *thesmoi*, and it was probably these that the *thesmothetai* were instituted to "set down," in the early days of Attic writing. Vinogradoff says that "they were originally magistrates formulating law as well as enforcing it."[105] But he gives no reason for supposing that they "formulated" law in any other sense than as all "initiative" officers habitually did so, when all the "law" there was, consisted of the *thesmoi* of such "initiators." Their number, six, is anomalous, fitting neither with the four-fold classification of kindreds in Attica, nor with the ten-fold arrangement, of which there are traces there early, as well as in the tribal reform of Cleisthenes. They are also the earliest recorded example of a strictly collegiate magistracy at Athens; and they are the first magistrates whose place of business (*thesmotheteion*) was named after them instead of retaining older associations in its name than those of its eventual use. The Athenian *Basileus*, for example, sat at the *Boukolion*, the "cow-shed" of some forgotten palace or sanctuary;[106]

the *Archon*, in the *Prytaneion* or "chief's house" itself; the *Polemarchos*, "at the Lyceum" (*Lykeion*), an old chapel on the drill ground outside the walls, rebuilt later for his proper use, but keeping the old name *Epilykeion*.

This is the more remarkable since the state archives were not kept at the *thesmotheteion* but in the *metrôon*, the temple of the Mother of the Gods. But their special premises and their abnormal numbers cohere when we remember that the primitive *arkhé*, the initiative chieftaincy of Athens, had been dissolved into its principal functions and was held in what may be described as "departmental commission." This is clearest in regard to the *Polemarchos*, or War-lord, whose special initiative was first conferred on him, so tradition said, when in an emergency there was a king "soft for fighting," over-age, that is (like Theseus when the people instituted the office for Ion, "sending for him when need seized on them"), or otherwise unfit for field service. It is implicit, too, in the account given of the *Archon*, and in his name, a present participle like the Latin "regent," signifying a provisional "initiator" whenever a king was, so to speak, "soft for business"; and consequently long a perquisite of the old royal family, the Medontid clan; originally quite supplementary, but, as

216

the *Athenian Constitution* puts it, "magnified by what was put upon it,"[107] a kind of official "maid-of-all-work," looking, for example, after disreputable foreign worships like that of Dionysus, which were quite beneath the notice of the high-priestly *Basileus*, and likely, moreover, to require the attendance of the chief constable rather than the archbishop, especially in the later stages of festivity.

Now, each of these collateral "chief executives" had, of course, judicial as well as administrative competence within the class of public business which came his way and was habitually propounding *thesmoi*, leading principles of behaviour, as well as *dikai* to interpret them in individual cases. And it was inevitable that, in time, cases which had several aspects, affecting, for example, individual or kindred rights or divine prerogatives as well as public security, were liable to be decided differently according as they were brought before a lay or military or religious tribunal, and were decided under the *thesmoi* of growing systems of civil, martial, or canon law. Moreover, the new art of writing was at first a rare art and mystery; how could the *archon* be sure that his clever "writer" had taken down his wise words accurately? Two pens being better than one, for exact record, the *thesmothetai* or "recorders"

217

were twinned: out of the notes of two wit-
nesses every word should be established. Consequently, there came into being, probably
at about the same time, three pairs of "recorders"; and from the first, with the same obvious
motive of securing co-ordination among the
three irresponsible jurisdictions, all six found
it convenient to meet and compare notes, and
were furnished with new premises as their
common office. Hence the first collegiate
magistracy at Athens, its custody of public
records, and its revisory function. Hence,
too, its eventual acquisition of judicial functions of its own; for, if you could find out from
one of the *thesmothetai* what *thesmoi* there were,
governing your case, what need for intelligent
men to trouble any of the three principal
"initiators"? The juridical functions of the
"recorder" in the City of London and other
ancient English boroughs illustrate the same
devolution of legal business from a chief magistrate to his scribe. Indeed, so fully occupied
did this board of "recorders" eventually become that they had no time to perform their
primary task of taking notes in court, and were
superseded by a new secretariat of six *paredroi*
nominated two-a-piece by each of the principal
justices to sit by them and record their rulings,
as the *thesmothetai* had done originally.[108]   But

it was only in Solon's time, when reform was in the air, and when also legal business was multiplying rapidly, that the six *thesmothetai* and the three principal officers began, or were enjoined, to meet all together, and became the anomalous board of "nine archons" which had general initiative in · Athenian administration during the sixth century. How easily such anomalies become accepted as part of the traditional order of things is shown by the fact that though the increase of public business, in the eighty years which separate the reforms of Solon from those of Cleisthenes, led to the creation of a first-magnitude "secretary," *grammateus*, this *grammateus*, though elected in the same way and at the same time as the other Archons, and a member of their "college," is never quoted as the "Secretary-Regent"[109] (as the *Basileus* was the "King Regent"); and the whole board of "regents" is never described as the "ten" but always as the "9 + 1"; the *Nine Archons and the Grammateus*.

There is no reason for assuming that the records of the *thesmothetai* were published at first. Indeed, if they had been accessible to all, it is difficult to see what was the meaning of that publication of *thesmoi* by Draco, at the end of the seventh century, which so closely resembles the publication of the *formulæ* by Cn. Flavius, at an analogous stage in the development of the legal procedure of the Romans, and the appointment of a "speaker" in the *Althing* assembly in Iceland, whose duty it was, being the most learned "law-man" available, to recite publicly all the law (or laws) that he knew, in the course of the annual session. Moreover, writing is an art which may be well known and habitually practised by those who need it, without being at all common otherwise. Even among a "musical" people, what proportion of persons can "write" music? But when such an art has begun to be employed for purposes of publication, by the few who can write, the number of those who can read, without themselves writing, increases rapidly. For one person, similarly, who can "write" music, there may be a hundred or more who can "read" it, to the extent of "singing from notes."

The Legal Code of Gortyna

It is a further question, not easily answered, whether what Draco published were the *thesmoi* of his predecessors, or those which he added to the traditional stock of *thesmoi* during his term of office, or substituted for them. But it is not of great importance, for, as the "giver of *dikai*" was required to give his ruling on every case submitted to him, it was only a matter of submitting a large variety of cases to obtain a whole code of rulings. And the knowledge that a clear-headed and unprejudiced man now had "initiative" in such matters was itself enough to bring into court many cases of injustice, where hitherto a "crooked" ruling had seemed a remedy worse than the disease. At this point the procedure at Gortyna is instructive,[110] for there, if the *dikastes* found either the facts or the law obscure, he fortified himself, as we have seen, with an "obligation" and delivered a *themis* which was added to the code; and at Gortyna the code was public by the time that we have any knowledge of it.

The mode of publication at Gortyna is worthy of notice. In its present form the *thesmoi* are carved, in roughly classified order of clauses, on the inner face of the wall of a circular public building, which we may presume to have been the courthouse, and probably the covered-in successor of such a "sacred circle of smoothed stones" as is described in the "Trial Scene" (pp. 203-4). As the inscribed building is of fine Hellenic masonry, not earlier than the sixth century, and as the clauses have been classified, it may be inferred that most of these clauses, which are drafted in the same hypothetical form as the *thesmoi* of Draco, had originated as *thesmoi* of this or that Gortynian *dikastes*, and had been simply painted or scratched on the bare wall of an earlier court house, just as the decrees conferring the status of *proxenos* on certain citizens and their descendants are found incised on the walls of the public hall of Aptera, another city of Crete, and as manumissions were registered on the terrace-wall below the Temple of Apollo at Delphi.[111] We are reminded of that minor functionary the "painter," *pictor*, who attended a Roman *prætor* and recorded his *formulæ*, his lists of assessors, and the like, on a "whiteboard," *album*, which has given its name in later times to any kind of scrapbook for miscellaneous notes. A generation after Draco the practice of immediate publication was well established; it is attested by the form in which Solon's "custumal," or collection of *nomoi*— in Roman terminology his *edictum*—was devoutly preserved by his successors, on those *kurbeis* and *axones*, the latter of which at all events are shown, by their name of "pivots" or "spindles," to have had some of the convenience of a modern "revolver" bookcase.

With *thesmoi* and *dikai* once published, and as we see them at Gortyna, roughly classified as opportunity occurred, "it was possible" at Athens after Draco, for example, "for the man who had experienced an injury (a 'failure of *dikê*') to send such information to the Council of Areopagus, making declaration, in despite of what *nomos* is his failure to obtain *dikê*."[112] In this procedure the injured person is presumed to know what laws there are, which of them applies to his case, and in what respect the *formula* of a public "giver-of-*dikai*" has failed to give effect to its provisions. Later, when the judicial initiative of the great "public servants" or "regents" had been reduced to preliminary formulation of the issues, and the decision lay with a popular tribunal (p. 233), the only remaining occasions for these "informations" against them, or any other official, were arbitrary acts in their executive capacity; but it seems likely that this was a proper mode—and, indeed, the only constitutional mode—of bringing an "unjust judge" to a reckoning in pre-Solonian days.

It is in this sense that the "Council of Areopagus" was "guardian of the *nomoi*, and kept continuous watch upon the [holders of] initiative (*arkhê*) so that they might initiate in accordance with the *nomoi*." For such a "public servant" to use his initiative otherwise was clearly a breach of order—of the way things

happen, under the customs of that state—
and this was the common and immediate
concern of all the corporator-clans. Consequently, it was for the responsible headmen of
all those clans to confer and take agreed action
on any such incident brought to their notice.
It was the acceptance-in-common of an agreed
"way of living together" by these corporator-
clans, which had constituted that city-state
itself in the past; it was the acceptance of the
arkhé, the personal initiative of an agreed individual, as the means for the enforcement of
that "way of living together" on ill-behaved
persons, which had made possible in course
of time the formulation, in detail, of what
that "way of living' was; and it is consequently
for those who had admitted the sufficiency of
this or that man's "initiative," not, indeed,
necessarily to inhibit his exercise of it, but to
verify his interpretation of the facts or the
law of a case, in which it is claimed that he
has "left something out" which the combined
memory and common sense of the "elders,"
in conference assembled may serve to recall,
so that truth—"unforgetfulness"—may be
established, and therewith the real "way of
living together." There resided, that is, in
the corporator-kindreds, and was expressed
through their headmen in conference, precisely

what Aristotle eventually described as an "initiative without frontier."[113]

For the moment, however, we are only concerned with what he goes on to describe as the "distinguishing" or "critical" aspect of this initiative, which confronts judicially a given event with the "way of living" to which such an event was expected and required to conform, and, as we say, "tries" the case, as we "try" a spare part on a machine. We must remember, however, that this reserve power of initiative had also another aspect, namely, the "deliberative" or quite literally that which is "tending to decision"; that is, to "make up the mind" what the way of living really is. For it is not necessarily the temporary holder of initiative who has "left something out of account;" it may have been one of his predecessors who formulated a "way" which was "not straight."

PUBLIC OPINION AS CRITICISM
OF *DIKAI*

The significance of this two-fold function of public opinion—if we may venture so far to anticipate its nature at this stage—begins to be apparent at the very next step in the development of public law at Athens.

In the procedure of Gortyna, the *dikastes* had to protect and fortify himself with an "obligation" on two distinct occasions, according as it was the law or the fact that was not clear. The remedy of an Athenian citizen against a decision which was wrong-in-law, was, as we have seen, an "information" laid before the Council of Areopagus, quoting the relevant "law," *nomos*. It is less clear what remedy he had if he challenged the decision on the ground that it was wrong-in-fact. But it seems clear, from the later procedure in those classes of enquiries which were still within the cognisance of the Council of Areopagus or its judicial committees, that both kinds of appeal had followed the same course and had been adjusted in the same way to the next phase of judicial development, with which we have now to deal.

In many disputes and breaches of normal order, the normal "way of doing things" was obvious, and the only question was one of fact, whether there had been such a breach of order or not. In such a case what the *dikastes* had to do was twofold: first, to formulate the normal order, and in the event of disturbance, state the normal way of restoring it to the satisfaction of all parties; and then to ascertain whether the facts were as stated by either side. In a civil case, affecting only the rights and interests of individuals, circumstances such as custom-of-trade, extent of damage to property, and the like, varied widely, and involved technical points beyond the personal competence of any ordinary "public servant"; and the obvious remedy was for the holder of "initiative" to refer such a case, (after his preliminary investigation, *pro-ana-krisis*, which revealed its special character) either to a single person or to a committee or panel of persons with more or less special knowledge of the matter, together with a *formula* summarising the points of law, and the statements of fact which had been established by the magistrate's *pro-ana-krisis*.

Similarly, in a "criminal" case, involving breach of the corporate unity of a kindred group, or the infringement of any customary observance or abstinence, with risk (as was believed) of retaliatory action against the community as a whole, the "public servant" or "initiator" of the necessary procedure for the restitution of normal order—in questions of homicide, and grave religious offences, the *basileus*, on whom had descended this prerogative of the heroic kingship—himself "introduced" the question to a conference of headmen of clans, or in later Athenian procedure, to a panel of "referees," *ephetai*, drawn by lot from its members, and left them to "utter their *dikai*" according to their view of the matter.[114] In the fourth century this session of "referees" was still held under the open sky, like the conference of elders in the Trial Scene; and its character as an assemblage of heads of kindred-groups is further emphasised by the statement that "the *basileus* when he utters his *dikê* takes off his crown;" for, though appointed by lot, as his predecessors had been since 487 B.C., the *basileus* still ranked as a co-equal among other chiefs of clans, as well as a public official bringing the breach of order to their notice; he was a member of the bench, as well as public prosecutor; but if he chose to act in the former capacity, as one of his own referees, he divested himself of the symbol of his public office. In the light of this Athenian survival it is easy to understand the solution adopted by the artist of the Trial Scene (p. 202), when he makes the disputants "hasten to the man-who-knows," to get a settlement, but describes them as arriving before a circle of elders without recognisable president. A *basileus* in the Homeric sense may well have been there; but to make him a member of the court the poet has "taken off his crown"; just as he has given the other elders only "the staves of heralds" instead of their family sceptres.

In matters which came within its competence—and very likely in some which strictly did not—the Athenian Court of Areopagus, like the "public servants" whose transitory rulings it eventually had made good its claim to review on appeal, had in the first instance unqualified "initiative": "the council formerly was competent to fine and to imprison and to kill."[115] But a new period of advancement opened with the challenge of Eumelides on behalf of one Lysimachus, "asserting that no one ought to lose his life without the cognisance of a panel," using the term *dikasterion* which was appropriated from the sixth century onward to the panels of ordinary citizens for the hearing of cases "previously examined" by one of the great "justices" as already described.[116] The result of this challenge was a new *nomos*, or formulation of public procedure—phrased, we should note, in the traditional *formula* of a supposed event—"if the Court condemns anyone (to death) for wrongdoing, or fines him, the *thesmothetai* are to submit the condemnations or the finings to the *dikasterion*, and whatever the *dikastai* decide by vote, is to stand." We note here, first, that the "new *nomos*" went far beyond the special case challenged by Eumelides, and included fines as well as the death penalty; secondly, that the proper persons to present the court's

verdict for confirmation or reversal by the new
revising body are the *thesmothetai* in their collegiate capacity; the reason being that as official
custodians of accumulated case-law they were
the body best equipped to lay the whole question, as formulated by the Court, before the
revising body, which by the conditions of its
origin was no panel of experts but a fair sample
of ordinary citizen sense.

Solon's Revolution in Judicial Procedure

Though it was only as applied to the committees of members of the ancient Court of
Areopagus, that the term "referees," *ephetai*,
survived in the judicial vocabulary of Athens,
the verb "to refer," and its substantive "reference," *ephesis*, remained in use to describe the
procedure by which Solon effected the greatest
of his three revolutions in judicial procedure.

The first of these, as is generally accepted,
was merely the substitution of a new *thesmos*
for the procedure previously customary with a
defaulting debtor—"not to borrow on personal
security." This was a change within the competence of any "giver of *dikai*," on any occasion
when in the fuller comprehension of all the
circumstances which was vouchsafed to himself, he declared, like a *dikastes* of Gortyna,

that he knew no *themis* applicable to this case, and proceeded to utter a new one. So, too, in Rome no *prœtor* was obliged to incorporate his predecessor's rehearsal of his knowledge of the law in his own "edict"; and no Icelandic "speaker" was bound by the recitals of earlier "law-men," though it was usually convenient and just that he should do so. A late but instructive Roman example is Cicero's drastic revision of the *edictum perpetuum* of his Cilician province: one of the first lawyers of Rome happening, by a political accident, to be put in charge of a frontier province which had suffered "justification" by the drumhead procedure of amateur governors, more or less corruptible, for a whole generation.

Solon's second innovation, "to allow anyone who wished to intervene in a case on behalf of those who were being wronged," was likewise within his competence as a "giver of *dikai*": for it amounted in principle only to the recognition anew of the Homeric volunteer-in-the-crowd, or *amicus curiœ*, "whoever along with them [the court-elders] should utter a *dikê* which should be most straightening"(p. 205). In its new context it had, indeed, a fresh meaning, as recognition of that reserve power of "initiative" in every citizen, which we are coming to see to have been fundamental in

Greek notions of political "freedom." But the notion itself was ancient, and it is noteworthy that it should have been in Attica, so backward in many respects, just because its social structure was in certain ways so archaic, that this ancient root of individual "initiative" should have blossomed into so early a flower.

But it is on Solon's third change that our authorities lay the greatest stress, "whereby they say the multitude chiefly acquired its strength, namely the reference to the *dikasterion*; for the populace when it is master of the verdict, becomes master of the state." There is no need to suppose that it was in itself an innovation in Athens for one of the great "justices" to refer a difficult or technical case to an assessor. The *Polemarchos*, at all events, who as "war-lord" necessarily dealt with all suits between an Athenian and a foreigner—because out of such quarrels arise the *casus belli* —the occasions of war—can hardly have avoided more or less formal "reference" of judicial curiosities to the consular representative (*proxenos*) of the foreign litigant's city, or to any knowledgeable citizen of it who happened to be within hail. But that was at the discretion of the "giver of *dikai*" himself. He might "disregard" the voice of the wise stranger, as a corrupt king "disregarded the voice of the gods." What Solon did was to make such "reference" obligatory in all serious suits; the great "regents," or "public servants," with their separate executive "initiative" merged for all great occasions in the collegiate competence of the "Board of Nine," found their judicial competence similarly merged by way of preliminary review of the facts and law of the case, such as is performed by a "public prosecutor," in the "frontierless initiative" of the whole "multitude" of citizens; exercised, it is true, normally by a panel of its members, larger or smaller, according to circumstances; but in these greater emergencies (of the abuse of magisterial initiative in its executive aspect) always reserved to be wielded, not by any delegacy, but by the "sovereign people" itself.

Gradually, as evidence becomes available, the extent to which the *polis* had asserted and extended its competence to prescribe a procedure for the repair of breaches of order becomes apparent, and especially its supplementary and regulative function. The breaches of order in such a community were necessarily in one or more of three classes: offences wholly within the kinship group, offences committed by a member of one group against a member of another, and offences committed by a member of one group against another group corporately; and the *polis* intervened, in each of these classes of offence, in a different way.

A breach of order within a kinship group was, in principle, a matter for the group itself to adjust through its own head-man, and in unconstrained tribal society it made no difference whether the offence concerned the personal property or economic amenities of the person concerned—which are a very small matter in the simpler and more communally conducted societies—or the total vitality of the group, when one of its members has been extinguished by the act of a kinsman. On such occasions of domestic blood-guilt we find the descendants of Heracles, for example, expelling Tlepolemus, and other Homeric examples of independent action of the blood relatives.[117] Once incorporated in a *polis*, on the other hand, such a kinship-group found its initiative overridden by that of the political whole, partly because the diminution of the man-power of the damaged group was a matter of "political" concern to the rest, partly because the damaged group was very ill protected by its own remedy of expulsion, if the "exterminated" person was able to take cover among friends and neighbours unconcerned in his blood-guilt. The banishment formulæ pronounced by Athenian or Gortynian or Roman "public servants" against such offenders extend the "fence," or *tabu*, which cuts off the criminal from his own group, to every member of any associated group who continues to tolerate his company. Expulsion thus becomes not only gentile but territorial; and the primary function of such "extermination," which was to remove rather than to annihilate the offender, is recognisable in the venerable procedure of the Athenian "Court of the Guild Hall," *prytaneion*, which dealt with deaths by violence, the cause of which could not be traced beyond the deadly weapon, found in or by the corpse: for in this event, public order was deemed to have been vindicated when that offending object had been ceremoniously and officially cast forth from Attic territory.

A breach of order in the second class, between individual members of two different groups, not infringing the vitality of either of the groups themselves, but only deranging the enjoyment of "external goods" by the parties, obviously concerned the political society in which those groups were corporators, both as a provocation to retaliatory or vindictive acts, and as a kind of offence for which it was in the common interest that the remedy should be uniform; and for which also the wider experience of the "political" society provided, from a very early stage, the larger store of *dikai* and *thesmoi* on which to base the desired uniformity. Nothing prevented the settlement of any such affair either between the parties, or through the good offices of their respective kinsmen and friends. It was only when these kinds of "first aid" failed to restore things to their normal course that the aggrieved party had his appeal to the "public servant," the "man who knows" in his official capacity, for the exercise of his initiative; in the best event, to utter a *dikê* (=*formulam dare*) which was sufficient guide to the "way to behave"; or, failing agreement of this immediate kind, through the uncertainty or complexity of the facts, to nominate a more leisured and expert *dikastes*, or a panel of such men, to go into the matter in all its bearings, and establish the facts, and therewith the practical effect to be given to the *formula*. In Persia, as we have seen, such *dikastai* were "royal justices," *basilikoi dikastai*, holding their commission from the monarch as sole source of public "initiative"; in a Greek state they might accurately be described as *politikoi dikastai*, "justices of the *polis*," their function being to interpret and apply in particular instances the general principles on which "our people" behave. The result of their labours, recorded in due course and codified from time to time by *thesmothetai, thesmophylakes,* and the like, was commentary and interpretation, ever growing, and also ever gently shifting, a body of case-law founded, indeed, upon traditional customs and habits of behaviour, and deriving their coherence and logical validity from them, but formally stating for the most part not these principles themselves but precepts, hypothetically expressed, for the restoration of public order in the event of almost every conceivable type of infringement which stupidity or malice had effected in the past.

In the third class of breaches of order, when the act of an individual member of one incorporated group infringed the vitality of another group and impaired its totality by eliminating or seriously damaging one of its corporators, intervention on the part of the *polis* takes a different form and initiates a quite different procedure. For this breach of order is an act of war, a reversion to the "turbulence" which the *polis* had come into being to preclude; and it is the first function of the *polis* to insure each of its corporator-groups against such state of war by provision for the co-operation of all those groups themselves against all aggressors, from within as from without.

Consequently, all the clans, through the joint initiative of their headmen in conference, take cognisance both of the facts and of the law of the case. It is significant, too, that this joint "initiative" was itself invoked by the primary and most venerable of all "public servants"; for, at Athens, for example, "it is the "king" (*basileus*) who introduces the case to the panel of elders, wearing royal insignia;[118] and it is he who—whatever part he may have taken as a co-equal "peer" among the other elders in the discussion of the case, "stripping off his crown"—resumes his royal function when the verdict is published, and is privileged to proclaim the exclusion of the criminal "from what is customary" among normal citizens. And it should be noted here, as illustrating what the distinction was between all this class of "criminal" offences, and the "civil" cases which only concerned possessions and other amenities, that the *basileus* had cognisance not only of homicide, manslaughter, and murder in all its degrees, including the picturesque "extermination" of the ownerless axe or spear which "did the deed," but also of all assaults upon the personal dignity of the citizen—all infringement of his *mana* or *orenda* (to recur once more to non-European analogies), his "frontierless initiative" as a "free" man of this *polis;* and, again, all acts such as arson and magical practices, whereby natural forces either were, or were believed to be, let loose to the detriment of a co-equal member of this political society.

Now, in all these aspects of its intervention to repair breaches of order, the *polis* was at the same time encroaching on the prerogatives and functions of the older kinship-groups and also facilitating concurrent encroachments by the "free" individual on the competence of his own kinship-group to control his personal initiative. Traditional solutions of internal disputes on old tribal lines were being challenged by appeal to the "public servant" and his assessors; tribal idiosyncrasies were being over-ruled and were disappearing; and out of a chaos of family usages a coherent system, and eventually a more or less completely written code of private law emerged; varying, no doubt, in detail between *polis* and *polis*, during the long centuries of comparative insulation, but seldom passing far beyond the stricter limit imposed by similar economic experience and ultimately geographical control, on the efforts of each group of kinsmen to make the most of their own plot (*kleros*) of Greek soil, which sentiment and inherited familiarity endowed with a personality like that of its corporate cultivators.

But it was not until the new opportunities both for the use and for the abuse of those *kleroi*, which resulted from the restoration of comparatively peaceful intercourse over seaways, that this encroachment of the *polis* on the kinship-group, in its economic aspect, became appreciable; and only in proportion as these abuses of corporate property become liable to lead to disputes between the groups themselves, and between a group and its own malcontents, does this kind of intervention and overriding of minor initiatives become common or significant. In civil cases, between a kinship group and its own self-seeking members, "political justice" gave guidance more imperious as well as wiser than the narrow and possibly prejudiced ruling of a clan chief, and was commonly invoked; whereas, in ordinary criminal cases between relatives, the old clan-procedure was not merely preserved but sanctioned by the *polis*, as may be seen in the fourth century case between Socrates' friend Euthyphron and his father.[119] State jurisdiction, in fact, had begun by being supplementary to that of the elements of the state; and never quite lost consciousness of its origin, or of its essentially regulative and remedial mission.

LECTURE V

THE GREEK NOTION OF LAW, IN THE WORLD AROUND US AND IN HUMAN AFFAIRS

WITH the institution of *thesmothetai*, and regular written records of the rulings of the principal "public servants," or "men with initiative," we have reached a point in the development of the Greek city-state, at which it became possible for intelligent and provident men to survey this accumulated experience, to take stock of its contents and classify them, as we have seen happening at Gortyna, and to supplement its omissions, as occasion arose. But these occasions were casual; they depended on the accident of quarrels and offences; and if the public justices were doing their work aright, every such question, accidentally presented to them for settlement, left one loophole the less in a growing network of case-law, for the most part of great antiquity, and by this time of anonymous origin. But there was little system or coherence in such a collection of *thesmoi* and *dikai;* and it was long before even the need was felt for such a rough classification by clauses as occurred, for example, at Gortyna.

It is in the new settlements in the west, along the coasts of south Italy and Sicily, that the first attempts seem to have been made to codify such case-law. Here the legal codes of Zaleucus and Charondas, compiled in the first instance for a particular colony, were adopted gradually by other states, from the moment of their foundation. They were probably in the first instance classified case-books, like the work of the nameless "recorder" at Gortyna, but they do not seem to have needed much revision or supplement; so we may assume that they were fairly extensive, and the fruit of long and varied enquiry. What gave them their value was not their philosophic basis, nor their convenient arrangement, but the massive foundation of experience wider and older than that of the states which adopted them; and the relative uniformity which they brought about between the legal procedure of neighbouring cities, in fairly free intercourse with each other. Some, if not all, of these more famous compilations had the sanction of the oracle of Delphi, perhaps even some revision of their contents in the light of the growing and eventually very wide and detailed knowledge which Delphi came to possess as to the doings of all kinds of Greeks. Of their contents we know almost nothing, except what can be gathered from the arrangement and substance of the Roman "Code of the Twelve Tables," the result of a revision of older Roman case-law in the light of experience of the contemporary working of the Greek codes gathered by a roving commission of Romans "learned in the law" in the years immediately before 450 B.C.

Except for the codification of Athenian case-law by Draco, late in the seventh century, the clauses of which bore the rubric *thesmos*, the word used to describe these early codes is not *thesmoi* nor *themistes* nor *dikai*, as might have been expected, but *nomoi;* and in later times there are innumerable appeals not only at Athens, where our information is fullest, but elsewhere, to the "ancestral *nomoi*" as to a body of rules of behaviour, positive and disciplinary, as well as precautionary, retributive, or remedial. We have met with the word once already, in Hesiod's comparison of the ways of men, who have *dikê*, with those of wild animals which have not; and this *nomos* is described as "given" by Zeus to man.

What, then, did the word *nomos* mean? How and by what stages did it come to be used in its eventual sense of a statute; and how, further, did it come to be used not only for the most inviolable standards of civic behaviour, the "*nomoi* of the *polis*," but also for the merely "conventional" observance of an agreed course of procedure, liable at any time to be resigned or revised by the parties to it or their political successors? And how does it come about that the rhetorical and even the philosophical antithesis to this revocable "convention" is not the "ancestral custom" which was, in fact, so generally and tenaciously observed, but a conception of physical growth, expressed by the word *physis*, which never formed part of the current political vocabulary but was borrowed from popular biology and became specialized as a scientific and naturalist rather than a political notion. This enquiry obviously will lead us rather far beyond the narrow scope of Greek political ideas, but it will soon be clear how imperfectly these can be understood without it.

The verbal substantive *nómos* itself does not occur in the Homeric poems, but the verb is common, and another verbal substantive, *nomós*, is used several times. The verb, used actively, means primarily to "pasture" a flock, as the Cyclops came upon Odysseus "pasturing his sheep";[1] it is used also for "distributing" portions of food at a feast,[2] and other formal shares,[3] and this appears to be the root meaning

244

of the substantives also. In the middle voice the verb means "to pasture oneself," or "graze,"[4] or, more generally, to "range over" or "inhabit" a district,[5] "exploiting" its resources[6] natural or man-made,[7] and occasionally in the sense of "ravaging" with fire.[8] These senses persist in classical Greek,[9] and in Herodotus we have the substantive *nomás, nomades* for men in pastoral life.[10] Thucydides contrasts "common pasture" of a frontier district by the herdsmen of two states, with sedentary "inhabitation" of it by either community.[11] But Æschylus has the middle voice for the assignment of a share,[12] and in Herodotus and Thucydides this derivative sense is common.[13]

Metaphorically, Herodotus has the word often for political administration, not, however, quite without suggestion of profit accruing to the ruler;[14] and Æschylus, for "handling" or "wielding" with appropriate skill a tiller, a shield, the tongue, or authority generally,[15] almost in the sense of the Homeric frequentative, *nômaô*. Indeed, it is not unlikely that we have here one of those elusive popular etymologies which deflect the significance of words and make it difficult to connect secondary and technical meanings with primary. We shall shortly find *theos*, "god," thus popularly derived from a stem meaning "to put," quite unconnected with it; and other quaint examples of Greek popular etymology will confront us later on pages 253–357. Of the three verbal substantives, *nomós* (oxytone) and *nomé* (also oxytone) need not detain us long. *Nomós* in Homer is simply "pasture"[16] and also more generally the "range" of a discussion. Hesiod has the word in the latter sense,[17] and for the "course" of the north wind.[18] A notable Homeric passage couples *nomós* with *ethea*, the "ranch" with the "haunts" of a drove of horses,[19] and Herodotus describes how in Scythia a shrine of the war god is established "ranch by ranch for each of the chieftaincies" and how "each nomarch or ranch-chief mixes a bowl of wine annually on his own *nomós*."[20]

Similarly, *nomé*, which is post-Homeric, is used both for "pasture" by Herodotus, Xenophon, Aristotle, and later writers;[21] by Plato for "fodder,"[22] and "pasture," and by Demosthenes, in more verbal sense, for the distribution of an inheritance. Herodotus has it in an important passage describing the functions of the gods, who are so called, he says (connecting the word *theos* with the stem which reappears in *themis* and *thesis*), "because, putting them in order, they held all things and all *nomai*," meaning all departments or "ranges" of activity, in which usage he is followed once by

THE NOTION OF LAW IN SOCIETY

Plato.[23] With *nomé* must be contrasted a word, *nomaia*, almost confined to Herodotus,[24] and used by him only in the sense of "custom," proper to the other substantive *nómos*, with paroxytone accent, with which we have next to deal.[25]

This other substantive, *nómos*, is not used in the Homeric poems at all; and in two of the three Hesiodic passages it cannot be quite certain which of the two forms is intended. For in one of them, where the Muses "sing the *nomoi* of all, and celebrate the good *ethea* of immortals,"[26] both terms echo the Homeric phrase about the "*ethea* and *nomós* of horses" in which it is their "haunts" and "ranch"-pasture that are meant. So, too, when it is said that "the son of Kronos assigned this *nomos* to men—to fish and beasts and winged birds to eat one another, since there is no *dikê* in them, but to men he gave *dikê*," there is at least a punning allusion to the meaning "pasture" or "sustenance."[27] In the third passage of Hesiod, however, there can be no mistake: "for now when any one of men upon the earth performing fair rites supplicates according to *nomos*, he calls on Hecate."[28] Here we have the same sense of "custom" as in the two other early citations, Chilon's advice to "obey the *nomoi*," and Periander's, to "use old *nomoi*

247

and fresh victuals."[29] The special musical use of the word for a "tune," as the "customary" intonation of certain words, is found also fairly early, in the Homeric *Hymn to Apollo*.[30]

Of the use of this word before the end of the fifth century there are not many examples. Herodotus illustrates the width of its colloquial meaning—as wide as that of *dikê*—in the repeated phrase "by *nomos* of hands" meaning, in "hand-to-hand" fighting,[31] which comes really very near to Æschylus' use of the verb for "wielding" a shield or other implement. Sophocles uses it in the sense of "natural law," the normal course of events on earth, which man in his pride of reason overrides; and he couples it with the "oath-bound *dikê* of the gods."[32] For a similar association with *dikê* in human affairs, Euripides makes Theseus say: "I make legal claim (*dikê*) to bury the dead, conserving the *nomos* of all Greeks."[33] The crucial passage, however, is in Herodotus' anecdote of the explanation of Greek discipline given by Demaratus to Xerxes: "free though they be, they are not free in all respects, for they have over them a master, even *Nomos*, before whom they are in awe even more than thy people are before thee, O king!"

From *nomos* itself there is also a derivative

verb, *nomizein*, to "treat as customary," or, more generally, to "hold a customary opinion" about a thing. The fatal charge against Socrates, for example, was, not only that he "spoiled" young men by his teaching, made them, that is, careless in their "observance" of Athenian custom, but that he "did not observe the gods whom the city observes" or accepts as customary.[34] And the popular sense is the same, in modern as in ancient Greek—to "expect" things, in ordinary course, to happen this way or that.

Though *nomos* in the sense of what is "customary" or "normal" does not appear in Homeric vocabulary, it has one Homeric cognate which deserves notice before we pass on to the legal conception which emerges in classical Greek. This word is *nemesis*, strictly a verbal substantive meaning "assignment" or "assessment" of shares, but already specialized in Homeric speech to signify the estimate formed by a bystander about a breach of normal behaviour. There is the less need to examine this usage at length, because it has been fully explained by Professor Gilbert Murray in his *Rise of the Greek Epic*,[35] and set in its proper light as correlative of *aidôs*, for which the nearest equivalent is what we call "self-respect." In simplest terms, *aidôs* is my feeling that this is a kind of thing that *I* don't do: *nemesis* is my feeling that this is a thing that *he* doesn't do if he is normal and "all right," and that even if he is doing it, he would not do it if there were not something out of the ordinary with him; and, similarly, *nemesis* is the other fellow's feeling that *I* am doing something which it is not mine to do, in the ordinary course of events.

How this special usage of *nemesis* came to be has been ingeniously suggested by Mr. Cornford,[36] from features in the cult of a personified *Nemesis* at Rhamnus in Attica. Here the goddess was represented by Hellenic artists carrying an apple or an apple branch with its fruit, and wearing emblematic stags in her hair. Moralised and personified thus, she is yet recognisable by these attributes as Our Lady of the Wild Places, and Wild Things, who "giveth them their meat in due season" and presides over their haunts, like Diana *Nemorensis* in her grove at Nemi in Latium with its "golden bough," and that Artemis *Agrotera*, "Our Lady of the Wastes," to whom a king of Sparta sacrificed at the outset of a military expedition,[37] a *rite de passage* before infringement of the no-man's-land between his country and the enemy's, where uncanny sounds and glimpses of its denizens, Pan and the Nymphs

who "range the wilderness," so easily spread
"panic" fear among a militia not yet inured
to warfare. In this aspect *Nemesis* not only
"assigns" to each of her fosterlings its "portion," but resents and repels encroachment.
So, too, in early Italy, the source of fertility,
Priapus, is also guardian of rural boundaries;
and in Attica his counterpart, Hermes, sanctions both possession and productivity in the
ordinary course of things, and blesses also the
"windfall" of unforeseen but no less provi-
dential events—good harvest, treasure-trove,
unearned increment of every sort and kind.
As *Nemesis* stands to *nomos*, in both its senses,
of "pasture" and "customary order," and as
Lachesis, "allotment," to *lachos*, a "share," so
Fortuna, no less verbally phrased, stands to
ferre in that she "brings" both normal maintenance and exceptional luck. What part
was played, if any, by the Lady *Nemesis* at
Rhamnus in specifically social affairs we do not
yet know, but it was not without reason that
Roman legend brought the first "law-man,"
Numa, to the Lady of the Grove for confirmation of his code of behaviour; or that the
men whom that "way of life" was designed to
bring together into normal relations of give-
and-take, of assignment and mutual respect,
were themselves congregated fugitives from

the crooked dealings of their own people, in
that *asylum* or outland sanctuary which, as
Livy described it later, was "the place which
is now fenced off as you go down the slope
between the two groves;"[38] a *nemus* like that
of "Our Lady of the Grove" at Aricia, and the
rural tree-sanctuaries described still later by
Pliny.[39] That *Nemesis*, personified, assigned
good things to men as well as evil is clear from
Pindar's description of her.[40] But it is quite
in accord with the political unhappiness of the
age of Hesiod that she is described already in
the *Theogonia* as "a bane to men."[41]

Of a widespread observance of such local
powers sanctioning allotment and peaceful
enjoyment of "nature's gifts," we have a
picturesque glimpse in Plato's occasional retro-
spects of the "Golden Age," as eloquent of
his acquaintance with the folklore of his
countrymen, as his brilliant geological sketch
in the *Critias* is of his knowledge of Greek
countryside. "Divine powers," he says,[42] "had
divided among themselves, like herdsmen, the
animals, by kinds and droves, each being self-
sufficient for all their needs to those whom he
pastured, so that there was nothing fierce
[literally, "like the wilderness"] nor any
eating of one another, and no war between
them, nor even party feeling at all." We

recall Herodotus' guess that the gods were so
called because they "set things in order" and
"held all pastures."[43]   And it was the function
of *Nemesis* to supervise and sanction this
apportionment: "all these, in the second age,
Nemesis joined respectively with spirits ancient
and earthly, the overseers of men's works, to
whom the divine ruler of all committed administration in the universe."[44]   "For gods once
upon a time allotted among themselves the
whole earth by its regions, not by strife; and
receiving what was akin to them [or "their
own"] by allotments of *dikê* they settled down
in their districts and, settling so their flocks
like herdsmen, they brought us up as possessions and nurslings of their own, . . . laying
hand upon us by persuasion of soul, according
to their own intelligence; thus leading us they
continued to guide all that was mortal."[45]   It
can hardly be doubted either that the fourth-
century philosopher is making philological play
with the two aspects of *nomos* and its cognate
words, or that his justification for doing so was
the general belief in earlier times, attested by
the cult of Nemesis at Rhamnus, that normal
order in human affairs cohered with order in
surrounding nature and derived its sanction
ultimately from a world-order which was one
and the same for all.

But how does man discover and recognise the "normal" way of behaviour, which renders to every man his due, and precludes *nemesis*, in its Homeric sense of a feeling that "this sort of thing won't do," or, more precisely, "isn't done" among people like ourselves? We have seen already that as early as Hesiod's time it is man's specifically human "assignment" from the son of Kronos, that he has *dikê;* that this *dikê* is "for the best" because it prevents men from "eating each other," as modern carnivora have lapsed into doing since the "Golden Age"; and that a *dikê* is the expression of man's ability to distinguish among conflicting practices what the normal coherent "way of doing things" is, and to express in a verbal and memorable *formula* that interpretation of these or those facts in the light of such a general "way" of behaviour, which, once formulated, makes the restitution of normal order not only possible but obvious and easiest for all parties.

PHYSIS IN EARLY GREEK

What, however, is it, which the discerning man appreciates as being at the same time "customary" or *nomos*, "obvious," when once pointed out in a *dikê*, and "initiatory" as a compulsive *arkhé* toward restitution and normal apportionment? The answer to this question must be found through examination of what in classical Greek comes to be the very antithesis of *nomos*, namely, the correlative notion or *physis*. Only once does *physis* occur in the Homeric poems; but its usage there is instructive, as all Homeric usages are, so long as we treat them fairly and squarely, as examples of very early Greek, and do not confuse our minds by comparing them with usages of classical times, separate by four centuries or more of time, and by a millrace of linguistic and cultural advancement unparalleled until the Renaissance, if even then. Hermes is explaining to Odysseus the *moly* plant, which is a magical (or was it to be a physical?) antidote to the magic potion of Circe, which changed men's "mode of growth" and caused them to become bristly all over and to grovel like pigs. "So speaking, then, he brought me a healing-herb (*pharmakon*), pulling it out of the ground, and showed me the growing, *physis*, of it." And then the plant is described: "at the root it was black, but the flower like unto milk."[46] Now, these two peculiarities stand, one at the beginning of the growing-process of the plant, the other at its completion. If you want to find *moly* in the dead season, you must look for a black root; in spring or summer it will have a milkwhite flower. The foliage apparently was not noteworthy. The *physis*, then, of the *moly*-plant is its proceedings while it is becoming a mature plant in full flower, from being merely a black root in the ground. Galen's comment that the word describes the "appearance" of the plant does not quite exhaust its verbal active significance;[47] it is not merely the resultant appearance but the sequence of events by which the *moly* comes to have such an appearance. Like other verbal substantives in Homer, it denotes the action or process signified in the verbal stem. The importance of this will become clearer as we proceed.

Hesiod does not happen to use the word *physis*, and, apart from late quotations from the Ionian physicists, the next usages which have been preserved are those of Pindar and Æschylus. Pindar seems to use *physis* in the same sense as its cognate *phyé*, which, both in Homer and in Herodotus, always means "growth" as the result of a completed process of "growing." Of one man, Strepsiades, he compares the courage and the "growth," that is, "stature," using *phyé*;[48] of another, Melissus, that he has not the *physis* of the gigantic Orion; that is, either, in the Homeric sense, the "way of growing" that a giant or a *moly*-plant has, or else the resultant "growth."

THE NOTION OF LAW IN SOCIETY

In a very corrupt fragment, also attributed to Pindar,[49] some commentators have assigned not only the famous phrase, "*nomos* is king of all" to the poet, but also the words "in accordance with *physis*"; others, however, more reasonably take them to be part of the fourth-century context of the quotation. In another doubtful fragment[50] Pindar is made to say that slaves "have compulsion to bear worries of other people, and a heart of alien *physis*"; that is, which has come to be what it is, like a *moly*-plant, by a different process of growing. More certainly[51] he compares men with gods in respect of "either (their) great intelligence or, indeed, (their) *physis*," namely, the way they have grown up and become fully men. For example, there was once upon a time an "infant Zeus," and in other respects also, such as sleep and other weaknesses, Zeus, according to the fables, was quite undivinely human.

Æschylus uses the word five times:[52] of the build of foreign girls, of Persians in the prime of life, of the effect of pestilence on the "original "physical process in normal men—the "way they grow"—, of the "right-handedness," in the magical sense, of certain birds "in the way they grow," and of the relations between the sun and the earth. Of these the last-named alone presents any difficulty. "No one," says the poet, "knows the facts, to recite them clearly, except the sun which nourishes the *physis* of earth." It has been suggested that this is merely a paraphrase for the earth itself, or for "the earth and all living things," but in view of early and widespread beliefs about the vitalizing effect of sunlight, there is no reason to hesitate to translate quite literally, "the sun which nourishes the growing of earth," namely, the process by which the earth, itself source of all terrestrial manifestations of life, comes to be what it is, by its own process of growing; a process as "original" or "originative" as that ascribed to men, in a previous passage, while yet unstricken by disease.

Now, there is no doubt that in the fifth and fourth centuries ordinary people used *physis* very loosely, as we use the word "nature" when we speak of "something of the nature of an accident," meaning simply "some sort of accident"; Plato, for example, speaks of "some other such *physis*," meaning "some other such cause," or "thing" considered as the cause (in this instance) of the degeneration of society,[53] though even among such examples many still retain a vaguely verbal implication. But it is no less clear from the rare early usages already noted that where it had any more precise meaning, it was that of the "process of growing," which we should expect from its verbal form.

PHYSIS IN HERODOTUS

This is especially clear in the usage of the word by Herodotus, on whose intimacy with Ionian modes of thought and literary idiom there is no need to insist. When the king of Æthiopia asked the messengers of King Cambyses, "What does the king eat, and how long a time, at most, does a Persian live?" they said "that he eats bread, explaining the *physis* of the wheat, and that eighty years were assigned to a man as the longest complement of life. At this the Æthiopian said that he was not at all surprised if they live only few years, making dung their food."[54] Now, the only point at which dung could have come into the argument was in the course of explaining how wheat was grown, and consequently the *physis* of wheat in this passage must either be, or include, the whole growth-process from seedcorn to harvested grain, precisely as in the Homeric account of the *moly*-plant. What was new to the Æthiopian, whose own victuals were roast meat with milk to drink, was that anything edible could be made to grow out of the ground, least of all with the aid of manure,

Similarly, in describing the hippopotamus [55] Herodotus says that it "exhibits a *physis* of a species of this kind: it is four-footed, two-toed, hoofs of an ox, snub-nose, with a horse's mane, showing jagged teeth, a horse's tail and cry, in size as big as the largest ox." Now, these characters are given in order of the significance of each as the creature grows toward maturity; a baby hippo is obviously four-legged, and on inspection exhibits two toes, but it certainly has not yet the "hoofs of an ox"; only later still does it acquire its adult tusks and mane, or attain the bulk of the largest ox.

Again, when an Egyptian priest is examining a bull to see whether it is of the sacred "Apis" sort, he "looks also at the hairs of the tail" to discover "if they have grown in accordance with the *physis*,"[56] that is, with the kind of growing which produces double hairs and shows the animal to be an "Apis"-bull. Here the substantive *physis* and its cognate-verb stand in the text side by side and in exactly the same sense.

Two other passages show clearly that for Herodotus *physis* was not confined to describing ordinary biological life but included both geological processes and the behaviour of men. Of the Egyptian Delta he says that "it is clear that the Egypt to which Greeks make voyages is land additionally acquired by the Egyptians and a gift of the river, . . . for the *physis* [mode of growth or extension] of the land of Egypt is as follows. When you first sail toward it and are still a day's run from land, if you heave a sounding-lead you will bring up mud, and be in eleven fathoms. This shows that there is a pouring forward of the earth to this extent," namely mud-bottom in eleven fathoms—a very rare occurrence off any Greek river.[57] The *physis*, that is, by which Egyptian territory grows larger, is a "pouring forward," a geological process of sedimentation; the word is a verbal substantive and nothing more.

Elsewhere, too,[58] Herodotus speaks of two Spartans as men "well begotten in *physis*, and risen to the first place in wealth," once again coupling the substantive with a verb expressing ordinary biological growth.

On the other hand, discussing the legendary attempt of the Egyptians to sacrifice Heracles, and his monstrous reprisals, he says that "when the Greeks say this they seem to me to be quite without experience of the *physis* and *nomoi* of the Egyptians, for seeing it is not permissible for them to sacrifice animals except such as are clean beasts, and geese, how should they sacrifice men? And further, how has it *physis*, that Heracles, being (as they say) alone, and still merely human, should slay so many myriads" as the story relates?[59]

Here, on both occasions of its use, *physis* signifies the normal course of events; Egyptians are men of a certain average size, and strength, and of a culture no less ascertainable, in which human sacrifices are just as unlikely to occur as an Egyptian either three feet high or thirteen.

But there is a further point established here from Herodotus' association of *physis* with *nomoi*. Thanks to the recent researches of Hecatæus, and nearly two centuries of commercial intercourse between Greeks and Egyptians, a good deal of the *physis* of Egypt and its people had been formulated by Greeks in general descriptions, which were in the same sense *nomoi* as the Greek practical experience that wine is sweet and vinegar is sour is a *nomos*, or an Athenian's political experience, since Solon's time, that if he had not taught his son a trade, his own claim on that son for maintenance in old age was disregarded. But though there was a good deal about Egypt in Hecatæus' *Journey round the World*, there were many things going on in Egypt itself that were not included. These, too, were part of the *physis* of Egypt—the way things

262

go on there—though neither Egyptian king nor Greek anthropologist or geographer had as yet formulated them into a *nomos*. So Herodotus, in order to be comprehensive in his condemnation of the ignorance of certain Greeks about Egypt, had to use the double phrase, and speak of the *physis* and *nomoi* of the Egyptians.

In view of this quite clear and simple conception of a *nomos* as man's transcript or formulation of some process which normally goes on in the world around us, considered as an element in that complex, all-embracing process which is the "course of events" in the largest sense, Herodotus' account of the sanction of custom deserves careful study. Customs, he says, vary widely.[60] Greeks burn their dead relatives; the Callatian Indians eat them; each alike would be horrified at the suggestion that they should do as the other does: and it was proof of the madness of King Cambyses that he set himself to ridicule rituals and customs: "for if one were to propose to all men that they should select as customs (*nomoi*) those that were best among all the customs there are, each people, after careful review, would choose their own: so much the best are each *accustomed* to think their own customs. Well, this has always been man's custom, and rightly Pindar seems to me to have spoken, in the verse *'Custom is king of all.'* " The sanction of custom, that is, is the observed formulation of that aspect of humanity which is its observance of customs; its tolerance, that is, of habitual modes of behaviour, because, whether absolutely the most efficient or not, they are for us here and now what we may count upon other people observing, and shape our own behaviour accordingly.

This aspect of *nomos* as man's formulation of a custom, habit, regularity of procedure, either in the outer world or in men's dealings with each other, is fundamental in the explanation of the Greek view of life, given by the deposed and exiled Spartan king Demaratus to Xerxes, and already quoted more than once.[61] For the reason given, for Greek reverence for law as formulation of custom, and for Greek conformity to it, is that "they do whatever it bids, and it bids the same thing always." How great a contrast to the "bidding" of a Persian king, like Cambyses or Xerxes, liable to whims or fits of temper! And how closely akin—had Demaratus, or Herodotus himself, been privileged to know the Persians better—to that "law of the Medes and Persians which altereth not," those "an-

264

cestral customs," which it was the function of the "royal justices" to interpret in its application to questions of everyday conduct!

In another saying of Demaratus, that interdependence of human and regional "ways of behaving," which is hinted but not fully expressed in the passage about the funeral customs of Greeks and Callatians, is explicit.[62] "Poverty is always our fellow lodger in Greece, and efficiency is a thing acquired," or "superinduced, wrought out by wisdom and overmastering *nomos*." Greece, that is, is so austere a region that it is only the right sort of man, stooping to conquer by conformity to its stern conditions, who can "make good" there; good impulses and initiative he may have had in the beginning, if he has been there always; good customs he may have had when he came into Greece from elsewhere; but, aboriginal or immigrant, the condition, not merely of goodness, but of maintenance at all, is that "in Greece he does as the Greeks do," and himself becomes Greek. This is the formulation as an "overmastering *nomos*" of that which every Greek, in his inward being, knew as the "handicraft of wisdom," and as his own *physis* or process of upgrowing into Greekness.

This is the conception of *nomos* as the reasonable formulation of *physis*, on which Heraclitus insisted that one must "insist," and for which one must "contend," as one fights for the walls of one's *polis*, "and more valiantly still."[63] For without such reasonable assurance of an orderly sequence and coherence among events, man has as desperately "lost his bearings" in the world about him, as in the capture and sack of his citadel and home.

This, too, is the "customary" in all things, as Empedocles called it, which "extends continuously through all-seeing sky and inexhaustible light"; not a substance, still less any kind of origin, but orderly processes, such as the codifier of ancestral customs in a human society could rationalize in the familiar *formula*, "If any man shall . . . , then let him . . . ," paying back, in accordance with this "straight-setting," whatever is requisite to restore all things and all persons concerned, as if there had been no departure from orderliness. It is in this sense that, for Anaximander, in the first dawn of Ionian "physical" inquiry, "that, out of which things, that are, had their coming into being, is that into which their dissolution takes place, in accordance with what is due"[64] *plus* balancing *minus*, credit balancing debit, just as in orderly course of business among men—"for they give *dikê* and reparation to one another for their breach-of-*dikê* in accordance with the order of time," the balance between the various factors inclining first this way, then that. Later commentators thought that Anaximander was using "somewhat poetical terms" in this passage; but were they more poetical than when a modern mathematician says that $(x+y)^2$ "equals" $x^2+2xy+y^2$; or when a chemist says that $2NaCl+H_2SO_4$ "equals" Na_2SO_4+2HCl in accordance with the order of time, in the sense that however "equal" the two states of things may be, in regard to total weight or otherwise, they cannot exist except in chronological sequence in regard to the same portions of chemical materials?

This insistence on the chronological or temporal aspect of custom as formulated in a *nomos*, and of *nomos* as an interpretation of some aspect of the process of *physis*, is conspicuous again in a well-known passage of Euripides:[65] "for it is slight cost to accept that this holds good, whatever be the divine, and the customary ever in long time, and what has come to be by *physis*." Once again we are reminded of the wide, cautious outlook of Herodotus,[66] where he illustrates the "growing-process" of Egypt by the comparison of the sediment-choked gulf, as he considers the Nile valley to be, with the gulf of the Red Sea, not yet choked, but destined (he thinks) to be so, as soon as the Nile Delta has become so much silted that the flood follows the "sweet-water canal" and falls into the Gulf of Suez. Unlikely enough, to the casual eye; but "in length of time everything might happen;" and, similarly, elsewhere he says, "what is said, I write; and everything *might* happen," the potentialities of the great course of events outrunning man's power to describe and formulate them.

In the same general sense of "the way things grow," *physis* is used also by Sophocles both of human upgrowing, as when Eteocles is described as "more recent in *physis*" than his elder brother, and of the process which makes such things as the sea continue to be as they are. Sometimes an adjective is added to show what particular growth-process is meant, as, for instance, "It was no mortal *physis* of men that gave him birth;" or, in a phrase of abuse, "you would provoke the *physis* of a stone," that is, make a stone behave otherwise than a normal stone does.[67] Not unnaturally there was a tendency, such as is common to all languages, to use the merely verbal substantive as if it were an abstract term; but among the physicists themselves Empedocles was vigorous in his protest against this, as when he says[68] that "there is no *physis* of all mortal things, nor even any end in destructive death, but only mixing, and separation of things mixed, and *physis* is a name given to those [processes] among men." To regard *physis*, either by way of first cause, or of fundamental substance, as any kind of entity, was for him at best a figure of speech, at worst a disease of language if not of thought. All that existed were things that mixed and separated; you might speak of processes, but not of qualities otherwise than as a jargon or slang for concisely describing processes. That is how it came about that while denying in this passage that there is any such "thing" as *physis*, Empedocles himself repeatedly uses the word in its strict verbal sense;[69] for example: "the *physis* of limbs has been distorted," meaning that in certain circumstances they do not grow straight; exactly as the normal growth of things is described by Hippocrates,[70] probably following the teaching of Heraclitus: "gods arranged the *physis* of all things, . . . and all that gods set in order, forever are straight, both things straight and things not straight;" some animals, that is, have crooked limbs, but that is because the process of growth which they exemplify produced crooked limbs in producing that kind of limb at all. Whether "in length of time" the corresponding limbs of subsequent individuals would be more, or less, crooked, was a further question, just as it was a further "growth," not to be excluded from Herodotean geology, for the Red Sea to change what Sophocles called the "sea's salt *physis*" and become a second Delta.

But if *physis* be a process of growing, and all *nomos* be man's formulation of such growth, how does it come about that, from the latter part of the fifth century onward, *physis* and *nomos* are contrasted and opposed, and Aristotle a century later has to discuss the question whether society and the *polis* exist "by *physis*" or "by *nomos;*" in the real world of things as they are, or by a conventional usage agreed among men, and alterable like any other such agreement, by a fresh convention to adopt another usage?

It hardly needs to be stated that man, while he has an exceptionally long infancy, which made some kind of stable family life, and political superstructure to protect and insure it, necessary if men were to continue to be at all, has also an exceptionally long maturity, during which, with few exceptions, men's characters and principles change very little, and their conduct follows and exemplifies the set of notions which they acquired during adolescence. In some kinds of external circumstances, as for example in pastoral societies, there is so little occasion for change, in view of the monotonous stability of their surroundings, and this early acquisition and long exemplification of principles of conduct is so closely in accord with the "way things happen," that it gives rise neither to inconvenience nor to discussion. There have been observed, however, other types of society, among jungle dwellers and hunting tribes, where conditions are liable to change rapidly, or where the community itself changes its circumstances; where, consequently, the race is to the swift, the battle to the strong, and the spoils of life to the pushful and brainy among the rising generation. In such a predicament the memory and experience of old age may well be at a discount; the old are despised, or even despatched; and the "way things happen,' may change rapidly, as the initiative of the momentary leaders may direct. And, thirdly, it has been repeatedly found that if, through excess of population over subsistence, increased facility for intercourse between communities of comparable but varied experience, or other changes of circumstance, a stable regime passes over into an unstable, an incongruity is perceived—which, indeed, had not even existed earlier—between the *physis* or process which now goes on in the surrounding world, and the *nomoi* or formulation of the suitable human response to it, which for a while past, at all events, had described it with sufficient accuracy to serve as a guide for conduct. That different communities attained the same general end by different means, and that often there seemed to be no very obvious reason for these differences, suggested that there was an element of human caprice, perhaps even of impish chance, in the forms taken by such local *nomoi;* and on the other hand, stern control of external, regional factors, in a country such as the Greek cradle-land, seemed to be perhaps even more responsible than it actually was, for the more fundamental similarities and the conditions which enforced them.

Also we have to recall at this point, what was only briefly noted at the outset (p. 108), that while the *polis* was encroaching from above, and from without, on the traditions and customs of its constituent kinship-groups, new opportunities for individual enterprise were being offered by more peaceful conditions and more frequent and easy intercourse, and were leading to similar encroachment on those uniformities of behaviour among members of any such group, which the austerer conditions of the "Dark Age" had imposed. More especially was this encroachment of the individual on the solidarity of the kinship-group facilitated, and even encouraged and provoked, by the new invention of metallic currency, and the discovery that it was possible not only to make wealth by individual "push" and "brains" far from home, but to realize it into an eminently portable form, and transport it at will into the owner's home city, or elsewhere, and so give him a personal consideration and influence quite other than fell, for example, to the lot of a younger son, however pushful and brainy, so long as the sole career open to him was to help cultivate the family freehold, which, however adequate to maintain its owners, was immovable, and also practically unrealizable, under the custom of the locality and the *polis* which protected and dominated it.[71]

PHYSIS AND NOMOS IN PHYSICS AND POLITICS

Now, it was in this difficult phase of transition from comparatively stable, not to say stagnant, conditions, to the rapid and complex advancement of the sixth and fifth centuries B.C., that the double problem confronted the

Greek people, of finding out what was "really going on" both in the world around and in their own city-state communities; of distinguishing between the confusing and perverse ways in which things actually *were* being done and the comparatively simple formulations of what *was* done with general consent on previous occasions, in view of the common habit of justices and other "formulators of *dikai*" to refer new cases to old customs which not only did not fit them and led to incongruous and unforeseen consequences when they were so applied, but also clearly had not been formulated themselves with any knowledge or experience of the kind of problem which was now to be solved. And these problems, as we have seen throughout, were themselves of two kinds—problems in the interpretation of the external world and problems in the interpretation of society and men's dealings with each other. In both kinds of problem it was only a matter of time and occasion for that incongruity between *physis* and *nomos* to become practically intolerable; and when that happened it was the *nomoi* that broke down and gave way. For it was matter of common experience that though things established by *nomos*, "conventionally," were alterable with comparative ease, there were other matters which were far more difficult to change. The result was a great period of investigation and criticism, in "politics" and "physics" alike; a generation of great lawgivers, *nomothetai*, "writers-down of customs," as the old *thesmothetai* had been "writers-down of ordinances" for public officials; and at the same time of what the Greeks called *physiologoi*, "describers" and "explainers" of *physis;* and it will easily be seen how the functions of researchers into law and researchers into the world around came to overlap and interlock along a broad front where it was difficult to say whether what needed readjustment was the human or the non-human factor in the problem.

Take, for example, Solon's reorganization of Athenian agriculture. On the one hand, he deals with political abuses, enslavement of a citizen for debt, abuse of the magistrate's initiative, restrictions in the interest of the kinship group on a man's freedom to dispose of his property by will, restrictions on that immemorial right of the private citizen to "speak up" in court on behalf of one party or another in a suit, and propound a *formula* which should settle the case. But, on the other hand, we find him restricting the production of grain, encouraging that of wine and especially of oil, for which physically Attica

is much better suited; insisting on a father's
obligation to teach his son a trade; readjusting
the system of currency so as to suit the new
trend of commerce which resulted from his
revolution in agriculture; and in the story of
his famous visit to Crœsus of Lydia we find
him presented as the foremost economist of
his age, called in to review the finances and
organization of the greatest merchant-prince
of that age, and advise him whether everything
had been done as it should be. From the
account of this visit by Herodotus—whether
the visit itself be a historical event or not—
it is clear that what was expected of such a
nomothetes or *physiologos*—lawgiver or research-
student in some branch of science—was that
he should first make himself acquainted with
the facts of the case, the processes which were
now going on, and leading to the current
problems, just as a physician is expected to
begin by diagnosis of the disease from its
symptoms; and then, on the basis of this
knowledge and his other experience of such
matters, to formulate fresh *nomoi*, or revise and
reformulate old ones, in such a way as to make
them accord with his new recognition of what
really goes on; and all this can be done and is
to be done, in the view of this phase of Greek
thought by rational inspection of the facts and

rational interpretation of them in their actual relation to each other. Only a generation before Solon, the Athenians had sought to cure their political troubles by the magic arts of Epimenides of Crete; so closely were the physical and the human factors believed to be intertwined in such affairs. Now, Solon's own account of his proceedings shows a purely rational and humane outlook and method "taking apart," as Heraclitus put it,[72] "according to its *physis,* and demonstrating how things stand." And Heraclitus, though apparently his work came eventually under the general category of books "concerning *physis,*" treated continuously the three topics "about the whole" and "about the *polis*" and "about the gods": it was described as an "exact steering-chart for the estimation of human life";[73] and the "steering" itself was achieved by that "one thing wise, to know judgment, which steers all things through all"[74] which is elsewhere called by him simply "common sense" or "straight thinking."[75] This "common sense" in ourselves corresponds *somehow* —for that "problem of knowledge" was not solved in Greek times any more than it has been solved in modern—with "that which surrounds us, being reasonable and coherent."[76] It is in this sense that for Heraclitus "all human *nomoi* are nourished by one, the divine; for it has force, to as great a degree as it wills, and is sufficient unto all, and yet there is more."[77] This "divine *nomos*" is clearly the gods' own formulation of all the reality there is, as they in their wisdom comprehend it. All human *nomoi* have their value and express some aspect or other of reality, of what really happens, insofar as they are transcripts from the same great original, the real order of events; and such is this great fabric of knowable reality that it is hopeless to expect human formulation to comprise or exhaust its meaning.

Heraclitus deals also in a very instructive way with the reasons why human *nomoi* are found to diverge so lamentably from this "divine law."[78] "For reason being common to all, most men live"—the word denotes only their physical, animal life—"as if they had a way of thinking of their own." Consequently, the "way men think" may diverge from the "way things happen." And then in a striking phrase he describes what really "straight thinking" or "common sense" achieves: "it is nothing else than the explaining of the fashion of the administration of the whole." Real genuine thinking, that is, whether about physics or about politics, is an intelligible presentation of the way in which things really go on.

THE NOTION OF LAW IN SOCIETY

The achievements, in detail, of this "real thinking" are what Heraclitus calls *gnomai*, "conclusions" or "opinions," acts of mental decision. His own treatise, or perhaps the political part of it, he described as an "opinion about habits," his conclusions about human character and behaviour. But he proceeds:[79] "man's character [or way of doing things] has not got *gnomai*, but divine character has. . . . Man—poor child!—listens to the deity, as a child to a grown man . . . To God all things are fair and good and in accord with *dikê;* but men have conceived some things as without *dikê*, and [only] some things as in accord with it." Yet by research, and above all by self-study, knowledge can come: "all men have their chance to come to know themselves and to think straight."

Thus, just as Homer and Hesiod, at an earlier stage, could speak of "crooked *dikai*," of a man-made justice which was itself unjust, so we have here the discovery that man-made customs, and public enactments based on them, may be as inaccurate and stupid a description of what human nature really is, as a child's attempt to understand and repeat the "grown-up talk" of its elders.

To this stage of Greek thought probably belongs a series of anecdotes like that of

Crœsus and Solon in Herodotus, reporting
various questions asked by Crœsus of other
"wandering scholars" and their answers to
them.[80] Crœsus asks Anacharsis, a great
traveller and naturalist, "What does he think
the most manly in the world?" Anacharsis
replies, "The most ferocious of the animals,
for they alone die, without hesitation, for freedom." This was surprising enough, and Crœsus asks again, "What he thinks most in accord
with *dikê*." The answer again is, "The most
ferocious wild beasts, for they alone live according to *physis*, not according to customs, *nomoi*,
for *physis* is the creation of God, but *nomos* an
ordinance of man, and it is more in accord
with *dikê* to follow [make use of] the inventions
of God, than those of men." Then Crœsus
asks again (to "pull the leg" of the sage, as
Diodorus unkindly says),[81] whether the wild
beasts are also the wisest creatures, and Anacharsis explains that it is the special quality of
wisdom to prefer the unforgetfulness of *physis*
to the ordinance of *nomos*. Here the point is
that only in *physis*, the real order of events,
is every circumstance included, so that "physical" truth is "unforgetful" of the smallest
detail, whereas man's legislation, as we know
to our cost, is often very badly drafted.

The "physical" philosophy, mainly of Ionian

origin, the main features of which we have been tracing here, passed over to Athens late in the fifth century, with Archelaus of Miletus.[82] His own teacher, Anaxagoras, had visited Athens some while before, but had been so imprudent as to declare that the sun was a mass of hot stone as large as Peloponnese, that is, some eighty miles in diameter; and he had had to depart quickly out of Attica. Socrates, who had sat under Anaxagoras, is said to have learned "physics" also from Archelaus, and it is quite likely that the allusions in the plays of Aristophanes to *physis* and "physical" learning generally, may be derived mainly from Archelaus, however amusing it may have been to palm them off as Socratic, at a time when Socrates was passing over to the alternative standpoint which was known as the philosophy of "behaviour." But, we are told, "Archelaus, too, dabbled in behaviour, for he has speculated about *nomoi*, good and in accord with *dikê*"—customs, that is to say, and their goodness and rightness; "from whom Socrates, borrowing, by his improvements was supposed to have invented this himself." Another symptom of advanced, or, rather, of late, over-mature opinions is the statement that he "tries to contribute something fresh about the coming into existence of the universe," a matter which his predecessors, more strictly "physical" in their inquiries, had left rather severely alone. Of his political and moral theories we only know[83] that he "used to say that righteousness and baseness existed not in *physis* but in *nomos*"; that is to say, like the abstract *physis* itself for Empedocles, they had no real existence in the world of real things, but were names superadded by men to describe this or that kind of behaviour when exhibited by men, which no one would call "just" or "unjust," "right" or "wrong," when exhibited by the wild beasts of Anacharsis.

The Notion of "Unwritten Law"

This may have been good "physics," but it had disastrous effects both morally and politically in Greece. For this depreciation of publicly formulated custom recognized no distinction between codified practice of the courts and the traditional morality and economy of old kinship groups, or between either of these and those "ancestral customs" to which statesmen and litigants alike made impassioned appeals without telling us very much about their content. It came, too, at a moment when the two opposite encroachments, of the *polis* from above and without, of the pushful individual from within and beneath, had nearly broken down the sanctions of old tribal society. Thus were revealed to each other a supreme form of society, the *state*, none too sure of its own ultimate sanction, beyond the fact that "ancestral customs," vaguely asserted, and instinctively or traditionally observed, had served it well enough in the past; and, confronting this state, the *individual*, conscious of his own immediate needs, aims, and abilities, fretted and antagonized by the last struggles of the clan and the house-father to keep him in leading strings along the "ancient ways," but very ill equipped to distinguish between obsolete custom and the new conceptions of purely political obligation, and purely moral self-criticism, which the Homeric literature, the oracle at Delphi, and all schools of contemporary speculation, were at one in inculcating, however greatly philosophic teachers differed as to the precise content of citizenship, or disputed the compatibility of good citizenship with an ideally good life for the citizen himself.

Was there, then, any distinction to be drawn between arbitrary man-made *nomoi* and such a *nomos* as had been proclaimed by Heraclitus, the one divine law, fully descriptive of man's place in the world, and of his path through it? Socrates seems to have thought so, if we may

judge from a conversation recorded by Xenophon,[84] but his argument is not very conclusive;
it demonstrates, rather, that the difficulty was
perceived, than that much progress had been
made toward finding a sanction. Socrates
begins by the assumption that *nomos* and
dikê are the same—what is according to one is
according to the other also. To this his friend
Hippias agrees. "Do you suppose, then, Hippias, that there are any unwritten laws?"
meaning by this, laws which represent in general the workings of human mind and character,
not the special reactions of particular groups
of men to regional circumstances. Hippias
agrees again: they are "those which are observed in every country in the same way,"
but he gives no instances, and it would, indeed,
have been difficult at that stage of geographical
discovery to demonstrate any such universal
principles of behaviour. "Would you say,
then," says Socrates, "that these laws were
enacted by mankind?" "How could that be,"
is the reply, "seeing that mankind could never
have come all together, and would not have
understood each other if they had?" "Then
whom do you suppose to have enacted these
nomoi?" Hippias adopts the current etymology, and says that he thinks the gods
ordained these *nomoi* for men. "For example,

among all mankind it is the first of observances, to reverence gods." Socrates adds another example, honour paid everywhere to parents. But what is the sanction of these "unwritten" laws? Hippias suggests the wrath of God, which he describes as the "greatest *dikê*," manifested in natural retribution; people who dishonour the gods and their parents perish miserably. This rather ingenuous view does not satisfy Socrates; he doubts even whether there is such a thing as an universal *dikê*, any more than an universal *nomos* of men's invention. Much more in accordance with experience is his second suggestion, that the penalties for breach of "unwritten" laws are social; an irreligious or unfilial man is avoided by his friends. This is the primitive Homeric doctrine of *nemesis*, public opinion, reinforcing *aidôs*, a man's own self-respect and good feeling. This, for Socrates, is where the gods come into the story; it is a divine provision that men should feel this resentment, when certain acts are committed within their ken. Thus the unwritten law carries its own sanction, in an automatic reaction of humanity, and man cannot be supposed to have made himself behave like that. What man has done, on the other hand, is to discover by experience of his own, god-made, predestined make-up that certain kinds of behaviour "do not do" and "will not do." This discovery he formulates as a *nomos*, as he ascertains the orbit of a planet, by trial and error. It is in this sense, for example, that Heraclitus had said, "I investigated myself," and that the God in Delphi enjoined every Greek to "know thyself."

But it is still left a matter for research, what observances are of this fundamental physical kind, based on the *physis* of men, and what are only seemingly so, and not universal or necessary but only very widespread because very generally convenient. A Greek, for example, honoured his father and bore his name; he also burned his body after death. A Callatian Indian ate his dead father; whether he honoured him in life, and how, we are not informed. A Lycian bore his mother's name, not his father's; did he dishonour his father thereby, and if so, how? Socrates himself, in the conversation with Hippias, is not yet very far beyond the standpoint of Archelaus, that "good" and "bad" are not qualities inherent in things themselves, but epithets applied by mankind to certain acts and situations as a result of their own experiences.

THE PHILOSOPHY OF MANNERS

It is at this point that Greek thought seems

to undergo a rather sudden conversion.
Hitherto it had been preoccupied with contemplation of the world around, as an orderly
intelligible whole, with humanity only less
easily intelligible because its orderliness rested
on relations between men and everything else,
including other men, more comprehensive and
varied than any other creature enjoyed. Now,
humanity itself loomed up between the thinker
and the rest of the universe, with the previous
questions, How do we know anything at all
about either ourselves or the world beyond?
And what is it that prevents both our knowledge from being accurate and complete, and
our reaction to what we know, from being as
effective in its results as our imagination and
will would lead us to expect?

There were reasons enough for this pessimism. The sixth century had ended with a
new political movement in full flood, to super-
sede old restrictions and intermediate loyalties,
and to set an emancipated individual face to
face with a disembarrassed state, in the new
type of institution which its supporters
described as an *isonomy*, "equality of apportionment," and its opponents—perhaps some of
its friends also—as *democracy*, "control by
the countryside" over war-lords, landlords,
money-lords, and all minorities alike. The

fifth century had opened with the wonderful deliverance of Greek lands from incorporation in the largest and most efficient administrative machine that the world had known, the Persian Empire. This salvation had in great part been wrought by the state which had gone furthest in the new political experiment; and it was in confidence that this Athenian state could be trusted to complete the work of liberation, in the years following the strategical defeat of the Persian forces, that the states which had most to lose, in case of accident or misbehaviour, put their fortunes deliberately in Athenian hands, and anticipated the Platonic notion of behaviour according to *dikê*, by "doing their own business and not meddling," while the Athenian fleet performed its part of the bargain, and kept Persian forces out of reach of the seaboard and its Greek cities.

But the century which had begun so hopefully ended in general disaster. Small abuses had been allowed to become the occasion of grave scandals; small quarrels had been aggravated into great wars; economic rivalries had masqueraded as differences of political principle; and political principles, defensible in themselves, had been applied in practice with results which would have been criminal in private life, and were appalling in their enormity even to people accustomed to real war. In particular, granted that in physics the one-pound weight has no claim or redress against the two-pound weight in the other scale, did it necessarily follow that the inhabitants of Melos had no *locus standi* before the tribunal of humanity in face of the inhabitants of Athens?

Clearly what was out of order here was not the world-in-general, with its physical processes, but man's outlook and aims, "enthroned in his *polis*, wresting aside the *nomoi* of the earth, and the oath-fenced *dikê* of the gods." What was wanted was what Heraclitus had tried to supply, a "judgment about manners," "an exact steering chart for the estimation of man's life." But it was not from the physicists of Ionia—not even from their latest disciple, Archelaus—that the next step forward was to come, though their physical studies were to bear fruit again in due season, as we shall see.

THE PHILOSOPHIES OF THE WESTERN GREEKS

Now, it was the claim of the "emancipated" individual, as against the "ancestral custom," that though custom represented fairly enough the "wisdom of our fathers," that wisdom was no longer a trustworthy guide; partly because our fathers' transcript of what was quite properly being done in the sixth or seventh century did not appear to accord with what the fifth century thought it knew about its own goings on, and consequently needed revision; partly because the external world was a more spacious and usable place than it had been in the early days of the colonial movement or before them. And not only did the world of sense seem different, more intelligible, and a better guide to human reformers, in the Ionian "physical" school; the western colonies, which had contributed so effectively to the codification of public and private law, in the sixth century or earlier, by their written codes, were introducing new methods of inquiry both into the problems of nature and into politics and morals, and a new standpoint and outlook, profoundly different from the Ionian, though Pythagoras, one of the greatest of these western thinkers, was apparently of Ionian origin, and though the Pythagorean use of analogy between physical and human affairs is itself a special outgrowth of views "somewhat poetically expressed" already by Anaximander. Statistical relations between a whole and its parts, or between the different parts of the same whole, can obviously be pushed much further when they are mathematically expressed than when they are in physical terms, as with Anaximander, or biological, as with Archelaus and Socrates, if only because experimental verification of a mathematical argument seemed neither practicable nor necessary. The Pythagorean explanation of justice as in some sense a "square number," or a property of such a number, began by being a refinement on the pre-Homeric notion of retaliatory reparation for abnormal behaviour; it ended as a philosophical sanction, either for democracy, because as a number is "square" so long as its parts remain equal, so a state was inferred to be "in accordance with *dikê*" if its parts (namely, its citizens and their functions) were equal; or else for aristocracy and a specialized hierarchy of abilities and functions, if we argue with Plato that justice is a principle of adjustment, but take differences of ability and training into account in assigning "to each his due"; or, if we go further and take account, with Aristotle,[85] of differences of motive in "corrective" justice as well as of personal quality in "distributive."

In its native West, this kind of reasoning seems to have had temporary vogue as the sanction claimed by political cliques of high-

brow politicians, first in Pythagoras' own
adopted city, Croton, later in Tarentum, where
Archytas managed to persuade his fellow-
citizens that his exceptional merits entitled
him to hold office seven times as often as
ancestral custom allowed. The same happened
also in Thebes, where "the city began to
flourish as soon as the rulers became philosophers";[86] and it was the contemporary fact of
"philosopher-kingdoms" of this kind that explains the remedy proposed in Plato's *Republic*
for contemporary political disorders, and also
the scheme of reform projected by him for
Syracuse, under encouragement from its tyrant,
Dionysius, whose estimate of his own merits as
a ruler was as seventy times seven.

But these western schools had a larger
importance indirectly than in these occasional
experiments in professorial administration.
And the reason for this is easily seen. As the
would-be-liberated individual launched out
into his campaign against ancestral customs,
he found himself very soon in the deep waters
of his own ignorance both of the "way things
really happen" and of everything else, except
the classical education, through Homer, Hesiod,
and other early poets, which was the only
training available. Then, in the latter half
of the fifth century, the demand for something

more efficient, in the law court, in the assembly, and in business, rather suddenly created the supply of students and teachers of "humanities" of various kinds; from grammar and composition, to natural science, morals, politics. Most important of all, attention was directed to a previous question, without some answer to which it was difficult to see how any other problem could be approached with any hope of a solution, namely, How do we know anything at all? What is the nature of truth? And how can the truth of any statement or conclusion about anything be ascertained, or demonstrated to others?

With the answer to these questions, which are problems not of politics but of logic and psychology, we are not here concerned, nor even directly with the more nearly allied questions as to the nature of goodness and beauty, inevitably raised by the Athenian claim, in the generation of Pericles and Phidias and Sophocles, to have discovered the secret of both; and by counter claims, of Peloponnesian artists in their masterpieces, and of Spartan statesmen in political life, that Athenian art was not the last word on the realization of beauty, nor the "gilded cage" of the Athenian Empire the last stage toward "self-sufficiency" and "equality" for Greek states. It needs hardly to be noted, too, that the collapse of the Athenian super-state, so closely followed by the failure of Sparta either to replace that regime by a better, or to guarantee to her neighbours the "freedom" for which many of them had been fighting throughout, left a large number of city-states in a position of precarious independence for which their long tutelage and lack of responsibility for large decisions had seriously unfitted them. What wonder, then, if there was a widespread interest in any fresh method that might be suggested, for increasing the capacity of the ordinary man for acting "in accordance" with that "real way" of behaviour about which everyone was talking, but about which most people seemed to know so little; while some of those who talked loudest or most fluently were most easily upset by a person like Socrates, who only professed to know nothing at all, but so obviously knew at least how to reduce other people to the same state as himself.

Among the excesses of the Sophistic movement, then, and alongside of the new birth of logically cogent reasoning on all subjects alike, what is significant in the political thought of Greece in the late fifth and early fourth centuries, is the general desire of the ordinary citizen to become better equipped both to form opinions of his own and to criticise opinions presented to him on matters of administration and conduct alike. This was quite compatible with an increasing willingness to hand over the responsible business of administration to the man who really knew; in warfare to the professional soldier, in law and medicine to the trained practitioner, in politics to more or less self-trained and self-advertised "public men," or, more accurately, "platform men," for the platform was too often their only sure ground in public life, and the scene of the habitual and rapid disillusionment of all concerned. Yet the instinct was sound, and the attempts that were made to provide this political craftsmanship were sound also, insofar as they were honest, as many "sophists" seem to have been, according to their lights. The common argument from the special arts to the supreme art of political leadership was sound also. It may be that in great crises "politics often demand instinct rather than scientific wisdom from the politician;" but is this not so also in war, and music, and in the practice of law and medicine? Or, rather, such political instinct is something superadded to the training and experience which is presumed as a matter of course in the leading men of every other profession.

THE INTERPRETATION OF LAW

Clearly what was needed was not so much a
fresh review and re-formulation of the "way
things happen" in physics or in politics generally, as a closer control by what was reasonable and consistent with this, in the make-up
of the individual citizen, over the desires and
impulses which he experienced in a world so
full of opportunities, and now so stripped of
safeguards and restraints such as had protected his fore-fathers within their kinship-
group and tightly organized *polis*. Æschylus,
whose memory could go back to days before
the worst estrangement had happened between
Persian and Greek, had sketched a dualist,
almost Zoroastrian, solution of the problem
of evil, with the Olympian gods, clean-cut as
in bronze or marble, on man's better hand, to
give him their help if he would accept it, but
with a shapeless, monstrous force on his other
hand, an *atê* external to him, like the gods, to
be admitted or excluded, at his own free will,
from his inner counsels. At most he attributes
to his own city goddess Athena—like a Hebrew
prophet exempting Jehovah from his condemnation of the "gods of the nations"—an
initiative in the war between Olympians and
atê, reinforcing human reason in the search
for a "why" which shall lead man clear of all

that. Sophocles, for whom the great struggle between the old canon law of Athena's tribunal, seated under the open sky on the Areopagus rock, and the new civil lawyers of the post-war generation, was but a memory of his boyhood, advances to the conception of a conflict of laws; eternal "oath-fenced" *dikê* of the "gods" facing man's extemporized expedients, so far from "unforgetful" that they neglect the greater matters on which the coherence of society itself depends: and the dark formless *atê* turns out to be the shadow cast by man's own opacity to light. With the ground thus cleared of the Zoroastrian "adversary," Euripides had little difficulty in disposing of the traditional Olympian statuary—gracious and cheering though it was—which cumbered the forecourt of the House of Reason, and reformulated "that which is divine" as an aspect of "that which is in accord with *nomos*"; and in the Platonic psychology the whole conflict of forces is transferred within the walls of the "city of Man-Soul," the counterpart of the faction-ridden *polis* of the fourth century. Principles of conduct, indeed, are assumed to exist, an ultimate "Idea of the Good," like those "laws of the Greeks" according to which even the ideal state will still make war on enemies; but there is once again the previous

question, first, how man can know what that
goodness is; and then how, even if he knows
it, he can bring the rest of himself into the
"way of behaviour" which leads thereto. It
is the counterpart, and in great measure the
explanation, of that lack of initiative—and
still more, of willing response to reasonable
initiative—in the political world, which had
been paralysing everything from the death of
Pericles to the accession of Philip of Macedon.

"PHYSICS" AND "MANNERS" RECONCILED
IN ARISTOTLE'S TEACHING

Only by way of reaction from extravagances
both of the "philosophy of manners" and the
western "philosophy of abstractions" does the
Ionian conception of *nomos* as the formulation
of *physis* come once again into view, in the
physical philosophy of Aristotle, and no less
in its moral and political counterpart; and
therewith the same "kinetic" conception of
physis as "change" rather than either "origin"
or "substratum." For in the "physical" philosophy of Aristotle the province of physics is
"existence not in itself, but, rather, insofar
as it participates in change"; and the word
used for this "change" or "movement"—or
perhaps, more accurately still, this "process"—
is explained as including all kinds of "proc-

esses"; changes of amount, and alterations of quality, as well as motions in space. Indeed, it might give the closest rendering of all to describe the subject of physics as "existence participating in processes." The student of *physis* has to become acquainted with it, not only in respect of the material in which these processes are manifested, but of the conception of "process" or "procedure" itself;[87] and seeing that every process initiates somehow, some-when, and somewhere, and by achievement gives place to some further process in the same material, the physicist has to be acquainted with all aspects of causation.[88] He is, moreover, specially qualified by this varied experience of processes in relation to one another, and of materials undergoing processes and participating in them, to formulate "hypotheses" or formulations of the procedure—the way things happen—implicit in this or that process, which, as Aristotle puts it, "string together for the most part" the facts of observation, on the connecting thread of the physicist's interpretation.[89] This habit of mind he is, moreover, at pains to contrast with that of the logicians, "who from their many explanations, *logoi*, are without practice in observing what actually goes on, and because they regard too few of the facts, come more easily to an explanation"; their explanations and their *formulæ*, however, are not "without forgetfulness" of all that is relevant, and consequently run the risk of not being true.

All things exist "in *physis*" which "appear to have in themselves an initiative [*arkhé*] of processes and arrest of processes—movements, growth and decay, and all forms of alteration."[90] Such *physis* is contrasted with human skill to make things move, or increase or diminish, or exhibit changes, in that "skill is initiative in another; *physis*, initiative in the thing itself, for man begets man,"[91] or, as Topsy still more precisely expresses it—"I 'spect I growed." Such things "in their growing"—to revert to our earlier rendering of the Greek phrase—"from some initiative in themselves, continuously exhibiting some process, reach some achievement, *telos*," in contrast with things which happen by coincidence, which are results of chance. So "when this or occurs always or usually"—and in physics it is in this sense "always" if nothing stands in the way—"it is not coincidence nor by chance"; and as an illustration of the "kind of life" which (in another passage) he describes the physicist as observing—"all the life which only coexists with matter"—he refers to "a man doctoring himself, for *physis* is like that,"

300

in the sense that in such a "process" we are lucky enough to be in a position to find out from the initiator himself, what it is that initiates the whole train of processes between the start and the finish of the cure. So too, if we could only see the other side of the shield, or get behind the tapestry of nature's weaving, we should see, he thinks, just as complete a sequence, not of effect on cause only, but of cause on motive, in the literal sense in which a "motive" is an initiatory *arkhé*. It is in this sense that Aristotle allows himself to say that "*physis* intends" or "wants" to produce certain results; and this in a political context[92] as to the "intended" physical superiority of free men over slaves, though he admits that we sometimes find the opposite. And, similarly, he regards all processes, human and social as well as physical, as "initiated" in this sense, that the *telos*, or achievement, is correlated with some *arkhé* at the initiative end of the "growth-process." "So every *polis* exists in a *physis*, at all events if the first associations did so, for it is the *telos* of them; and their *physis* is a *telos*. For what each thing is when its coming into existence has been achieved (has reached its *telos*), this we say is the *physis* of each thing—man, horse, household, for example."[93]

What the student of *physis*, then, has to do
is to propound *arkhai;* to express, that is, in
language the various kinds of initiatives which
result in processes and lead to achievements
or results in the world about us.[94] The "order"
or "system" which emerges looks, as he graph-
ically puts it, like the organization of an army,
neither wholly inherent in the material in which
such "order" is exhibited, nor wholly imposed
from without; in an army there is discipline,
a certain relation between man and man, and
between them all and the *telos*, which is success
in war; but there is also the fact of the commander, and that is an initiative and a "living"
force manifest in this material and not otherwise.[95] And Aristotle goes so far as to give
the greater initiative, in this instance at least,
to the personal living force; "for he does not
exist because of the system, but that system
because of him." With another general, that
is, the army would be differently arranged; it
would, indeed, be a different army.

The cautious description of the physicist's
generalisations as linking up his observations
"to a great extent" is further explained by the
discussion of monstrosities, biological and other.
For *physis*, like God (who is the "general" of
nature's army), "makes nothing uselessly,"
and "always makes, of what is possible, the

302

best."[96] Yet there are exceptions, which need to be explained. "The monstrosity, *teras*, is one of the things beyond [outside] the way things grow, *physis*, but not beyond [outside] all *physis*, but that which mostly happens," and it only occurs when the process-of-growth, *physis*, n accordance with the particular kind, *eidos*, does not dominate that according to the material." This attribution of an impish "kind of life not exhibited except in the material," though we have already encountered something of the kind as the proper study of the physicist, is so little in accord with the more normal representation of the "material" in Aristotle's philosophy, as to look as if in despair he were having recourse to an almost Zoroastrian dualism, with a perverse force counter-working against the orderly initiative which makes things grow as they "mostly" do. Spontaneous variation from one *eidos* to another, of which he gives reputed examples among plants,[97] and border-line forms of life, like some sea-creatures which might be either plant or animal,[98] illustrate an evolutionary aspect of the "process" which is *physis*: it "passes continuously from the lifeless to the animals through things which are alive but not animals, such as sponges;[99] and leads to the conclusion that between animals and man, too, there is gradation: an animal's function is not only to perpetuate its kind but to know something about its surroundings, "for they have perception, and perception is knowledge of a sort."[100] Of habitual ways of behaviour there are "traces" already in all animals, more clearly in those which have what he calls *ethos*—a temperament susceptible to training —and, most of all, in man; "for this [human *ethos*] has *physis* brought to full achievement."[101] Current disputes, he adds, about the homogeneity of all life or the significance of the differences which some had detected within its whole range, are as inconclusive as they are, because the disputants seem to have confined their observations to humanity, and neglected the forms in which the process of growing has not gone so far.

For two reasons it has been necessary to describe in some detail the "physical" philosophy of Aristotle. The first is that it is the background and presumed substructure of his moral and political philosophy and deserves greater attention than is commonly paid to it by interpreters of these other parts of his system. And, secondly, it is this side of Aristotle's teaching that is most clearly appreciated as a reconciliation of the "philosophy of behaviour" with the Ionian "philosophy of growth-processes." His examination of human conduct begins with a formulation of the popular notion of well-being in terms which are purely biological. Man, like all other beings, has a specific function, as well as the generic animal function of maintaining and perpetuating a particular kind of *physis*; this specifically human function is the maintenance and perpetuation of a particular kind, complexity, and intensity, of perceptions, desires, intelligence, in a growth-process—a human lifetime—which achieves utmost efficiency by reasonable co-operation of all these manifestations of the kind of life-in-a-material, which a human being is. It presumes not only normal surroundings—and by normal are meant the physical conditions of Greek lands, such as we have already seen them to be—but also normal neighbours and associates, on whom to practise consideration, benevolence, and in its fullest and highest aspect that "friendship" without which an earthly paradise were but a Crusoe's Island. And it recurs to the biological mode of presentation at the highest point, where clash between rational generality and impish particularism might seem to be least liable to recur; for "this is the *physis* of the reasonable man, a re-establishment of *nomos*, where it falls short by reason of its generality."[102] Even on the human plane, growth-processes can only be formulated with what might be justly described as a biological degree of accuracy. "Monsters," that is, are still liable to occur, where by some freak of chance the "growth according to the type does not keep its hold on that according to the material." Men are "mostly" humane and reasonable, but not quite always; a few men seem, to our unaided knowledge, to have been "made in vain'; the idiot with "a way of thinking of his own" is as little amenable to normal treatment as the genius whose "way of thinking" is also peculiar to himself, so that he takes into account things which we others have left out, and so "sees true." On such occasions and in face of such anomalies, the rigid accuracy of a general *formula* or *nomos* necessarily leaves out of account the very facts which are of the essence of the problem; and to take these into account, and devise a new *formula* which will express them in their true relation to the other facts in the case, is the *physis* of the "reasonable" man; a "reestablishment of *nomos*" by "setting straight" this particular disturbance of it.

And it is not wholly accidental that this recurrence to biological, "physical" terminology follows closely on a discussion of the meaning of the popular word *dikaion*, which strictly and originally meant "in accordance with a *dikê*." The Pythagorean or "logical" school of abstract dogmatic speculation had started quite reasonably with that primitive custom of retaliation as offering the typical *formula* for the restoration of outraged order.   Whether their source was Babylonian, Confucian, or the more accessible *ius gentium* of Italian peasantry in a "state of nature"—like Montesquieu's "Iroquois" and "Huron," or Rousseau's "Carib on the banks of the Orinoco"—does not concern us here.   What is important is that this notion of *physis* is mathematically abstract: theft or damage to the amount of "2" demands precisely "2" of retaliation, and so forth.   But, as Aristotle has no difficulty in showing,[103] such abstract justice breaks down when applied to the facts of daily life; neither in "distributive" nor in "corrective" procedure will "retaliation" or "reciprocity" re-establish order. When we are measuring commodities and can obtain agreement as to a ratio of exchange between them, reciprocity is the foundation of civil society, "for by doing in return what is proportionate the *polis* holds together."   But in matters of conduct, not of produce, Pythagorean retaliation brings us back abruptly to the Homeric Trial Scene: "The one said that

307

he paid in full; the other, that he was not taking any;" the law was clear, and the facts; yet decision tarried, and two talents lay there for the man who "along with" the interpreters of the law should so formulate the issues as to "straighten things out." "And this is the *procedure* of the reasonable man, to re-establish the rule, where it falls short through its generality."

THE GREEK NOTION OF LAW IN ROMAN JURISPRUDENCE

In the mind of the Greek "man-in-the-street," then—no less than in that of the professional citizen-justice in the courts, and of the philosopher who so nearly risked default in his duties as a citizen at all—"law," "justice," "equity," "self-respect," "public opinion," and whatever other aspect or procedure established normal relations between man and man, or re-established them after infringement, was an attempt on the part of human reason and intelligence to wrest from the surrounding world its secret, of "how things really happen," as a Homeric king "wrested" from the mind of Zeus his "ordinances" for the guidance of men to fulfilment of his will-and-pleasure. In this sense, "politics" and "morals" are no more and no less than two chapters in the same code, two "tables" of the same "law," formulating, and ever reformulating, the one a man's duty toward his neighbour, and toward his neighbours collectively in a city-state; the other what we can best interpret as his "duty toward himself."

It is remarkable and conclusive evidence of the contribution of Greek thought to Roman law that the definition or, rather, group of accepted descriptions of law · in its essential features, prefixed to Justinian's *Digest*,[104] differs only in a single word—the substitution of the Christian "God" for the Olympian "gods"— from the text of a well-known passage in Demosthenes' speech in the case of Aristogeiton. "This is law, to which it is proper that all men should conform, for many reasons"—and we note at the outset, as in so many other connexions, that the relation between the Greek and that law which was his king was not that of master and servant, but of teacher and pupil. Then follow the reasons, which are essentially four: "chiefly because every *nomos* [rule of law] is a discovery and gift of God [or 'gods'], an opinion of sensible men, a restitution of things done amiss, voluntary and involuntary, and a general compact of a *polis* in accordance with which it is proper for all in that *polis* to live." Each of these aspects of

309

law deserves separate examination in the light of conclusions already tentatively reached.

First, in law as *"invention and gift of gods,"* we recognise, as immediate prototype of those gods, the Platonic "spirits," *daimones*, special providences giving to all kinds of beings in their respective environments all things needful to normal self-sufficient maintenance "in accordance with the way things grow"; under supervision of *Nemesis*, indisputable because in accordance with all the facts, and leaving nothing out of account; and behind this looms up the Herodotean notion of gods as "those who set all in order and held all feeding-grounds." No less we recognise the operation of supreme and unfettered intelligence, investigating, analysing the "way things grow," and literally discovering its processes, and their irrefutable because all-comprehending coherence. This divine code, if we may so describe the complete result of this divine observation and analysis, being itself the all-wise formulation of what actually happens, is also the all-beneficent "will of Zeus," because Zeus himself does not, will not (for he knows all and knowledge is goodness), and—to contemplate momentarily what is almost unthinkable— *cannot* override that Necessity which is the realisation of things as they have come to be, because so they were. It is the "gift of gods" to men, because now, as of old, men can, if they will, "extort" the will of Zeus and express it in their own words; and every such formulation of what really happens is a *nomos*, proper for men to observe. All human *nomoi*, that is, are "nurtured," as Heraclitus said, "by one *nomos*, the divine"; from this they derive their initiative, their driving power; in politics, as in physics, "speaking with intelligence, it is for our good to fortify ourselves in that which is common in all"—the general formula—"as a *polis* fortifies itself in its *nomos*, and far more firmly."

Secondly, law is an *"opinion of sensible men."* They, too, like poets and minstrels, are "nurtured by one *nomos* which is divine"; for the musician has his *nomoi* with their own canons. And their "opinion" has value, in two senses. Isocrates expressed both, when commending to the court "among laws, the most ancient (original), among arguments the most recent." The most "original" among general rules he commends because these have stood the test of more varied application, and have, moreover, "originated" more processes of restitution, exercised wider influence, and acquired higher esteem. For it is not their age—venerable though they were—that counted, but

their efficiency.[105]   On the other hand, among
the applications of general rules, in argument
and conference, to fresh circumstances as they
arise he commends "the freshest" because these
are the pioneers of our experience of the unexhausted meaning of those "originative" phrases.
It was the sound advice of a well-known English
counsel to his juniors to "look up that new
case"—the most recent embodiment of old
principle in practical guidance.   And this more
especially is that "common sense" or "practical
wisdom" of which a *nomos* was the "opinion"
in Demosthenes' phrase; though the other is
not excluded, and, indeed, was itself once
"freshest," when the paint was wet on Solon's
revolving notice-boards.   For it is one of the
strangest paradoxes in the history of Greek
laws and constitutions that in an age when
society, as has been said, was "moving like
quicksilver," an importance which at first
sight seems exaggerated was attributed to
traditional and often very ancient *formulæ;* and
much ingenuity was expended in interpreting
these older phrases and notions so as to cover
the facts of contemporary business.   Hence
the frequent appeals of the pleaders, in the
fourth century, to the "*nomoi* of our fathers,"
and the care with which the ancestral custom
of Athenian public life was reconstructed, when

312

sanity with normal circumstances returned
to the survivors of that orgy of constitutional
experiment which began among the friends of
Antiphon, and ended with those of Critias.

Thirdly, in law as *"restitution of things done
amiss, voluntary and involuntary,"* we have
explicitly the same notion of the procedure of
justice as a restoration of an outraged order—
an initiative force which sets things straight
and free to go on as usual, when they have
somehow by force become "crooked" and
jammed—which we have been following from
Homeric antiquity, and meet again in Aristotle's description of justice, *dikaiosynê*, as
"an excellence whereby each man holds what
is his own, and as is the custom, *nomos*";[106]
whereas its opposite—*adikia*, "where there is no
dikê"—is "that whereby he holds what belongs
to another and not as is the custom." Law
and justice, that is, "restore" the state of things,
normal and customary, which has been disturbed in "absence of *dikê*," by behaviour,
that is, which is the negative and contradictory
of the "way" of straight-living, which could
be described in such a *dikê* or *formula*. Justice, that is—to amplify Aristotle's phrase—
is not only "distributive" but "re-distributive";
of law-in-operation, redress of grievances is a
primary characteristic.

313

And law-in-operation is not limited to crimes or things "done amiss" deliberately. It is a process of research, supplementing the current stock of knowledge and experience, no less than of redress, applying that store of *formulæ* to defeat the schemes of abnormal persons. We are reminded of those not infrequent cases, in modern law, where a disputed point is "taken to court" in cool and friendly fashion in order simply to discover by experiment "what the law of the matter is." And in this sense the Athenian courts, at all events, like English courts of justice, were literally "making law" all the time; confirming, defining, refining, the case-law of the past, itself the "opinion of sensible men" applied to the primitive "invention and gift of gods"; and providing the material in the hands of the college of *thesmothetai* for their annual report to the sovereign people, on the working of the "*nomoi* of their fathers," and for the schedule of formal and material amendments appended to it, which it was the first regular business of the Athenian mass meeting to discuss at the New Year.

And this process of research—inevitably, however unconsciously, cumulative—into the working of "customary" behaviour in a world which was expanding rapidly, and enriching its inhabitants with unprecedented interchange

of commodities, and amenities, and ideas, gave
expression, within each field of its operation,
to a complex of traditions, expedients, and
aspirations, in the shape of an explanatory
analysis of their assumptions and implications,
which varied from city to city in its partic-
ulars, but was prevented from more than such
almost accidental divergences by the general
uniformity of the conditions of life, and of the
initial structure, or lack of structure, of the
communities themselves, which we were forced
to recognise at the outset. Here, indeed, we
have another reason why the "most original
nomoi were best," for the further back an
observance or a *formula* could be traced, the
more surely was it found to cohere with similar
early solutions of the same elementary problems in other but similar societies, and the
broader, therefore, the basis of divine invention and human concurrence therein, on which
this consensus appeared to rest. The significance of this we already had occasion to recon-
sider (p 282,) when we came to the "unwritten
nomoi" as the fourth-century philosophers
conceived them. Meanwhile, within the broad
guiding lines traced by geographic, economic,
and ethnic uniformities, each such "complex
of ethical rules" as formed the "custom of our
fathers" in a Greek city-state, was demon-

strably relative—once anyone took the trouble to examine it—not merely to the *ethos*, in the Aristotelian sense, of the men who observed it, but also to their *ethea* in the Homeric use of the word for habitual abode.

Fourthly, and finally, law is the *"general compact of a state, in accordance with which it is proper that all in that state should live."* Here we have explicitly the recognition of the regional and particular quality of Hellenic law, to which we have already been led, and to its character as an agreed body of descriptions of the "way people behave," the things that "are done," in a particular city and its territory. To put the matter in a phrase, "custom exists by custom," observance by being observed. The same conclusion is presented, not quite unexpectedly—as we are now able to see, after our analysis of the relation between *nomos* and *physis*—by Aristotle in his discussion of the validity of contracts. "For a compact is *nomos* of a sort, special [between individuals] and in matter of detail: and it is not the compacts which make the *nomos* valid, but the *nomoi* which make valid the compacts in accordance with them. And, inclusively, the *nomos* itself is a compact of a kind, so that whoever breaks faith or makes void a compact is making void the *nomoi*."[107] Individual breach of

316

individual compact in a particular matter
implies and involves breach of the *nomos* or
general observance, that compacts once made
are observed. And that general observance
is itself, for Aristotle, a compact between you
and me to observe compacts; an agreed assumption not so much that this shall be our
common way of behaviour in respect of each
other, as a scientific discovery, by comparison
of our respective behaviours, that we *are*
creatures of that sort, by whom certain kinds
of things, and among them contract-breaking,
"are not done"—a discovery which no one but
a lunatic would profess to have made as between himself and "fish or beast or winged
birds," because, as Hesiod expressed it long
ago, there is no such "way" in them, [108] whereas
it is the *nomos* or formulation of human behaviour that men as a matter of observation
do "customarily" keep faith; just as they
"customarily" tell the truth according to the
knowledge that they have.

In this respect it may be suggested that
Greek reflection on this matter anticipates and
even transcends the description given recently,
by Professor de Montmorency, of jurisprudence as the study of human *principia* or "laws
of motion" in the Newtonian sense, as descriptions of the way things actually happen.[109]

Of these human *principia* he formulates the first as follows: *Fides est servanda*—"Troth must be kept"; or, in other words, *ius suum cuique*—"To every one his due." Now, this accords well enough with the Kantian notion of the moral and political world as a "realm of ends," wherein each fellowman is an end like his fellows, including myself their fellowman, not a means either to my ends or to the ends of any other man. But does it quite attain to the Newtonian objectivity of the "first law of motion" in physics, that "movement *continues* [rather than *must* or *should* continue] in the same direction and with the same speed"? And is not the physicist's observance of the *physis* of man—the way, that is, in which normal men normally behave—more precisely formulated in the words, *inter homines fides servatur*, than in the commendatory or imperative form to which reference has been made? This, indeed, is the *dikê* uniquely peculiar to mankind. If you found a creature behaving so, you could not but dissociate it from anything fishy or bestial; you must rank it unerringly as man.

LECTURE VI

THE NOTION OF FREEDOM, *ELEUTHERIA*: THE MAN AND THE CITIZEN

WHEN the head of a Roman household formally released from his own paternal authority —from observance, that is, of his initiative in all family affairs—a son who was of mature age and sound judgment, and thus permitted him to become in his turn *pater familias* like himself, he was said *liberare*, to "make *liber*"; and a man's *liberi*, accordingly, are his grown-up, independent sons. And when such a son became *liber* he entered into a new direct immediate personal relation with the state: he was no longer *in manu patris*, under the hand and guidance of his father; he was in the fullest sense *civis*, "domesticated," or "disciplined" to considerate, tolerant conduct to other *cives* of the same *civitas*; but, above all, he was *liber*, "grown up." For other members of his father's household—a slave, for example—might be "put out of hand," *manu missi*, or "liberated" as he had been; and, given the same personal "grown-up"-

319

ness, though their entry into full relationship
with the *civitas* was postponed in consideration of alien ancestry, and only befell their
children. They were *liberti*, not *liberi* like
the freeborn.

Now, though the Greek city-states of which
we know most had a family life far less rigidly
"stable" and accorded far greater freedom of
action to grown sons during their fathers'
lifetime, the Greek language had nevertheless
the precise linguistic counterpart of the Roman
liber, only slightly disguised in the form *eleu-
theros*; and its primary meaning was exactly
the same: it meant "grown-up"—able, consequently, to take care of yourself; competent
to take care of others in the four physical
associations recognized by Aristotle, and by
Greek legal practice long before his time; to be
responsible for wife, children, slaves, and the
estate; literally, under the last heading, for the
"land of his fathers," or whatever portion of
it fell to his share in due course. To realize
how a well-bred and well-educated young man
regarded these responsibilities, read that most
gracious and humorous essay on "How to be
Happy though Married," the *Œconomicus* of
Xenophon.

But to whom was this "grown-up" citizen
responsible? In regard to his wife, there was

the wife's family; and their remedy, in case of misconduct or ill treatment—if remonstrance, outward symptom of their *nemesis* against his behaviour, failed—was to take the facts to a public justice and ask for a *dikê*, which should set that straight in the fashion already familiar from our Lecture IV. He, similarly, could bring home to her and to her kinsmen responsibility for misbehaviour on her part. And, besides, in many a Greek *polis*, flighty or unseemly behaviour of a wife, if it occurred in public, brought her into disciplinary collision with the initiative of the public "wife-warden," and the majesty of ancestral *nomoi* on the subject of woman's place in the state. Similarly, if his children were neglected, or noisy, or otherwise abnormal in their lives, the "child-warden" was at hand to set that matter straight too, like the "beadle" in an old English village. His slave, too, was no more at his mercy than a modern costermonger's donkey: he was entitled to apply for a *dikê* from the proper official in the event of ill treatment, and to be transferred to another master if the facts made this the most prudent precaution for the future. And for neglect of his farm, in addition to the criticisms and complaints of the neighbours—another aspect of *nemesis*— and his own arrears of taxation, there was the "field-warden's" initiative, to keep him up at least to the minimum of intelligent effort.

There is no reason to believe that an ordinary Greek householder in the fifth century was more seriously worried by this kind of public supervision than a modern citizen is by the education officer, the Board of Agriculture, the Society for the Prevention of Cruelty to Animals. He had been brought up to conform to a way of behaviour which had, at all events, stood the test of about five centuries— as long as from the Italian Renaissance and the invention of printing to our own time. Of this the normal citizen was proud enough; and it had stood also—though this he could hardly be expected to realize—the test of slow reasonable remodelling in detail, as manners matured, and needs multiplied, together with the means to satisfy them. In its general features this way of life resembled those which prevailed in some hundreds of other city-states, large and small, so that a Greek whose business made it necessary for him to "lodge," as he expressed it, in another city, either temporarily, or as often happened, habitually, found no more difficulty in making himself "at home" and inconspicuous than an American in Cape Town or Sydney. Yet quite apart from differences of dialect, which were quite as recognisable as between English and Lowland Scottish, and the more superficial and intelligible contrasts between the great seaports and industrial centres, such as Corinth, Ephesus, or Miletus, and the very numerous cities which had had no such exceptional fortune, there was not a *polis* in Greek lands which had not that all-pervading individuality of behaviour, and outlook, which made its ordinary citizen, enduring the ordinary surprises and accidents of foreign travel, thank God, like the Pharisee, that he was not as other men are, men of Sicinos or Pholegandros, or even those impossible fellows in the next bay to his own; or praise Zeus and the Graces, on his return, because, after all, "there is no place like home." Truly, as Herodotus wrote, "if all men were free to select the best among all the customs there are, you would find that each people chose their own, as being best in accord with their own way of behaviour."

The great majority of the Greek people did not wish things otherwise; they groaned under no "tyranny of custom" any more than they consciously idealized the "reign of law." And Anacharsis did his countrymen injustice when he said that only the beasts of the field fought without reserve for freedom (p. 280). Heraclitus' advice to fight in behalf of the *nomos* of the *polis* as one fights for its fortress wall, only put into words the natural instinct of the citizen and the house-father. For the *polis*, which had come into being to keep men alive, had in essentials achieved a higher purpose, the supreme end, indeed, of all society; it existed to insure to them felicity, all the felicity that was possible to men—and, indeed, this was much—in Greek lands and under a Greek sky.

Wherein this felicity was thought to consist, by Greeks of the fourth century, we have already seen, in Aristotle's summary of current opinions (p. 52). And, indeed, in essentials, the first and widest of them, "prosperity with efficiency," does not fall far short of Plato's ideal of behaviour according to *diké*— which is the code of rules for the great game of life—"to do one's own business, and not meddle with other people's," combining, as this does, both tables of the law, as they were engraved upon the temple at Delphi, "Know thyself" and "Nothing in excess." For to do one's own business one must have taken one's own measure, as well as the measure of one's fellows; all "meddling" is "in excess" of one's own business in life, and sure sign of inefficiency, as well as of an excess of "push."

But while there was general agreement as

to the object of society, the "end of the *polis*," there was wide difference of opinion how it was to be realized. For the means were partly material, partly formal, partly personal; and in regard to each there was controversy.

MATERIAL RESTRICTIONS ON GREEK FREEDOM

For a while, the material means of well-being seem to have increased concurrently with the population and its material needs. Terrace-agriculture increased the cultivable area; tree crops, such as vine and olive, supplemented cereals, milk-products, and meat, as the basis of subsistence. Temporary over-population, when there was no more land at home to be exploited, was relieved first by colonisation, then, as in Solon's Attica, by more specialised agriculture, and various manufactures which intercourse with the colonial regions made possible; and commercial wealth, due to individual initiative, held more completely at the personal disposal of its creators, and made portable, as we have seen already, by the adoption of metallic standards of value, gave the individual an enhanced value and significance, which was cumulative. In societies inevitably so small and incapable of extension, such individual efficiency and capac-

ity for initiative became and remained a
source of serious anxiety, not unknown in
other types of community in other countries
and periods of history. If "initiative" displayed the man, it was "wealth" that made
him, in the sense that it gave him wherewithal
to display such initiative as he had. And for
"wealth" the Greek language, concrete and
concise as ever, used a plural form meaning
literally "things that help" or are "useful."[1]
No one disputed in Greek any more than in
Hebrew cosmology that though the Son of
Cronos had not given men a *nomos* which contemplated their eating one another, he had
assigned to them as their "portion" all that
earth holds: "unto you it is given for meat,"
so far as human initiative should exploit and
domesticate it, "wresting aside the *nomoi* of
the earth," winning metals from stones, grain-
crops from Scythian prairies, Milesian carpet-
wares from the wool of Phrygia and Cyrene;
utilising, too, for their own ends the labour
of such other men as were unable to make good
their claim to use their own labour as they
pleased.[2] Such men were not *eleutheroi*, "free-
men," because they did not seem quite
"grown up"; that a Greek should catch them
young, and give them a sporting chance to
"work up" to grown-up-ness and self-mastery

326

like his own, was in his view not as much reasonable as obvious; even if this philanthropy was hard to distinguish from the labour-hunger which beset the great centuries of Greece, as it beset the first stages of our own "industrial revolution."

With the procedure of industry and commerce, Greek political thought, even in its closest approaches to a "political" economy, was almost unconcerned; less because it knew and thought very little about it than because the question for statesmen and thoughtful citizens was not, as in our own industrial revolution, how to acquire wealth, but what to do with the "usable things" which existed already. In this respect Greek political thought, in those phases of it which we can best follow, in the writers of the fourth century, is a whole stage ahead of our own, and for that reason specially deserves our attention. For the period of the individual fortunes, relatively vast, in comparison with the resources of the state, seems to correspond rather with that of colonial exploitation; and the moneyed "boss" in political life to the "age of tyrants" in the seventh and sixth centuries. There were very rich men, it is true, in the fifth century—Cimon, Callias, Nicias, to name only Athenians—but their wealth was not a

public danger, and it was only on the out-
skirts of the city-state regime that private
wealth dominated a political situation, in
Thessalian and Macedonian dynasts, in Maus-
sollus with his Carian barony superposed on a
Hellenic *polis;* in Evagoras of Salamis, merchant-prince in Cyprus as well as twenty-
second in descent from a "divine born" king
of the Heroic Age; in Dionysius of Syracuse,
who had "struck oil" in the supply of merce-
naries, the most marketable of commodities
in a generation of incessant warfare, and used
both his capital and his stock-in-trade to
exploit the Greek West as well as to defend it
against national enemies and rivals, old and
new.

PRIVATE WEALTH AND ITS OBLIGATIONS

There were good reasons for this material
restriction on the "utilities" or "external
goods" at the disposal of the Greek individual:
the physical poverty of the country, a land
of thirsty limestones and dusty schists; the
simplicity and backwardness of the customary
methods of agriculture; the shortage of labour,
due to perennial shortage of sustenance; the
difficulty and insecurity of communications,
mountain passes and seaways being alike no-
man's-land infested by outlaws and "advent-

urers";[3] the precariousness, moreover, of all
wealth, in a world where accident, disease,
violence, not to speak of the political sport
and gamble of regular war, made the "act of
God" a far more serious matter than could be
covered, as with ourselves, by a clause in an
insurance policy.[4]   Then, more remediable, had
a little common sense been devoted to it, there
was the sentimental restriction on the alien-
ation of family estate, that inherited injunction
"not to hand on diminished" what the living
trustees had received from the last dead ancestor, for the maintenance not of themselves
and their living issue only but of their successors
for all time.   There was also the childishly
elementary notion of finance and "management," which saw no reason why the "progeny"
of a borrowed mare or cow should not be returned in part at least to the owner along
with the "principal," but boggled at the notion
that a loan of current coins could "breed
money,"[5] by way of interest, for which the
business-word was still *tokos*, "progeny."

On the other hand, as has been hinted
already, every Greek knew well enough how
hard it was to accumulate wealth, and how
monstrous an advantage "realisable utilities"
gave to their possessor in the daily struggle to
"live well," and he consequently kept a very

watchful eye on any neighbour who seemed to
have "utilities" at his disposal. Among the
natives of British Columbia, in quite recent
times, a man's only secure investment for the
profits of hunting or mere labour in a lumber
camp or canning factory, was to distribute it
among the members of his own community;
for only so was he sure of the help he was
certain to require sooner or later, when the
luck was no longer his way. And this is no
isolated instance. So, for example, Crœsus literally showered gold upon Alcmæon the Athenian, confident that if the kingdom of Lydia
ever needs Athenian help, it will be for Alcmæon to do "what is done" by a man in his
position. It was a bad bargain, as things
turned out, for when Crœsus wanted help it
was not the Alcmæonidæ, but Pisistratus, who
was in control of Athenian affairs, and Crœsus
failed to liquidate his investment. So, too, he
gave gold to the Spartans, when they came
quite prepared to buy in the Lydian gold-mar-
ket, but he expected something in return "by
and by," and when the Spartans found that
they had inopportunely lost their field army,
just when Crœsus put up his signal of distress,
they took the only honourable course that
remained to them, collected subscriptions,
and repaid the loan in gold.

Similarly, in a Greek city, wealth of all other kinds, like landed property, was in trust for reasonable provident use; it was an affair of "utilities" and no man was expected, any more than in the similar circumstances in Palestine, to "keep his talent in a napkin." That was indeed one of the grievances against the new portable wealth which commerce and, above all, money-lending, created. If a man's farm prospered and he began to lay field to field, it was a process which the neighbours could watch—and stop if it went too far for general convenience. It might, on the other hand, be good policy to bring impoverished estates and landless capitalists together, as Solon did, financing Attic agriculture out of the "invisible imports" of Attic trade and shipping, and turning dangerously volatile "utilities" into the fixed assets represented by barns, oil-presses, fruit-trees, and the like.

But what "was done" in ordinary circumstances was something simpler, humaner, more gracious, and in the highest sense "politic," namely, what was courteously known as a "public service," or *liturgy*. Among ourselves the word *liturgy* has been reduced to signify public acts of observance and recognition to the Giver of Good. In Greece the giver of good was the *polis*, which included the gods as well as the citizens—sleeping partners, perhaps, those gods, and a little liable to be asleep, or pursuing, like Baal of Mount Carmel, when you put up your signal of distress; but in older days they had helped the city, and if their worshippers remembered them, "as is done," it was not in the nature of things that they could utterly forget. So it was to the *polis* that the prosperous individual was led to turn, by example, by precept, by his own self-respect, and the force of public opinion in support of "what is done." Customarily, whole departments of what we should now consider the "public service" were financed and administered by way of such "benevolences," much as Tudor and Stuart kings attempted to direct the new-made wealth of English merchants and adventurers into public channels by similar though less successful euphemisms. Ships of war, for example, public festivals and especially musical and dramatic performances, public buildings, monuments, and "utilities" of every kind, were equipped and maintained by this substitute for a supertax on individual prosperity. The custom, it is true, hardened as time went on into a system and a schedule, and eventually, in Athens, at all events, showed signs of breaking down; but throughout the great days of the *polis* it was the means whereby the personal abilities and still more the personal tastes of the citizen were enlisted in the public service, in addition to the state's reasonable share in his "utilities," that is to say, his realizable wealth.

PUBLIC WEALTH AND ITS RESPONSIBILITIES

But though the private fortunes of Greek citizens in the fourth century were not usually allowed to become large enough to achieve political domination for their individual possessors, there was nevertheless sufficient range of difference between the richest and the poorest to make the old question urgent, "How is private wealth being used, and does it contribute, in proportion to its amount, to the general well-being?" Considering, that is, the "number of the state" in population, and in estimated amount of "usable things," is this or that *polis* as near to "prosperity with efficiency" or whatever other definition of felicity was locally preferred, as an economist like Solon, or a "physiologist" and engineer, like Empedocles, might be expected to figure it out to be? As in the regime when Crœsus "had the initiative," it was necessary to "look to the end," and not the chronological termination only, but the consummation of that

333

process of achievement, the "way things grow" in this or that society.

In the supreme example of great and well-earned wealth in Greek hands—this time in the hands not of an individual but of the *polis* of the Athenians—criticism took the same line and asked the same question. Everybody knew what the original bargain had been, after the defeat of the Persian invaders of Greece. The primary condition of security was naval supremacy.[6] Athens undertook to relieve allied states of the personal service necessary for this end, in consideration of an agreed (and very modest) annual levy. Athens fulfilled her obligations, and (so long as no third party interfered, with other occasions for war) had something over out of the levy, as well as her agreed compensation for her management. No question, however, seems to have been raised as to the propriety of this management; the trouble came over the uses to which the Athenians put their accumulated balances. Now, this, as in all other instances where there was wealth to be applied and expended, was a matter of initiative in the spender. He might "know himself" and "do his own business" without "meddling" or "excess," or he might act in such a way as to infringe the competence and opportunity of his fellows to do the same.

THE NOTION OF FREEDOM

Now, in the political as well as the economic circumstances of the Greeks, accumulated wealth was exceptionally difficult to use; and also, poor as the country and the people generally were, it was usually difficult to avoid occasional "windfalls," just because the chapter of accidents was so rich in unforeseen episodes. The problem, too, was complicated by traditional belief in divine jealousy of human affluence, still more, of human initiative, and by customs based on those beliefs, which made certain kinds of expenditure for the conciliation or merely the felicity of the city's gods a heavy first charge on fortune's gifts. It was not everybody who, like the Alcmæonidæ, could first conclude a contract for the rebuilding of the temple at Delphi, then acquire the reputation of having employed marble where only limestone was in the bargain, and escape detection for over two thousand years, through the excellence of the cement which they substituted for marble.

The Persian Incubus on Greek Freedom

A further material limitation on the "grown-up"-ness of the Greeks resulted from the historical accident of the rise of Persia, and the restriction of the field of colonial enterprise to those few regions which escape absorption into the Persian Empire. Consequently, the struggle for existence became suddenly severer, and the competition keener between the Greek states already most irrevocably committed to foreign enterprises on any very large scale; consequently, again, the temptation, more severe to some *poleis* than to others, to throw in their lot with the new imperial regime, and enjoy at all events some of the old facilities which had resulted from similar dependence on the Lydian kings of Sardis. We have only to read in their literal sense the more historical phrases about the "servant of the Lord, even Cyrus," in the later chapters of the book of Isaiah, to realize what prospect of peace and prosperity opened before the Hebrew remnant at the close of its Babylonian exile; and the political significance of those repeated appeals to the "islands" to hear the good news and come into the Persian fold. And Miletus, at all events, did come into the fold, at Cyrus' first invitation, and remained hand-in-glove with the new masters for nearly half a century.

It would be out of place here to trace in detail the tragic stages by which the misunderstanding of each other deepened between Persians and Greeks, and the nationalist and parochialist trend which was given thereby to the great advance in Greek political thought which was already taking place when Cyrus and his Persians appeared on the scene. That the Persian was not incapable of "understanding democracy" was believed by Herodotus at all events; but the policy, or lack of policy, of the more democratic states threw the Persians into the arms of the reactionary elements in Greece, with even more momentous results than the same situation produced later, during Rome's initiation into the Greek political world.

For in the mere pursuit of efficiency, in dealing with these small but energetic and superficially turbulent communities, the Persian government made one fatal mistake; by "recognising" as its permanent instrument of local administration either the chief "public servant" of the moment, or the citizen, whoever he was, who seemed to have the greatest capacity for initiative, and the widest personal influence, Persia literally "stopped the clock," and deranged the customary circulation of opportunities for public service, and—it must be added—for the abuse of such occasion for initiative; and the dismay and desperate courses that this error of policy provoked are conclusive evidence that Aristotle's diagnosis of citizenship as "the capacity on either side of

initiating and being initiated for" was as true
of the sixth century as of the fourth.

Now, it was this "equality of allotment"—
isonomia, as Herodotus calls it—which was the
political equivalent of "grown-up"-ness, in the
Greek use of *eleutheria*. It has other aspects
too: "equality in public meeting" and "in
public speech"—for *isegoria* may mean either,
and probably did connote both—and *isoteleia*,
"equality of performance," more especially
in regard to the assignment of the less agree-
able occasions of public service, such as drill
and payment of taxes. Those superficial restrictions and interferences in private affairs
with which we began were as innocuous as they
appeared to the ordinary Greek householder,
less because, on the whole, they were reasonably and charitably enforced, than because
they were enforced by men who had private
affairs of their own and interpreted "ancestral
nomoi" in the light of their own experience of
such administration before their brief term
of public service, and with the knowledge that
at its close they were to come under the similar
inspection and admonition of other citizens as
ordinary as themselves. In such an administration "to do one's own business, and not
meddle" was a high standard of public service,
yet not impossible of attainment, and very close

indeed to any conceivable ideal of "justice," if "justice" was to be, as its Greek name implies, the quality of accordance with *dikê*, the normal "way of doing" whatever has to be done, the remedial way of "straightening out" whatever has been done "crookedly."

MINORITY GOVERNMENT

There were, of course, differences of degree between one *polis* and another, in respect to the attainment of this "grown-up"-ness by the whole of the adult male population; quite apart from the disastrous wrench given by the Persian interference to the contemporary trend of political evolution among the Greeks. In the conquest-states of Mainland Greece (pp. 86-88) large elements even of the legally free population were very far from "grown-up" in the political sense. In many more a minority variously constituted and distinguished, by birthright, hereditary landownership, acquired-wealth, skill, or discipline in war, monopolized "initiative" in regard to all ordinary occasions, and used it, as such minorities frequently do, to obstruct political initiative outside the privileged circle. Some of these "oligarchies" probably deserved the condemnation poured on them by their actual victims, and by dispassionate philosophers too, as governments "in the interest of the governors"; but we begin to know enough of the public work of some of them to realise that, for ordinary circumstances of the kind usually found in Greek lands, this kind of government was indeed in a true sense "government in the interest of the whole"; and that in point of thoroughbred descent, homogeneity of experience and outlook, and efficient conduct of the small amount of public business which came before them, they were truly "aristocracies;" states, that is, where power was in the hands of the "best people." Certainly, it seems to have been in some of these minority-ruled states that the general welfare of the population was best maintained, and that stability, which almost all Greek states so pathetically desired, and seemed in general so little able to secure in detail, was best guaranteed. Notoriously it was in such states that most attention was paid to the strict upbringing of the young; and Aristotle's description of the "aim" of this type of *polis* as "education" is borne out by the few instances in which anything is known of their public provision for it. It was not, indeed, so much a system as an ideal of conformity to type that was set before the young people, boys and girls alike. As a Greek "economized" finance by benevolences,

340

so he anticipated teaching by habituation; in the grave "respect" shown by elders to children, no less than in that required of children toward adults, we have a striking example of that "will-to-behave" which employed for "obedience" the word for "being persuaded," yet regarded a father as possessing "in the nature of things" initiative in respect of his sons, at all events, until habits of right initiative were firmly implanted in them too. And we must remember that in so simple and austere a mode of life as was imposed on the Greek people by its circumstances a very much larger part of life than among our indoor-living selves was spent in the public view. The primitive arrangements of a Greek private house made such privacy as it afforded the privilege of the women and children, who might, indeed, be heard on all hands, but were very little to be seen, and fairly drove the men out of doors from breakfast, or before, till bedtime, so that a man who merely "looked after his own affairs" was regarded as eccentric or defective.

In such conditions it is easily seen that "education," as an aim of public life, and of the *polis* which made it possible, was by no means confined to states which were "aristocracies," in the constitutional sense. Conformity to a type of behaviour was doubtless easier to maintain among citizens of homogeneous descent; but it was the boast of the greatest of the Athenians that "our city as a whole is an education for Greece, and our citizens, man for man, have no equals for freedom of spirit, versatility of achievement, and entire self-sufficiency of body and mind."[7] The difference was less in the ideal of the *polis* as a school of character than in the conception which this or that city formed of what the type of character should be.

While the "aristocracies," by which Aristotle and his contemporaries meant the states in which birthright remained more or less absolutely the condition of political privilege, not unnaturally concentrated their attention on this educative function, that main alternative type of minority-rule, which popularly was "oligarchy," but strictly its "timocratic" variety—because a man's "assessment" in the financial sense was accepted as evidence of his political utility—has been consigned to rather ill-considered disrepute on the ground that its "object" or ideal was the accumulation of wealth. That this is an incomplete analysis of the facts seems to follow from the consideration that neither as political wholes, nor in anything that we know of their citizens indi-

342

vidually, does any state fully exemplify the description; though it must be admitted that none of our information comes from within such a state, and much of it from unsuccessful or, at all events, resentful rivals of states such as Corinth and some of the western colonies which had allowed their birthright limitations to lapse without falling into the other extreme of "democratic" promiscuity. But it is noteworthy that for one of the six formal types of government which Aristotle's analysis establishes,[8] there is not only no example quoted but even no name that could be applied. Yet government "by the majority, being the richer, in the interest of the whole," can hardly have been unknown among so many grades of privilege and qualification as are actually found.

Quite apart, indeed, from the lack of instances of Greek states which either deliberately hoarded, or allowed their leading citizens to accumulate wealth, such a situation is so unlike anything which the behaviour of the Greek people would lead us to expect as probable, that allowance must be made for misinterpretation. Very many states in the Greek world, it is true, had very little use for great wealth; they could build temples and public monuments if they had a good

343

harvest or a successful raid on their neighbours; but beyond such elementary luxuries neither their territory nor their population could be improved by capital expenditure: and the same causes which restricted investment made it almost impossible that they should habitually have surplus wealth to invest.

But in the few states which were really launched on a career of economic exploitation, things were very different. On the one occasion when we should have expected Corinth to liquidate accumulated wealth, if either she or her citizens had it, namely, when the obvious method of defeating the projects of Corcyra was to outbid her for control of the new colonial venture at Epidamnus, we find the Corinthian government frankly going into such money market as there was, and raising the necessary cash by debentures secured on land allotments in the projected settlement.[9] How much of this issue was taken up by Corinthian citizens we are not informed, but the advertisement at all events was public; the shares, so to speak, were not underwritten. And the reason presumably was, not that the community as a whole was poor, but that, as in other mercantile communities, all the wealth there was at any moment was employed as fast as it was made in enterprises like that which had created it. In such a community, ancient or modern, the more tolerant public opinion becomes of great wealth in comparatively few hands, the better for everyone concerned. "Capital," it has been cynically said, "is a term of abuse for the other fellow's savings when employed to create opportunities for labour"; and at Corinth labour was welcomed, encouraged, and rewarded, because this was more nearly a capitalist state than most of its contemporaries.[10] Nor is there any reason to believe that the race-feud which had embittered the earlier history of Corinth was replaced by a class-feud after the fall of the tyranny; we may perhaps infer that what was left of the landed-families after the reforms of Pheidon[11] found consolation in the victualling of the industrial and mercantile population.

In aristocracies, in the stricter sense, where citizenship remained a birthright, the total numbers of the class thus born to govern were in any case small, and became relatively smaller whenever local facilities attracted resident aliens in any number or allowed the natural increase of the peasantry, free or serf, on the countryside. And it became absolutely smaller when the gradual exhaustion of the soil, destruction of fruit trees and other invested capital by war, and the diminishing value of the produce, in competition with oversea supplies, made life relatively harder and increased the temptation to restrict the size of the free families, which is already recognisable in Hesiod's time, and was widely recognised as justifiable in public law.

In the timocracies, on the other hand, numbers were only limited by the material prosperity of the whole community, and by the way in which its material wealth was distributed between the richer and the poorer citizens. The qualification for privilege being external and fortuitous, could be made stricter or laxer by agreement, to increase the fighting force or the popularity of the governing class; or, on the other hand, to prevent the governing body from becoming unmanageably large. The lack of homogeneity among the members of such a state was compensated by close community of material interests; but this community of interests, just because it was material and fortuitous, risked economic cleavage of a disastrous kind and was a main cause of that confusion of majority government with government by the poor for the poor, which makes the history of Greek constitutions such monotonous and yet such obscure reading in the period for which we have most evidence.

THE NOTION OF FREEDOM

DEMOCRACY AS MAJORITY GOVERNMENT

Of only very few democracies have we at all adequate records, and of only one is our information sufficiently detailed to demonstrate how completely democratic it was. For the tribal reforms of the Athenian state by Cleisthenes, in the last years of the sixth century, replaced a rigidly hereditary citizenship by a form of government which was as new as it was precisely described by what may have been the new word *demokratia*—government by all free inhabitants of the countryside. Attica had retained, as we have already seen, in exceptional degree its pre-Hellenic settlements in small open townships—described, in quite Homeric fashion, as *demoi* (p. 73)—either unfortified always or, at all events, dismantled when the *polis* protected by Athena on its precipitous table-rock became the one citadel of the whole Attic peninsula. Many of these open townships bore the names of clans; some far up-country probably still consisted mainly of the members of such a clan, but in time there came to be resident aliens in most of them, liberated slaves in all; and, further, members of one township and clan were free, by the federal custom ascribed to the initiative of Theseus, to settle in any other township as business or acquaintance

347

prompted. These *demes* Cleisthenes accepted as they stood, with their actual free population, whatever its antecedents, in substitution for the old kinship-groups; he associated these local constituencies apparently quite arbitrarily in new larger groups, and these (with special precautions to separate neighbouring *demes*) in ten new tribes, which were now the immediate constituents of the political *"Polis* of the Athenians."* The result was literally *demokratia*, government by the country-side population of Attica, in an unusually literal sense, unbiased by ties of either kinship or neighbourhood or individual wealth. How complete was this fusion of old and new personal interests and loyalties is illustrated— and no doubt this was intentional, as Herodotus observes—by including among fictitious "ancestors" of the new Cleisthenic tribes (all the rest of whom are great names of early Athenian tradition), Ajax, the prince of Salamis in the "Heroic Age"; "and him he added, though he was a foreigner, because he was a neighbour to their town and a good fighting friend."[12] For the sole and absolute criteria of a man's worthiness to be enrolled in an Attic *deme* were to be *bona fide* residence on Attic soil, and loyalty to the defence of the Athenian *Polis*.

THE NOTION OF FREEDOM

It is an interesting question, and not without importance as an illustration of Greek political thought in this period of climax, what the provisions of Cleisthenes and his collaborators were, for the perpetuation of this "democratic" regime. We know that in the fourth century a candidate for political "initiative" had to show, in ancient form, that his parents and grandparents had been by birth Attic citizens of this or that *deme;* but beyond this point he had only to show in what *deme* his ancestor's hearth-fire and family tomb, and consequently his domicile, had been.[13] This formula no doubt goes back to a period when many genuine citizens would have been unable to show any *deme* of which their great grandfather had been a birthright member, because he had been one of 'Cleisthenes' people" who had been registered on the strength of loyalty and *bona-fide* domicile only. But why was not this formula changed when the terms of admission to the archonship were altered in 458? Yet by that time, fifty years or so after the revolution of Cleisthenes, there can have been hardly any survivors of the original "people of Cleisthenes" who were admitted on their "hearth-fire" qualification; and it is at least an open question whether the retention of the original formula in 458 does not point

to the continuous admission, after Cleisthenes'
time, of new citizens qualified by residence
in a *deme* and attested by loyalty, but not
of Attic descent, much as Solon had encouraged
this kind of "desirable alien" to settle in
Attica with some implied prospect of incorporation in due time. That about this time
there were in Athens many such citizens,
imperfectly qualified by descent, is clear from
the drastic revision of the citizen-roll about
451, which excluded a large number of persons
who would have been qualified by residence,
if the Cleisthenic terms of admission had been
retained;[14] and it is significant that this revision
occurred just two full generations after the
revolution of Cleisthenes, and consequently
at the earliest date when it was possible to
insist on the rule of descent "from citizens on
both sides," without hardship to descendants
of the original "people of Cleisthenes." The
pretext for this reactionary revision was that
there were too many citizens already; but the
occasion of this discovery was the distribution
of a benefaction of foreign foodstuff, and it is
clear from this that Athens had already out-
lived the period of relatively cheap food supply
which followed the defeat of the Persians and
the organization by Aristides of a defensive
league under Athenian management.

THE NOTION OF FREEDOM

We have only to contrast with this "failure of nerve" on the part of the Athenians at this time the effects of the opposite policy pursued by Rome at the corresponding stage in her political history and we shall realise how narrowly Athens missed the chance of becoming an "inclusive" state, of the Roman type, and thereby providing a quite different sequel to her really revolutionary past, from that which actually befell. That ideas of this sort. were in the air in Herodotus' generation, which is also that of Pericles, is clear from his wise words about an earlier scheme of Thales for the cities of Ionia, "that they should have one place of common council . . . but that the *poleis*, though inhabited as before, should rank as if they were *demes*";[15] a plan which would have been "profitable even before Ionia was ruined"; and profitable, too, for Ionia in the writer's own day, if citizens of an Ionian *polis* had been free to qualify for membership of an Attic *deme* after *bona-fide* residence therein, and so to become corporators in the "United States of Attica," instead of contributory members to its defensive league.

JUSTICE IN ATHENIAN DEMOCRACY

That, with these mongrel antecedents, "democracy" as practised in Attica necessarily

351

stood for a wide toleration of individual peculiarities goes without saying: its political
"object," in the Aristotelian sense, was inevitably "freedom" in a sense unknown and
almost inconceivable before. Yet the leading
case, for those who had followed the whole
course of events, was in Attica itself in the days
when it was the asylum and sorting-ground
and mother of "homes-away-from-home" in
the islands and beyond. Herodotus, as we
have already seen, takes quiet pleasure in
disclosing the foreign origin of one great
Athenian family after another, Pisistratid,
Alcmæonid, Gephyræan, and the worshippers
of a "Carian Zeus" to whom Isagoras belonged,
himself the leader now of the opposition to
Cleisthenes. To fill in the detail of this picture of the new fusion of old and new customs,
in every *deme* of Attica, we have only to
remember that both before and after Cleisthenes, Attic and non-Attic *nomoi* were liable
to be different in almost every point of detail;
and that for this very reason all legal disputes
in which one of the parties was a foreigner
came, not before the "Archon," whose competence was solely in the "ancestral custom" of
Attica, but before the "Polemarch," or War-
lord, because he might, at all events, have
some notion—or be able to acquire it at need—

of how they settle this sort of thing in Thebes or Megara or Ægina. With the Cleisthenic enfranchisement of every willing and respectable "metic" or resident-alien in Attica, the Polemarch's court became for a while a solitude; but heaven help the Archon! No wonder that the old habit of referring cases of unusual difficulty from the "public servant" to a more expert assessor (*dikastes*) or panel of such assessors, opportunely converted by Solon into an obligation, gave rise in this new crisis to a mass of interpretative *dikai*, which reconciled the old legal traditions of the Athenians to the varied expectations and claims of "Cleisthenes' people" who might have been brought up anywhere and under any sort of customs. Can we wonder that the habit of believing that the Athenian panel-courts were steadily "making law" as well as interpreting it, came to be deep rooted?

That this aspect of judicial procedure was clearly and steadily recognised at Athens, and that for this very reason regard should be had to the public interest of the *polis* itself as well as to the spirit of ancestral custom which the court was to interpret, is clear from such a passage as this, from Demosthenes' speech in the case of Dionysodorus.[16] "Do not forget that, in formulating a single *dikê* now, you are

353

drafting a *nomos* for the whole of our trade,
and there are here many who have made
seafaring their career, watching how you
decide this affair. For if you take the view
that agreements made between people ought
to be binding, and treat those who break them
without mercy, those who have capital to lend
will be the more willing to provide it, and
thereby your trade will be increased." In this
instance, obviously, honesty was the best
policy, a high standard of behaviour its own
reward, and decision relatively easy. For
equality is easily measured, and, as Aristotle
puts it, "in contracts, that which is in accord
with *dikê* is a kind of equality, and that which
is not, is inequality, not taking other matters
into account, but numerically; for it makes no
difference whether it was a gentleman who
deprived a cad of his due, or a cad a gentleman."[17]

But there was always a risk, especially in the
assignment of "public" advantages or benefits—meaning by this, those which it was in the
power of the governing body of the *polis* to
distribute as it pleased—to "take into account"
such other matters as the personality, circumstances, or even the opinions, of those
entitled to participate. Aristotle, indeed,
accepts this, apparently, as inevitable, and

certainly the practice was widespread.[18] Historically, the reason for this view is obvious, for the earlier distributions of this kind were emergency-grants from public sources in alleviation of widespread distress; and there was the same reason for graduating a dole of food in accordance with the need of the recipient, as for graduating the levy on food stocks, from which it was issued, in accordance with the reserves in the rich men's barns.

Economically it was defensible, insofar as the acknowledged occupants of fertile territory or a convenient port were at liberty to make their own terms with persons from elsewhere for a share in the enjoyment of those "external goods," or with those of their own countrymen who were profiting most from such enjoyment, for a corresponding share in the responsibility for defence. And politically there was reason for the claim, on the part of each person admitted to be exceptionally qualified to sustain the burdens of defence and maintenance, to have a corresponding voice in administration and the general trend of public policy. "Equality of apportionment" was the most beautiful phrase in the language, as Herodotus had said long ago,[19] but it was also the most gaseous, unless some agreement existed as to the points in which equality was to count.

Or was it the only remedy that an individual who thought that he was not being treated by his neighbours with the kind of "proportionate equality" that his self-respect demanded, should "take his own belongings and depart whither he pleased,"[20] taking the quite real risk that no other community wanted to have him at all?

The answer was, of course, that in affairs so complex as those of human associations no formulation of "what really happens," in a general rule, was applicable without qualifications to the occurrences of everyday life. "*A nomos* could never prescribe the best procedure and most in accord with *dikê* by comprehending accurately in its terms what was the best at the same time for everybody. For the dissimilarities among men themselves and among the things they do, and the fact that (so to speak) nothing ever keeps quiet in human affairs, do not permit any kind of skill whatever to yield any unqualified result in any matter, under any circumstances whatever and over any period of time."[21]

The Greek Notion of Equality as "Reasonableness"

For this inapplicability of formal rules to the feckless diversity of men's actual doings, there was only one remedy, a quality the Greek word for which is almost untranslatable, though its meaning is evident from Greek usage. What *epieikeia* meant in the first instance is not quite clear, for there are two verbal stems with either of which it seems to have been popularly connected; and, as often happens, it matters less historically whether a thing is true than whether it is believed to be so. Whether, then, the primitive *epieikes* was the man who *yielded more* than there was formal justification for yielding in a contentious matter, or the man who *saw more reason* than the others—and made them see it too—in the way of behaviour which he proposed, his peculiar efficiency lay in the fact that what he said and did was "in accordance with *dikê*, not, however, along the lines of a *nomos*, but of re-establishment (or rectification) of what is in accord with both *nomos* and *dikê*."[22] Elsewhere the same quality is described as that which is "in accord with *dikê* but against the written *nomos*," a state of things which results sometimes from defective observation on the part of the authors of laws, sometimes from their inability to give a clear definition at all points, so that they have been obliged "at one point to speak in universal terms, at another point not, but only in general."[23]

This, then, is the *physis,* the mode of procedure, of the "equitable" man, "a re-establishment of *nomos,* at the point where it falls short through its universality; for this is how it comes about that everything is in accordance with *nomos,* namely, that about some things it is impossible to formulate a *nomos,* so that what is needed is a special decision. For in matters which are indefinite, the rule too is indefinite."[24]

Here we find used in a quite general sense of a "special decision" in equity, the technical term *psephisma* for one of those "votings" or "resolutions of the whole house" by which the sovereign people, at Athens, and presumably in other democracies, carried on directly its current public business, at the same time adapting its customary practice to particular incidents as they occurred, and also providing through its secretarial archives the materials for that annual review of the "ancestral *nomoi*" themselves, by the *thesmothetai,* with the object of just such a "re-establishment" or "rectification" of those *nomoi,* immemorially sacred as they were, if in any point they were discovered to have formulated inaccurately or obscurely the *physis* of an Athenian, or of Athenians in general; the "way things are done," or "not done," in the *demes* of Attica.

THE NOTION OF FREEDOM

There were grave risks in such a procedure. Suppose "the mob took the initiative," as Herodotus puts it,[25] were its "votings"— however expressive of its own impulsive "way" of behaviour at the moment—any more "in accordance with *dikê*" than the "orders" of an unscrupulous or misguided king?[26] Clearly not, and Athenian public procedure at all events recognised this, and made it a fundamental principle that the citizen whose "frontierless initiative" had prompted him to such a proposal was personally responsible for the consequences of its adoption by his fellows; and this responsibility remained with him until the *thesmothetai* in their annual review of public proceedings absolved him on the ground that there was nothing in ·his proposal that was "contrary to the *nomoi*." But meanwhile, mischief might ensue that was irreparable: and, further, such an error of judgment as the Mytilenæan decree or the condemnation of the generals after Arginusæ might be formally "in accord with the *nomoi*" and yet a very grave departure from the "way things are done"among normal and reasonable people. It was indeed the risk, and the historic occurrence, of irreparable mistakes of this kind which led to wide-spread distrust of a type of constitution in which the "frontierless initiative" of the ordinary citizen came so near to "mob-rule," in default of just that spirit of "reasonable" equity which, according to the defenders of democracy, had nowhere else such boundless scope for its exercise.

THE STATE AND THE INDIVIDUAL

Here then we come, once again, to the point at which that unqualified and unprecedented encounter between the state and the individual, emancipated alike from the "ancestral customs" of the tribal society and its kinship-groups which had intervened between them so long, became a matter of very practical concern to statesmen and of anxiety to political thinkers.

The remedy was obvious, as we have seen; that the general rules furnished by the state should be applied to the enterprises and aspirations of the individual, so infinitely and perplexingly various, so as to "re-establish" reasonable order without infringement of reasonable freedom. But how was the remedy to be applied?

The question has been often discussed how it came about that with political ideas so clearly and early defined, and such endowment of natural ability, the Greek people had a political history so checquered and disappointing, and in some respects even so futile. Look-

ing back as he was already able to do, over the
most brilliant period of political construction,
Aristotle supplies, at all events, an outline of
the answer. If men are to be good and useful
individuals, and therewith good and useful
members of a well-ordered state, three things
are indispensable—breeding, training, reasoning.

EQUALITY IN BREED

By breeding he still means what the older
aristocracies had so jealously maintained, purity
and homogeneity of descent, as the best
guarantee for sureness and uniformity of reaction to circumstances.[27] Now, it was precisely this homogeneity which most Greek
communities had lost, by Aristotle's time,
through the relaxation of kinship-grouping,
and the temptations of a "rich match" outside the circle of long-established corporator
families. And of this modern promiscuity,
Athens, the type-specimen of extreme democracy, was at the same time the conspicuous
instance. In its purely biological aspect this
great experiment has been discussed by Doctor Bateson.[28] The effects of the crossing of
pure strains are already well known from
experiments on many species of plants and
animals. Among the "first-crosses" there are

certain to be many individuals of unusual qualities and exceptional vigour, some reproducing characteristics of one of the parental strains, some those of the other. But there is no security that these "sports" will themselves breed true, however carefully mated with their like, and in the next generation, among the "second-crosses," there will no less certainly be a large proportion of individuals who are in every sense of the word "ill-bred"; of poor physique, incomposite, dysharmonic build, uncertain temper, and unstable character.

Now, this had been precisely the experience of Athens in the generations following the revolution of Cleisthenes. Down to this point in their history, with very few exceptions, such as the marriage of Megacles, son of Alcmæon, with the heiress of the tyrant of Sicyon, not merely the Attic "nobility," but the population of every Attic *deme* had been of purely Attic descent for some five centuries. Then the bar to mixed marriages was abruptly removed; and in the generation which was growing up after the Persian Wars, there was an outbreak of exuberant energy in all ranks of life which has seldom been equalled, if ever. It was not only that in the positions of political initiative there were men like Cimon (who was partly Thracian, and not quite Greek either in appearance or in temperament), Thucydides, son of Melesias, and Pericles; it was the same among the potters, the sculptors, the bronze-workers, above all among the soldiers, seamen, and traders who made the reputation which the Athenians retained until the outbreak of the "great war" in 432. But in the course of that war we find Socrates raising the question whether human efficiency is hereditary, answering it in the negative, and illustrating his pessimism by the examples of those same men of exceptional ability, whose own children were of quite ordinary ability, if not even an anxiety to their friends.[29] And here, too, what can only be described as a loss of "nerve" or "tone" was general. To the new shock of a general war the "second-cross" Athenians reacted quite otherwise than their grandfathers had done in the Persian crisis. Their tempers were uncertain, their judgment clouded by panic and prejudice, probably even their physique upset in a way that made them easier victims to war-crowding and insanitary surroundings than they might otherwise have been. Above all there was a notable lack of men of initiative and leadership, together with a superfluity of ill-balanced, temperamental enthusiasts, cranks, and wind-bags; the one really able man, Alcibiades, belonging to the same ancient and exceptionally original family which had thrown up Pericles among its own "second-crosses," and hereafter disappears from public life. What wonder if people began to take note of these signs of the times, and if Sparta was thought to owe much of its success in the great war to its abstention from that facile receptivity which had blotted the escutcheon of Athens.

EQUALITY IN TRAINING

Aristotle's second requirement for good citizenship is training: and in this respect, too, the state which had been the pioneer in political experiment had been the victim of recurring accidents. For any public system of education family solidarity was still quite unprepared down to Socrates' time; Alcibiades' treatment of his teachers only put the fine point on the practical problem of moulding this human quicksilver at all; and the only contemporary sketch of a schoolmaster is the more eloquent because it is humour, not caricature.[30] Consequently, such education as was possible was the business of the father and the boy's elder relatives, for the women, under the economic handicap of Greek society, could do little for him after the nursery stage. Even Alcestis, Euripides' ideal of what a Greek

mother might be, worries herself but little
about the future of her boy, though a good
deal about the future of her girl.[31] But three
times during the fifth century Athens endured
the ravages of a general war—against the
Persians, against the League of the Land
Powers from 460 to 445, and again against
the World of Reaction after 432; not to mention
the grave losses sustained by the way, between
476 and 400, in the "little wars" incidental
to the reparation-period after the Persian
retreat. Seldom, in the history of any community, has the young generation had to
face its responsibilities earlier, or with less
of that habitual, imperceptible, and most
potent discipline of seeing "how father does
it." Seldom, consequently, has there been
greater need of some professional substitute
for that home-training, or greater alacrity of
response to the offers of foreign teachers, when
they began to come. That the "sophistic"
movement centred in Athens as it did is the
clearest proof both of the severity of the strain
on Athenian intellect and temper, imposed
by those amazing experiences; and also of the
"will-to-learn" exhibited by the young Athenian, and, on the whole, tolerated (and rightly)
by his elders. What is instructive as well as
pathetic about Strepsiades in the *Clouds* of

Aristophanes, is not that the old man knows nothing about education himself, either in theory, or to practise it, but that he is all too ready to register his son in the first "thinking-shop" he comes across, to make good his own omissions. Similarly, the whole plan of Plato's *Republic*, and still more of his *Laws*, presumes a general interest in educational problems among ordinary people, casually met, which has no parallel in literature until 'the Revival of Learning, and perhaps in our own time.

EQUALITY IN INTELLIGENCE

But both "breeding" and "training" are for Aristotle preliminaries only, in the creation of a good man and a good citizen. They are the conditions for that freedom and facility with which the mature "grown-up" individual is expected to use his own reason, both in personal and in public affairs. This rational intellectual ideal of citizenship is exemplified in the notable word regularly used to characterize the "desirable alien" whom a city-state from time to time "delighted to honour" by enrollment among the men of its own sort. Let breeding and training have been what fortune gave, what made a man acceptable for incorporation in a society so exclusive as every Greek city was in principle, was that

he was "of a good intelligence toward us."[32]
Not sentimental loyalty, or physical heroism,
or magnificent benevolence, but an honest,
impartial man's application of hard common-
sense, business acumen, "unforgetful" states-
manship, to the city's occasions and perplex-
ities, was his title to this "order of merit."

Nor was this an easy task, for, as we have
seen, the ideals of political "initiative" stood
high. On the one hand there were the "ancestral customs" which had brought the city
through great perils in the past, sometimes a
"written" constitution, though the latest and
completest example of a rechartered constitution shows how little of the "ancestral
customs" it was thought necessary to re-
hearse in detail on such an occasion;[33] sometimes a traditional code, precariously extorted
as case-law from the "public servants" or the
"council of elders," as the *themistes* aforetime
were "wrested" from the mind of Zeus. On
the other was an ever-changing world of rival
states and groupings of states, rival enterprizes
of individuals and associations of narrower
scope than the state, and beyond all the Persian incubus, the Carthaginian incubus, in
due time the Macedonian incubus, of which
no one was qualified to say whether it was,
as Isocrates hoped, a revelation of the mind

of Zeus for the undoing of Persia, or, as Demosthenes feared, a leviathan whose devastation of the Greek culture which the city-state had created and was maintaining, could be averted only, as Heraclitus had phrased it, by insistence on the custom of the city, as on the fortress wall, and yet more insistently.

Between those customs—different for each city, and rightly differing, as all agreed, because no two city-states were, or could be, quite the same—and these circumstances, no less differently affecting each several state, in its relation, for example, with the leviathan of the moment—adjustment was possible only by the exercise of that "good intelligence" which was so valued in the foreign benefactor, and so hard to ensure in the home-bred and home-trained. For it was precisely the revelation to this later phase of Hellenism, of that "gift of the Muses" which Hesiod had celebrated in the "salt of the earth," as he perceived them in the Early Iron Age. In the individual, both in his private affairs and in his discharge of public obligations, it is what is described uniformly as "reasonableness," or "equity," in the sense already described; as the will to take less, and give more, than the strict normal "way of doing things" presumed or required that you should. It was the quality most admired and valued, just because it was the hardest to exhibit, for people with the stern upbringing, intellectual alertness, and abounding vitality of the Greeks. It is the re-interpretation to a more ruthlessly rational age, of what *aidôs* and *nemesis* had expressed in days when the risk of disturbance was less from skill and subtlety than from exuberant "will-to-power." Pericles claimed this reasonableness as the characteristic of Athenians as he idealized them, believing democracy to be capable of this and predisposing men to it; and in the fourth century the opponents of democratic shifts and excesses claimed it for themselves, in mitigation, at all events, of the charge that because they made both ends meet in their own concerns they were "enemies of the people," who were taking such care that those ends should not overlap by much.

REASONABLENESS IN PLATO'S *LAWS*

If we ask how an exponent of "reasonableness" thought this kind of efficiency, no less moral than political, might be attained and propagated, we find a rather striking answer, less in the *Republic* than in the *Laws*. It is the old answer that man, like any other animal, has a *physis*, a way of growth throughout life, of his own; that this process of growth can best be observed, and can only be counted on for normal reactions, in well-bred examples and homogeneous groups; that its reactions vary in detail according to external circumstances, and that consequently only the most general rules of conduct can be regarded as universally valid, while apart from these the *nomos* in each state is the "general opinion" of the community.[34] Training to conformity with established custom is based on the assumption that doing a thing right is itself a source of satisfaction, and that this "joy of well-doing" can be cultivated from infant days;[35] there is a right way and a wrong way, or, rather, a truly human way as distinct from a puppylike or goatish way of skipping and prancing; man, indeed, might be described as the only "dancing animal" in the same sense as he is the only "political animal," because, as Hesiod said, there is no *dikê* in those others, no recognition of a "way" of doing things as being alone truly efficient, because in accord with all the conditions. And so throughout the whole scheme of reform. To give only one instance, of momentary interest, observances in regard to the consumption of alcohol are to be formulated by men of experience in such matters, acquainted with the real properties of liquor, accustomed to use it without abuse, and in that special sense "reasonable" that they know how to communicate their own moderation to the rest of the drinking-party.[36]

This is "going back to nature" with a vengeance; but it was the return to nature not of the savage but of the scientific anthropologist. The Athenian speaker in the *Laws* is uniformly respectful to the prohibition-laws and other peculiarities of his Spartan and Cretan friends; if they are good customs, they will reveal their goodness by conformity with the circumstances which gave rise to them; and meanwhile they have the benefit of the doubt, while he expounds a more excellent way, as he sees it. And the Spartan pays the Athenian in return the well-deserved compliment that when an Athenian is good, he is very, very good, just because[37] "they alone are good without compulsion, spontaneously, by divine endowment, genuinely, and in no way artificially;" while the Cretan, more ingenuously, grounds his own devotion to them on the historical fact that they more than justified a Cretan expert's diagnosis that they were indeed "all right."

GOOD MAN AND GOOD CITIZEN

This is indeed something to set against the stock complaints of politicians and other cartoonists against Athenian democracy. It was in fact a question of degree, as well as of the chance that we know more, both for good and for evil, about that great experiment in political freedom; about the only city-state in which the individual was really allowed to be "grown-up" even if he grew up to be noisier, more flighty, more impracticable, in his political behaviour, than his best friends had hoped, or than those who annoyed him could endure. And the reason why democratic Athens held together at all was the same, only in larger measure, as that which maintained the smallest and closest "aristocracy," namely, the conviction that above and beyond all "ancestral custom," all regional controls, all personal leadership of public servants, there remained in each individual corporator an "initiative, frontierless, deliberative and critical," the voice of human reason facing facts, opinions, and traditions open-eyed and open-minded, and in a very real sense "making the best of them," in confidence "that it might be well with the *polis*" of Athens, or of Pholegandros, in which his lot was cast. Not always very reasonable in retrospect; sometimes very unreasonable, as its possessors could on occasion realize within twenty-four hours and repair their folly as the Athenians did over the revolt of

372

Mytilene; but always in principle, and usually in practice the best that ordinary men, under ordinary circumstances of political emergency, could be expected to offer to their state, on whose security and efficiency their own chance of a "good life" depended.

Greek "Reasonableness" at Work

Indeed, what is impressive, in the practical, every-day working of the Greek states, oligarchies and democracies alike, is the great amount and fine quality of the routine work of administration, of judicial business, of political deliberation about emergencies as they arose, which resulted when Greek political ideas, of which an outline only has been attempted here, were applied under ordinary circumstances to the ordinary maintenance of these highly specialized communities. It was not every day, nor once in a century, among some hundreds of such cities, that there was a debate on revolted Mytilene, or a trial of the generals after the spoiled victory of Arginusæ, or a condemnation of Socrates for "observing gods whom the city does not observe." It is in the speeches drafted by the professional advocates, and, among these, rather in the closely argued pleadings in private cases, than in the gaseous or impassioned appeals of politicians, that we make the acquaintance of the "reasonable man," speaker and audience alike. It is even rather in the crisp incisive drafting of those "resolutions of the whole house" which political theorists regarded as so dangerous and insidious a rival to "ancestral customs" that we realize how an Athenian citizen earned his modest compensation for the loss of a day's work attending to "public business." For those phrases are of amateur drafting, reviewed by a government of less than a year's experience of office, and not only adopted but amended by a mass meeting in the open air, on a crowd-worn hillside, with an amateur platform committee, and amateur speakers "for the bill" as well as against it. Only a high sense of public efficiency on the part of amateur "public servants" in all sorts of civil-service business, as well as among the panels of ordinary citizens who reviewed the year's work of such men, kept the routine administration of a city like Athens from chaos. Only a sense of public responsibility far more highly developed than is commonly attributed to Greek councils and mass meetings could have kept direct personal administration going at all, however lamentable the workings of panic or prejudice on certain crucial occasions, or in a few classes of accusations on which we have usually only the comments of those who sympathised more or less strongly with the condemned. And where the "enemy upon the frontier" stood, in the great political issues, we must remember that the "enemy within the gates" was to be suspected and feared in such trials as that of the "corn-dealers" for profiteering at the expense of a "sovereign people," on a margin of subsistence between plenty and famine such as the modern world has not known, but of which the Irish "potato-famine" or the Lancashire "cotton-famine" in the last century, and occasional shortages in India or Russia, give us even now some impression.

Even in such instances of political austerity or economic panic it must be remembered that the measures proposed, and even taken, were deliberately preventive, not vindictive; and that this explains why such severity was shown at times in the democracies. Extreme liberty of action, discretion, opinion, in the ordinary affairs of life, was a high privilege and a public trust, for the abuse of which no deterrent penalty could be too severe; even if the blow did not always fall on the right head, it kept bad heads under; and moderately good heads could look after themselves. The jests over "sycophancy," in the comedians, are in part at least the equivalent of the pantomime policemen and the detective story among ourselves. That they were amateur detectives made it all the more necessary that the court should be severe if they made a good case; and the "sycophant," we may remember, had his nickname from a popular form of contraband.

POLITICAL TYPES IN MORAL PHILOSOPHIES

The attempt has been made in what precedes to supplement the representation given of Greek political ideals in the writings of great fourth-century philosophers, by illustrations of their practical working from more ephemeral sources, and side lights on the circumstances of their origin, and especially on their simple descriptive terminology.

But with the practical working of the mature constitutions which those philosophers knew by experience or from contemporaries, we reach a turning point at which those philosophic analyses began to have a fresh and more individual interest. It is sometimes difficult to see whether the hackneyed analogy between the individual and the body-corporate is intended to illustrate primarily the one or the other. Even of Heraclitus the "physicist" some Greek critics believed that his "physical"[38] chapters were incidental to his "political" argument. And there was a reason for this. Wider scope was offered in economic and other non-political directions to a man of "push" and intelligence; and after Alexander's conquest a new world was thrown open to these same capable people. On the other hand, we have encountered again and again the failure of all types of Greek constitutions and most conspicuously of the most "grown-up" among them, to retain in political life the best abilities and energies of its corporators, in face of the freedom allowed to so many, less well bred, less well trained, and—to be frank—less well meaning and less "reasonable" in that high equitable sense.

But "equity" in that sense was by no means limited to political matters. It was indeed only another aspect of that "behaviour in accordance with *dikê*" which was recognised in Hesiod's day as the specific behaviour of man in all his activities and aspirations. In the *Republic* the two enquiries as to righteousness in politics and in morals proceed side by side; in the *Laws* the preparation of the state for the reception of the good man begins by eliciting, among the skippings and chirpings of infant *joie-de-vivre*, those "rhythms" which will transform the good child into the good citizen; in the *Politics* the question, formally left unsolved, of the compatibility of the life of the "good man" with that of the "good citizen," is really answered by the presumption of the same "equity" in both; and that "equity" is in essentials no more and no less than this; an "unforgetfulness" of all relevant circumstances, an ability to "see life steadily and see it whole," and to see life also as a process of growth, in which things now immature and inadequate may be "counted happy on the ground of their hope," and in which, above all, "we feel joy in doing things well." To life, as to its material and external goods, such a diagnosis of human nature brought the transforming salutary touch of the Greek spirit; out of the cradle of the Greek city-state sprang that amazing never-ageing child, the Greek conception of humanity.

We have seen that the political experience and, above all, the political tragedies of the fifth century left to the fourth-century alternative political ideals—"aristocratic" and "democratic," to adopt the catchwords of the time. The one frankly despaired of making the great mass of mongrel stupid humanity much better than gods or nature evidently intended it to be, and concentrated its attention on the discovery or the creation of a minority of experts, to whose wisdom, when found or prepared, the state might be entrusted confidently. The other, in the largest sense far more "reasonable" in its humanism, hoped for the best, as the founders of the first *polis* must have hoped for the best, when they looked round on the human wreckage which was all the material that they had for rebuilding society. But in proportion as their hopes were great and their patience long, they had to lay all the greater stress on the need for training to supply the defects of breed, and subordinate unruly desires and impulses to the reason which they believed was there, if it could only be given free play. These two tendencies—to look for the expert and leave the state to his care when found, and to insist on more careful preparation of the ordinary citizen for deliberative and judicial business— both distinguish the more cautious and disillusioned thought and practice of the fourth century from the climax of political instinct and enthusiasm in the fifth, and go far to explain the first signs of a transference of interest from politics to morals, which gathers strength as the fourth century passes into the third.

For with political life becoming so complicated and specialized, and ordinary business becoming more intricate also—in an overcrowded and restricted world between the Persian Empire, the rude protectorate of the king of Macedon and Thrace northward, and the rival imperialisms of Carthage, Rome, Syracuse, in the west—the stipulation which had been tacitly recognized as fundamental became more explicit, that "equality," to be worthy of the name, must be "among equals." It was by observing a standard of intellectual honesty beyond the comprehension of many of his fellow citizens that Socrates came by his death, in spite of scrupulous conformity to political routine, and, indeed, because of it; for had he been willing, he could have escaped death by merely leaving Attica. On the other hand, the tolerance of various forms of personal rule, which distinguishes the fourth century from the fifth, implies widespread indifference to that positive "equality of apportionment" which had formerly replaced so many sixth-century tyrannies by more or less completely popular governments, and illustrates the growing conviction that to "do one's own business and not meddle" was political prudence if not political wisdom.

STOIC AND EPICUREAN

In proportion, therefore, as the difficulty became greater, of being at the same time a

"good man" and a "good citizen," these two
ideals drifted apart, and, moreover, each
became specialized into corresponding pairs
of alternatives. To the citizen of the old
"conquest-state," exclusive in his birthright,
indifferent to "this people that knoweth not
the law," unconcerned with the use, or even
the scientific comprehension of an external
world in which he is, so to speak, a stranger
and a sojourner, corresponds the Stoic ideal
of individual behaviour, self-sufficient, self-
controlled, self-sanctioned and approved—a
Spartan character, in a world where the "arrows
that will cover the sun" are those of a Hellenistic dynast or a Roman emperor, and concern
him as little as those of the Persians.

To the freespoken, tolerant, inclusive type
of citizenship, of which Athens as reformed
by Cleisthenes, and Cyrene reconstituted by
Demonax, are mature examples, with its intent
utilitarian outlook on a world in which it is
good to live, because there is so much to do to
make it all Greek and a home for Greeks,
corresponds the keen interest in physical
science, the cheerful resignation of Olympus to
the old gods, provided that man be free to
exploit the plains and shores below, the conception of self-development as consistent with,
and, indeed, inseparable from, wise steward-

ship of "external goods," and reasonable
intervention in the affairs of city and regional
state—which are fruits of the philosophic
teaching of Epicurus.

PHARISEE AND SADDUCEE

In later Hebrew philosophy and behaviour
it is not difficult to recognise the same alternative reactions, as soon as the little sanctuary-
state which was reconstituted after the Cap-
tivity found itself deprived of the patronage
extended to all small peoples and cultures by
the wide tolerance of imperial Persia. For
between conflicting outlooks and policies Jeru-
salem ceased to be "a city at unity with itself";
between the Pharisee, standing in the ancient
ways, obdurately insistent on the "law" that
he had received, and the "tradition" that
interpreted it, as infallible guides, and the
Sadducee, "following the works of the heathen,"
already more than half-Hellenized, even while
he shed those elements of his own culture
which obstructed his outlook on a modern
world, or his enjoyment of its gifts, or his co-
operation with whatever secular power seemed
to offer the best prospect of such enjoyment.
So closely do Greek and Hebrew thought take
parallel courses in their later history when their
immediate political missions among their own

countrymen pass over into their missions to mankind.

THE MEDIÆVAL ECLIPSE OF GREEK POLITICAL IDEAS

It only remains now to account for the long eclipse of Greek political ideas in the later stages of ancient culture and in the earlier history of the next cycle of political experience. And here, what is most noteworthy is the separation between the physical and the political outlook which had begun, indeed, when the study of politics began to lose interest in presence of new and deeply orientalized kingdoms; and physics, as the Ionian observers had understood them, gave place in popular esteem to "Chaldean," "Syrian," and other oriental expressions of a magical as distinct from a scientific outlook on the world around. Greek "physical" observation occupied itself with the proper subject of "physics," namely, "things as they grow" and actually behave; only occasionally did it think backward up the time-stream of events to some kind of beginning, and only so much as this because the genealogical scheme imposed on its analysis of nature's processes narrowed upward to some first "pair of opposites" or other, themselves conceived as due to some unexplained flaw or polarity in universal chaos. Greek "political" inquiry similarly busied itself with the *physis* of man, his actual movement toward fuller humanity "in the way things actually grow"; if it looked backward at all, it was either to a perspective rendering of its own sociological analysis, as in Aristotle's sketch of the "first" family, prior rather in conception than in time to the "first" state; or else transcended any such apparent beginning, as in the prehistoric anthropology of the *Laws*, by the hypothesis of destructive spasms, undoing by physical cataclysm what earlier men of like *physis* with ourselves had laboriously won and constructed. But the notion of "origin" seems to be as remote as that of "substance" or underlying foundation, from the Greek conception of *physis*; and the Greek physicist was as free as the Greek political philosopher to follow the course of events backward in observation, or forward in inference, from the one sure point, "that which is around us, being reasonable and intelligible" in the present.

The Latin Notions of *Natura* and *Lex*

But with the necessary translation of Greek philosophical nomenclatures into Latin grave disaster happened. One aspect of this we have already noticed briefly (p. 164), the con-

fusion wrought by the substitution of *principium* for *arkhé*, and of *finis* for *telos*. Another
and far worse pair of blunders translated
physis into *natura*, and *nomos* into *lex*, and
fifteen hundred years of obscure and perverse
thinking followed, before the Greek conceptions
of *process* and its *formulation* were recovered
and the modern scientific movement could
begin.[39]

The word *natura*, like *physis*, is a verbal
substantive; but it means not the "process of
growing up," but the "act of being born."
Its primal meaning, therefore, stops just at the
point where that of *physis* begins. Its use
inevitably distracted attention from processes
and events which are going on now around
the observer, and beckoned away to a point
necessarily outside his ken, when things as we
know them either were not yet at all, but were
"coming into being" somehow; or else, if they
were then as we know them now, left the
moment of creation fashioned and immutable
by God or man—obviously, a very difficult
statement to demonstrate, in either event,
and dealing with a question which did not
belong to the province of the physicist at all.
Lucretius, at the very outset of this period
of confusion, perceived the difficulty and spent
much labour in the attempt to connect the

creative or originative act denoted by *natura*
with the start-less and end-less process described
as *physis* by Democritus and other Greek
"physicists."

With *nomos* and *lex* things were even worse.
The Roman state had come into being as the
result of a series of bargains and treaties, no
mere "Social Contract" inferred from actual
institutions, but a *Lex Sacrata* of which the
date and drafters were believed to be historically known. And a *lex* meant to a Roman
primarily, not what we mean by a "law," or
the Greeks by a *nomos*, formulating what
actually happens, but a creative initiative
bargain, providing that whatever may have
been the practise in the past, "henceforward
there shall be but one Use," sanctioned by
penalties for failure to conform, but itself
liable to repeal or amendment on grounds as
arbitrary as those which determined its original
terms. Hence Roman *leges* were habitually
identified by the name of the magistrate who
propounded the draft to the mass meeting of
citizens, and obtained their consent to abide
by its terms.

Now, we have seen that it was a reasonable
and accurate way of describing man's formulation of the "way things grow" or otherwise
"happen" in any department of the world

around us, to call it a *nomos* or formal description of the *physis* of whatever process it described; and it did not lead seriously astray if the *nomoi* of a Greek city were described in terms appropriate to a *Lex Calpurnia de pecuniis repetundis* or a *Lex Cornelia de vi*. But what was the meaning of a *Lex naturæ*, the "contract of a birth-process"? Between what parties was this contract made, and when? On whose proposition and with whose acceptance? Under what sanctions was it binding, and for how long? What *lex*, for example, was involved in the *natura* of water? Under what penalties for non-performance did oxygen and hydrogen agree together to combine in the proportions of 16 to 2? Who drafted this bargain, and ratified its completion; and could he, being in some sense the author of this "nature" of water, or of "nature" in general, dispense this or that particular sample of water from its "natural" obligation, and permit or command or force it to become wine, or to break out from a dry rock, or stand upon an heap on either side of an extemporized track? All these were notions and hypotheses in which we trace old Italian animism, Babylonian magical theocracy—"wind and storm fulfiling His word"; Persian notions, even, of an almost-all-embracing kingdom of God, in which all "good" things, at all events, like all "good" men, work together to fulfil the divine purpose. But they are, at all events, not Greek ideas, and to superpose the conceptions of "origin" and "contract" on the Greek notions of "process" and "formula" was to create confusion. It was a proper theology, or metaphysic, for a world the thinking portion of which had, in fact, become Stoic and resigned itself in politics to glum acquiescence in the "benevolent despotism" of a *princeps* and an imperial bureaucracy "fulfilling his word" by "rescripts" and "edicts"; for an age in which physical science was dying out, under the grip of a despotism in external things no less arbitrary because it was believed to be beneficent in the long run; of a power outside and beyond the "way things happen" whose ways were so wholly "past finding out" that there was no good reason left for believing that they would ever happen again as they did last time.

We have clearly travelled a long way here from the "reasonable that surrounds us" in Ionian and Aristotelian thought; and it was a long way to travel back at the Renaissance before attention was recalled once more from origins to processes, from speculation about arbitrary or contractual *leges naturæ* to the old Greek notion of the inherent reasonableness of the "way things grow" and patient observant detailed description of the way they grow, with a view to the formulation of those processes in terms so general and so coherent in their implications that we rely upon their "unforgetfulness" in the old Greek sense of that memorable word for truth.

THE RETURN TO THE GREEK VIEW OF NATURE AND SOCIETY

So, too, in politics, the first challenge to traditional notions of the origin of man, and his present distressful disqualification for fulfilling his own need of humanity, came from the discovery of a "New World" suspended between West and East, and peopled with inhabitants of indisputable humanity but no discoverable affinity in descent or culture with the "seed of Adam" which had acquired that "nature" and fallen under that "law" of disinheritance. And the first attempt at a solution of that problem came through the recognition that here, and by analogy also in the manifold culture of the familiar Old World, what was operative in all these regional provisional attempts to solve the same specifically human problem of "living well" was the same "common sense" and common humanity; the same common appreciation of the "rhythm" and orderliness of events, as reason analyses them and recognises the reasons for them; the same conviction that in man's doings too there is a real "way of behaviour" and that with honest persistence it can be and will be found out and made clear to others; and, further, that between the great "laws of the earth" and "oath-fenced way of the gods" on the one hand, and the perverse perplexing trivialities of daily intercourse on the other, there stands, as there stood in the Greek city-state at all happy moments in its varied career, one saving source of grace, the "reasonable," "equitable" individual, "re-establishing custom where it falls short through its universality," illuminating by his own behaviour, "gently and quietly" as Hesiod saw him, his gospel, "we feel joy when we think we are doing things well." For such men as he "alone are good without compulsion, spontaneously, by divine endowment, genuinely and in no way artificially."[40] And in the city of such souls the Good Man and the Good Citizen are one.

NOTES FOR LECTURE I

[1] H. Diels. *Die Fragmente der Vorsokratiker.* Berlin, 1912,[3] p. 69, ἀκριβὲς οἰάκισμα πρὸς σταθμὴν βίου. According to Diogenes Laertius, 9. 12, this superscription was suggested by the grammarian Diodotus, but its appropriateness is confirmed by Heraclitus, fragment 41. Diels, εἶναι γὰρ ἓν τὸ σοφόν, ἐπίστασθαι γνώμην ὁτέη ἐκυβέρνησε πάντα διὰ πάντων.

[2] Note that the northern end of the Nile Valley has two perils: Asiatic intruders east of the Delta, Libyan intruders west of it.

[3] Herodotus, 1. 153, and 7. 104.

[4] Demosthenes, *Aristogeiton,* 774. 16.

[5] Aristotle, *Rhetoric.* 8. 5. 3.

[6] Democritus, fragment 119. Diels.

[7] Aristotle, *Politics* 7 (4), 13. 1331 b 25ff.

[8] Aristophanes, *Clouds,* 1078, χρῶ τῇ φύσει.

NOTES FOR LECTURE II

[1] Aristotle, *Politics,* 1. 2. 1252a 31.

[2] Il., 9. 419. 15. 257 αἰπεινή; Od., 3. 130 αἰπή; Il., 2. 501. 505. εὐκτιμένη; Il., 21. 516. εὐδμήτος; Il., 2. 12, Od., 22. 230. εὐρυαγυίη; Il., 13. 815. εὐναιομένη; Il., 15. 737. πύργοις ἀραρυῖα; compare Od., 6. 263. ἦν περὶ πύργος ὑψηλός.

[3] Il., 8. 52. εἰσορόων Τρώων τε πόλιν καὶ νῆας Ἀχαιῶν.

[4] Od., 6. 9. ἀμφὶ δὲ τεῖχος ἔλασσε πόλει, καὶ ἐδείματο οἴκους, καὶ νηοὺς ποίησε θεῶν, καὶ ἐδάσσατ' ἀρούρας.

[5] Il., 20. 217. ἐν πεδίῳ πεπόλιστο, πόλις μερόπων ἀνθρώπων.

[6] Il., 1. 366. 7. 20.

[7] Il., 2. 117. 9. 24. Compare 6. 327.

[8] Il., 9. 24.

[9] Il., 21. 540. ἰθὺς πόλιος καὶ τείχεος.

[10] Il., 6. 95.

[11] Il., 16. 549. ἔρμα πόληος; 17. 144. πόλιν καὶ ἄστυ σαώσεις. Compare Od. 6. 176–7: 14. 472–3.

[12] Il., 9. 593.

[13] Il., 18. 512. κτῆσιν ὅσην πτολίεθρον ἐπήρατον ἐντὸς ἔεργεν.

[14] Il., 14. 230.

[15] Od., 1. 170.

[16] Il., 15. 558.

[17] Il., 22. 429.

[18] Od., 7. 130–1.   17. 205–7.

[19] Il., 16. 69.

[20] Il., 8. 522.

[21] Il., 5. 473. φῆς που ἄτερ λαῶν πόλιν ἑξέμεν ἠδ' ἐπικούρων.

[22] Il., 18. 509—24.

[23] Il., 18. 497. λαοὶ δ' εἰν ἀγορῇ ἔσαν ἄθροοι.

[24] Il., 18. 503. κήρυκες δ' ἄρα λαὸν ἐρήτυον.

[25] Thus we have πτολίπορθος, περσέπολις, but ἀστυδάμας, ἀστυάναξ; compare ἀστυγείτων "neighbour to the town," ἀστυβοώτης, "calling through the town," of a herald, Il., 24. 701: ἀστυνόμος, "police-commissioner," dealing, like the Roman *aedilis*, with buildings, streets, and open spaces, as well as with public order.

[26] Thucydides, 2. 15.

[27] Il., 11. 242. ἀστοῖσιν ἀρηγών; Od., 13. 192. Aristotle, *Politics*, 3. 5. 8, distinguishes between ἀστοί, "residents," and πολῖται, "corporators," in a Greek πόλις.

[28] The same word is used of uncultivated land, Thucydides 3. 106. and for wild varieties of fruit trees, Plato, *Laws* 844 D. 845 B.

[29] Pindar, *Ol.*, 7. 165. *Herodotus*, 2. 160, 3. 8. uses ξένος.

[30] Another term of mere "multitude" is ἀλίη. For ὅμαδος contrasted with λαός, see Il., 7. 306.

[31] With λήϊτον compare the Athenian λειτουργία where a wealthy citizen undertook as a "public service" the production of a drama, the commissioning of a warship, and the like. Probably ληίζειν originally meant "to let loose one's *laos*" upon a district; in later times this was only done by robber bands, λῆσται, not by respectable communities. For this and other philological matter, see S. Feist, *Kultur, Ausbreitung und Herkunft der Arier*. Berlin, 1913. Much of

the very suggestive commentary on Greek political terms in
O. Schrader, *Real-lexikon der Indogermanischen Altertums-
kunde*, Strassburg (1901), and in his earlier *Prehistoric Anti-
quities of the Aryan Peoples* (English Translation, London,
1890) is out of date, and must be used with caution. V. G.
Childe, *The Aryans*, London, 1926, is the only recent general
book in English.

32 Il., 5. 710; 16. 437. Λυχίης ἐν πίονι δήμῳ.

33 Il., 3. 50; 24. 706.

34 Od., 11. 14; 14. 43.

35 Ἔδοξε τῇ βουλῇ χαὶ τῷ δήμῳ . . . . ὅπως ἂν εἴη βέλτιστον
τῷ δήμῳ. For examples, see Hicks and Hill. *Greek Historical
Inscriptions.* Oxford, 1901². Nos. 36, 40, 49, etc.

36 Hicks and Hill *l. c.* No. 32.

7 *Inscriptiones Graecæ*, ii. 5. No. 18b.

38 Thucydides, 5. 18.

39 Il., 11. 372 alludes to the "tomb of Ileus, son of Dardanus, a demos-elder of long ago," παλαιοῦ δημογέροντος:
compare Il., 3. 149.

40 Il., 1. 231. δημοβόρος βασιλεύς, ἐπεὶ οὐτιδάνοισιν ἀνάσσεις.

41 Od., 19. 197.

42 Od., 15. 80–85. Menelaus proposes to Telemachus to
make a tour among his vassals and collect presents for his
guest.

43 Stesichorus, fragment 37. Bergk, quoted by Aristophanes
Peace 798, χαρίτων δαμώματα.

44 These names are, of course, late examples, for the most
part; but Demodocus is Homeric.

45 Od., 17. 383; 19. 135. χηρύχων οἳ δημιόεργοι ἔασιν.

46 Homeric *Hymn to Hermes*, 98.

47 Il., 9. 544.

48 Il., 11. 716, a λαὸς is collected for a war; 16. 129 for
a battle; 2. 438 for a mass-meeting, ἀγορά.

49 Od., 9. 112.

50 Il., 11. 807-8. ἵνα σφ’ ἀγορή τε θέμις τε|ἤην, τῇ δὴ χαί σφι
θεῶν ἐτετεύχατο βωμοί.

51 Il., 3. 213. ἀγόρευε, of Menelaus; 1. 248, Nestor is λιγὺς

POLITICAL IDEAS OF THE GREEKS

Πυλίων ἀγορήτης: another verb, ἀγοράομαι, is used both of the speaker and of the audience, Il., 4. 1; 1. 253.

⁵² Il., 9. 32–3, Diomedes claims the right of free speech: ἦ θέμις ἐστίν, ἄναξ, ἀγορῇ. σὺ δὲ μή τι χολωθῇς.

⁵³ Od., 24. 413ff., especially 421–2. Here the use of ἄθροοι in its primitive sense of "with one voice" (compare ὁμηγέρεες, and the unusual colourless passive ἥγερθεν), mark the proceedings as confusedly spontaneous. It is a naïve attempt to express the workings of the "common sense" of a whole community unaccustomed to corporate initiative, and is all the more notable, whatever the relative date of the passage.

⁵⁴ *Nomen* in Latin is used for a status (*nomen Latinum*) or for a political aggregate (*nomen Ætolorum*).

⁵⁵ Il., 2. 867. Κᾶρες βαρβαρόφωνοι; Od., 8. 294. Σίντιες ἀγριόφωνοι.

⁵⁶ Od., 19. 173ff. With ἔθος, ἦθος, compare ἕσμος, "swarm."

⁵⁷ Compare the Greek use of ἡλικίη, "age," for a man's contemporaries. For ἔθνος, of birds, flies, and military contingents, see Il., 2. 459–69.

⁵⁸ The meaning of γένος includes both the larger divisions of the Greek people, such as the Δωρικὸν γένος, and the clans with kinship demonstrable at law, such as the Alcmæonidæ at Athens.

⁵⁹ In Homer the form φρήτρη is used, Il., 2. 362; but φρατρία in Attica is archaic.

⁶⁰ *Phyle*, φυλή (in Homer φῦλον), is probably akin to φύω, "grow"; it is used for other creatures as well as for men. Il., 19. 30 (flies); Sophocles, *Antigone*, 343 (birds); Il., 9. 130, the whole sex of women.

⁶¹ Od., 14. 68. φῦλον Ἑλένης; 14. 181, φῦλον Ἀρχεσίου.

⁶² Il., 2. 362ff.   ⁶³ Il., 2. 212–278.

⁶⁴ Od., 4. 174–6 μίαν πόλιν ἐξαλαπάξας | αἳ περιναιετάουσιν, ἀνάσσονται δ' ἐμοὶ αὐτῷ. We almost hear the voice of Roger of Sicily passing the word to Robert of Normandy to leave those storm-ridden coasts of the Narrow Seas and come down into fair Sicily: "I'll soon sack a town or so, of paynim-men, vassals of mine though they be!"

NOTES

[65] Thucydides, 3. 94.
[66] Thucydides, 3. 105.

[67] Thucydides, 2. 81.
[68] Herodotus, 1. 146.

[69] Whether these "houses" at Megara were the first "shanties" of the invaders, or the deserted "palace" of the last Minoan dynasty, there is no evidence to decide.

[70] Thucydides, 2. 15.

[71] Herodotus, 1, 170.

[72] A good instance is the law of Draco at Athens, to which Demosthenes appeals in his speech against Macartatus (1069); it defined the limits of kinship within which the relatives were authorized to "pursue" and prosecute the murderer; associated with them all other members of the political unit (*phratria*) to which the dead man had belonged; and provided procedure for "appeasement" otherwise than by literal "pursuit" and destruction of the offender.

[73] Aristotle, *Politics*, 1. 1. 1252 a. 5.

[74] Herodotus, 5. 57. 61.

[75] For this Carian sanctuary of Zeus Stratios, "God of Armies," see Herodotus, 5. 119. Strabo, 659. My information as to the ruins at Labranda is from my friend and fellow traveller, the late William R. Paton; but I can find no reference to the site in his published work.

[76] The ceremony was called ἀμφιδρομία, "running around" the hearth.

[77] U. von Wilamowitz-Moellendorff. *Staat und Gesellschaft der Griechen* (in Hinneberg, *Die Kultur der Gegenwart.* Berlin, 1910), p. 35.

[78] Common names for such political units are φρατρία, πάτρα; more peculiar are χιλιαστύς, "thousand" at Ephesus; πύργος, "tower" or "block-house" at Teos.

[79] See note 77 above.

[80] The word συνοικισμὸς itself occurs first in Polybius (4. 33. 7), but the verb συνοικίζω and its verbal substantive συνοίκισις were in use in this political sense in the fifth century (Thucydides 1. 24, 2. 15, 3. 2–3, 6. 5.) and Thucydides is authority also for the name Συνοίκια for the festival which commemorated the reorganization of Attica by Theseus. Like other

political terms, συνοικίζω had also a popular meaning, probably its original one: Herodotus 2. 121. has καὶ οἱ τὴν θυγατέρα ταύτην συνοικίσαι,, "and to give him in marriage this daughter": the fundamental meaning being here too the same—to "make to live together" persons who were not blood-relatives.

[81] Aristotle, *Politics*, 1. 2. 1252 b. 29. πάσης ἔχουσα πέρας τῆς αὐταρκείας.

[82] Compare the Homeric description of the destruction wrought by a freshet in such a valley among the "works of man" along the stream banks.

[83] On this subject of agricultural organisation see Heitland, *Agricola*, Cambridge, 1921.

[84] Aristotle, *Politics*, 1. 2. 1253 a. 30, ὁ δὲ πρῶτος συστήσας μεγίστων ἀγαθῶν αἴτιος.

[85] To such an *oikistes*, οἰκιστής, the same honours were paid as to a local hero; he had his chapel, altar, and priesthood, and annual "founder's day" ceremonies.

[86] Compare the passage Hesiod, *Theogonia*, 81–97, discussed in detail in Lecture III, p. 155.

NOTES FOR LECTURE III

[1] The Greek terms are ἐταῖροι, "companions"; θεράποντες, "attendants"; βασιλεῖς, who "make the people to go"—perhaps a popular etymology of some word like the Phrygian βαλήν, "king"; ἄνακτες, "masters"; φῦλα, "clans," composed of narrower φρῆτραι, "brotherhoods" of blood-relatives.

[2] Il., 2. 73.

[3] Il., 11. 807ff. (see Lecture II, note 50, above).

[4] Od., 9. 112, τοῖσιν δ' οὔτ' ἀγοραὶ βουληφόροι, οὔτε θέμιστες.

[5] Od., 9. 214–5, ἄνδρ' ἐπελεύσεσθαι μεγάλην ἐπιειμένον ἀλκήν, l ἄγριον, οὔτε δίκας εὖ εἰδότα, οὔτε θέμιστας.

[6] From the stem θε- we have the verb τίθημι, "put"; θεμερός, "steadfast"; θῶκος, "seat"; θεσμὸς, θέσις, θέμεθλον; similarly, νῆα θέμωσε, "set the ship on her course." Od., 9. 486. 542.

[7] Plato, *Gorgias*, 505C.

[8] Il., 11. 779; hospitality; 2. 73, trial of morale.

NOTES

[9] 9. 132–4, evidence of chastity; 23. 581, absence of foul play.

[10] Il., 9. 32. 33, freedom of speech.

[11] Il., 24. 650–2. There is no suggestion here of a *themis* equipment in Achilles' tent like that in the *agora* of Odysseus' camp; the slight tone of boredom with the whole proceeding shows that it was the will-and-pleasure (*boulé*) of Achilles personally, that his visitors wanted to know, in order to make up their own minds.

[12] Il., 23. 44.

[13] Il., 14. 386–7.

[14] Il., 16. 796.

[15] Od., 16. 403.

[16] Il., 2. 204–6. The word here used, xοίρανος, is now found to have been an official title of the great Achæan chief Atarysias (probably Atreus), who gave much trouble to the Hittite government between 1250 and 1225 B.C. Probably the later Greek word, τύραννος, "tyrant," which the Greeks themselves thought to be Lydian, is another version of the same pre-Hellenic title; and it is worth noting that the founder of the Hellenic dynasty in Macedon, to which Philip and Alexander belonged, was called Caranos.

[17] Il., 1. 233.

[18] The vase from Hagia-Triada is figured in A. Mosso, *Palaces of Crete*. London, 1907, pp. 77–8, fig. 33. 34: G. Glotz, *The Ægean Civilisation*. London, 1925, p. 155, fig. 27.

[19] Il., 9. 156.

[20] Il., 1. 239.

[21] Herodotus, 2. 136., 3. 30.

[22] Pindar, *Nem.*, 7. 99.

[23] Od., 19. 481.

[24] Il., 22. 351.

[25] Od., 3. 268.

[26] Od., 16. 459.

[27] Il., 21. 230.

[28] Od., 23. 82.

[29] Il., 8. 21.

[30] Il., 16. 388.

[31] Od., 9. 214–5. The history of this word *dikê* (δίκη) is discussed in Lecture IV.

[32] Homeric *Hymn to Apollo*, 394ff.

[33] Homeric *Hymn to Apollo*, 253; compare 390. His "dwelling-place," νηός, is the classical word for a "temple," or "god's house."

[34] Il., 9. 156.

[35] Od., 9. 114.

[36] Od., 11. 568–71.

[37] Od., 14. 56ff.

[38] Il., 15. 119. *Deimos* (Horror) and *Phobos* (Fear) are personified; and *Ossa* (Rumour), literally a "voice," in Od., 24. 413: and the "expulsion of *dikê*" by bad kings comes very near the same standpoint.

[39] Od., 2. 68. λίσσομαι ἥμεν Ζηνὸς 'Ολυμπίου ἠδὲ Θέμιστος l ἥ τ' ἀνδρῶν ἀγορὰς ἠμὲν λύει ἠδὲ καθίζει.

[40] Miss J. E. Harrison, *Themis*. Cambridge, 1912, p. 481–5. Compare an early Roman invocation in Livy, 1. 32. 6, *audi Jupiter, audite fines, audiat fas;* and Ausonius' express identification, *prima deum fas quæ Themis est Graiis*. Techn. Idyll, *De Deis*, 1–2.

[41] Il., 20. 4.   [42] Il., 15. 78–99.

[43] Aristotle, *Politics*, 3. 4. 15. 1277b. 15.

[44] Il., 9. 69.

[45] Il., 7. 286; compare 11. 472, 15. 559, 16. 632.

[46] Od., 22. 437; compare Il., 1. 571: also with a participle, ἦρχε λεχόσδε κίων, Il., 3. 447.

[47] Od., 5. 237, ἦρχεν ὁδοιο, though Od., 8. 107, has ἦρχε δὲ τῷ αὐτὴν ὁδὸν ἥνπερ οἱ ἄλλοι. Il., 17. 597, ἦρχε φόβοιο, compare 24. 723. γόοιο: Il., 20. 154. ἀρχέμεναι δὲ δυσηλέγεος πολέμοιο. The genitive is also used of a body of persons "put in motion" by their customary leader, such as the military contingents in the *Catalogue*, and the brigades in Il., 12. 93–98, 16. 173ff.; Od., 10. 205, τῶν μὲν ἐγὼν ἦρχον: 13. 266, ἄλλων ἦρχον ἐταίρων.

[48] Od., 10. 205; 14. 230; 23. 370, 24. 501; Il., 2. 805.

[49] Il., 15. 95, ἀλλὰ σύ γ' ἄρχε θεοῖσι δόμοις ἐνὶ δαιτὸς ἐΐσης.

NOTES

50 Od., 8. 107.

51 Od., 1. 28, τοῖσι δὲ μύθων ἦρχε (very commonly).

52 Il., 1. 144, ἀρχὸς ἀνὴρ βουληφόρος; compare ἀγοραὶ βουληφόροι, Od., 9. 112.

53 Od., 14. 446, ἄργματα θῦσε θεοῖσι.

54 Il., 2. 837, ὄρχαμος ἀνδρῶν; Od., 3. 400.λαῶν.

55 Il., 7. 324; 9. 93.

56 Od., 1. 367.

57 Od., 14. 428.

58 Od., 8. 499, ὣς φάθ', ὁ δ' ὁρμηθεὶς θεοῦ ἤρχετο, φαῖνε δ' ἀοιδήν.

59 Od., 1. 188; 2. 254; 11., 438; 17. 69.

60 Il., 11. 604 ἀρχὴ κακοῦ; Od., 8. 81. πήματος; Il. 22. 116. νείκεος.

61 Od., 21. 4; 24. 169.

62 Od., 19. 13.

63 Od., 21. 31–38.

64 Il., 3. 98–110.

65 Æschylus, *Prometheus*, 64. 908; Herodotus, 6. 92. αὐθαςής.

66 The normal sense of πελεμίζειν is "to make to vibrate" a spear, Il., 16. 612; but it is also used of men "rattled" by violent blows, Il., 4. 535.

67 The verb is εἴρω to "link together"; εἴρη is a "place of assembly." Il., 18. 531; and εἰρήνη, the state of peace, when one thing follows on another in orderly fashion.

68 Il., 9. 156; compare p. 129.

69 Demosthenes, 1455. 15, ἀρχὴ ἄνδρα δείκνυσι.

70 Od., 10. 38.

71 Quintilian, 3. 7. 6.

72 Suetonius, *Tiberius*, 43.

73 Virgil, *Georgic*, 1. 99.

74 Tacitus, *Germania*, 26.

75 Ovid, *Metamorphoses*, 2. 118.

76 Terence, *Eunuchus*, 2. 2. 21.

77 Plautus, *Amphitruo*, 3. 3. 1.

78 Virgil, *Æneid*, 5. 726.

79 Cicero, *de Republica*, 2. 13.

POLITICAL IDEAS OF THE GREEKS

[80] Ennius, *Annales*, 3. 4.   [81] Acts, 19. 34.

[82] R. H. Codrington, *The Melanesians*, Oxford, 1891, p. 118ff.

[83] E. Tregear, *Maori-Polynesian Comparative Dictionary*, Wellington, N. Z., 1891, *s. v. Mana*. R. R. Marett, *The Threshold of Religion*. London, 1909, p. 121.

[84] Miss A. C. Fletcher, *The Omaha Tribe*, Washington, 1911. E. S. Hartland, *Proceedings of British Association for the Advancement of Science* (York), 1906, p. 675ff.

[85] For example, F. M. Cornford, *From Religion to Philosophy*, London, 1912, pp. 83–87.

[86] Hesiod, *Theogonia*, 81–97. For further illustration and commentary, see A. E. Zimmern, *The Greek Commonwealth*. Oxford, 1911, p. 92.

[87] We should note that, for Hesiod, the greatest of these Muses, who especially cares for kings and singers, is Calliope, "our lady of the fair voice." Later she confines her operations to epic poetry, that "fame of former men," with which she charms away care in this passage. That the word has probably a quite different philological derivation, from ὄψ. "face" (Miss G. H. Macurdy, *Troy and Paeonia*, New York, 1925, p. 220), does not affect the Greeks' own belief as to its meaning.

[88] Pindar, *Nem.*, 3. 16, ἄρχειν ὕμνον; Sophocles, *Electra*, 553. λυπηρόν τι; fragment 337, ὕβριν. This construction with a direct accusative is in Homer (Od., 8. 107), but seems not to affect the sense of the verb. With the genitive as in Homer, Thucydides, 5. 19, has ἄρχειν σπονδῶν; with the dative, Pindar. *Isthm.*, 6. 55, has σπονδαῖσιν.

[89] Pindar, *Nem.*, 5. 45.

[90] Thucydides, 1. 107.

[91] Xenophon, *Cyrus*, 8. 7. 26; Herodotus, 3. 80.

[92] Herodotus, 1. 96.

[93] Herodotus, 5. 71.

[94] Herodotus, 4. 147; 1. 96–101.

[95] Ennius, *Annales*, 3. 4.

[96] Herodotus, 1. 95.

NOTES

[97] Thucydides, 3. 90.

[98] Examples of such "lords" are ἀρχιθάλασσος, ἀρχίφωτος; of "leaders," ἀρχιληστής, ἀρχιθιασίτης, ἀρχιτρίκλινος. (St. John, 2. 8.)

[99] Plato, *Politicus*, 259E. where the ἐργατῶν ἄρχων is contrasted with the mere ἐργατικός.

[100] Thucydides, 4. 128.

[101] Herodotus, 3. 97.

[102] Herodotus, 1. 174. χώρης τετραμμένης ἐς πόντον . . . ἀργμένης δὲ ἀπὸ τῆς χερσονήσου τῆς Βυβασσίης.

[103] Herodotus, 4. 60. σπάσας τὴν ἀρχὴν τοῦ στρόφου.

[104] Il., 3. 291; 16. 630.

[105] Il., 3. 309 τέλος θανάτοιο; 9. 411, 13. 602, θανάτοιο τέλοσδε.

[106] Od., 20. 74.

[107] Il., 21. 450-2. μίσθοιο τέλος. In later Greek, ἐντολή means any "injunction" intended to be fulfilled.

[108] Il., 16. 83.

[109] Il., 18. 378-9.

[110] Il., 10. 56. ἐλθεῖν ἐς φυλάκων ἱερὸν τέλος; 10. 470, ἐπὶ Θρηκῶν τέλος ἴξον ἰόντες; the whole army bivouacs ἐν τελέεσσι; 11. 730; 18. 298.

[111] Herodotus, 2. 64. ὀρνίθων τέλεα: 1. 103, of territorial levies; 7. 87, of cavalry; Æschylus, *Persæ*, 47, of chariots; Thucydides, 1. 48, of ships.

[112] Il., 24. 660. τελέσαι τάφον Ἕκτορι δίῳ.

[113] Il., 14. 195.

[114] Il., 18. 426. εἰ δύναμαι τελέσαι γε, καὶ εἰ τετελεσμένον ἐστί.

[115] Il., 9. 156. τελέουσι θεμίστας: 1. 5. Διὸς δ' ἐτελείετο βουλή.

[116] Il., 13. 377: the word translated *fulfil* (375) is τελευτήσεις, but in the answering clause (377) τελέσαιμεν is used.

[117] Herodotus, 1. 32. παντὸς χρήματος τήν τελευτήν.

[118] Euripides, *Supplices*, 1137. ἄυπνα τ' ὀμμάτων τέλη.

[119] Cicero, *Ad Fam*, 3. 2; 3. 3; *in Pisonem*, 21.

[120] Livy, 2. 40.

[121] Cicero, *pro Sulla*, 18; *pro Cælio*, 26.

[122] Æschylus, *Eumenides*, 743; compare *Agamemnon*, 908.

POLITICAL IDEAS OF THE GREEKS

[123] Cicero, *de Legibus*, 2. 14. 36, *initiaque ut appellantur ita re vera principia vitæ cognovimus.* Elsewhere, *Academica*, 2. 36. 116, he speaks of the "principles" of exact science, as *illa initia mathematicorum, quibus non concessis, digitum progredi non possunt,* and of the physical "elements," with a farmer's metaphor—*inde est indagatio nata initiorum et tanquam seminum unde essent omnia orta, generata, concreta. Tusc. Disp.*, 5. 24. 69. These *initia* were, indeed, in all probability once what a Greek called ἀπαρχαί, *aparkhai*, "first fruits," or "preliminary" rites, of the farmer's year: as Varro says (*De re rustica*, 3. 1. 5.), *initia vocantur potissimum ea, quæ Cereri fiunt sacra*; and it was the same with a new reign: *novis initiis et ominibus opus est.* Curtius, 5. 9.

[124] Cicero, *de Fato*, 15. 34. *Causa ea est, quæ id efficit, cuius est causa; ut volnus mortis, cruditas morbi, ignis ardoris. Itaque non sic causa intellegi debet, ut quod cuique antecedat, id ei causa est, sed quod cuique efficienter antecedat.*

[125] *De Finibus Bonorum et Malorum*, literally rendered into Greek, becomes περὶ τέλων καλῶν τε καὶ αἰσχρῶν. The word τέλος, as we have seen, can mean a "public office," a "squad" of soldiers, a "flock" of birds, a "tax," or a "conclusion"; it might perhaps, on Homeric analogy, mean "death," but certainly not whatever comes after death.

NOTES FOR LECTURE IV

[1] Miss J. E. Harrison, *Themis*, Cambridge, 1912, p. 517, paraphrases "the way of the world, the way things happen."

[2] Od., 24. 254–5.

[3] Od., 4. 691.

[4] Od., 3. 244, ἐπεὶ περίοιδε δίκας ἠδὲ φρόνιν ἄλλων.

[5] Od., 9. 215.

[6] Od., 11. 570.

[7] Il., 16. 542.

[8] Il., 18. 508.

[9] Il., 3. 109–10.

[10] Il., 16. 386–8.

[11] Il., 23. 542.

NOTES

[12] Il., 19. 179ff.

[13] Il., 1. 237–9: see p. 128.

[14] Od., 11. 184–6.

[15] Od., 9. 106; 8. 575; 13. 201.

[16] Od., 2. 282; 3. 133; 13. 209.

[17] Od., 20. 294; 21. 312.

[18] Od., 18. 414; 20. 322, illustrating Il. 19. 181–3. *Hymn to Aphrodite* 20. The general qualities of the *dikaios* are illustrated also by Homeric *Hymn to Earth* (xxx). 6ff.

[19] Il., 11. 832.

[20] Il., 13. 6. γλακτοφάγων, ἀβίων τε, δικαιοτάτων ἀνθρώπων. To take "Abioi" as a tribal name is to disrupt the portraiture and lose an essential feature. No "means of livelihood," such as sedentary folks practise, had these curious people; they just drank milk! And it may be questioned whether δικαιοτάτων does not refer as much to the monotonous similarity of "thoroughbred" people to each other, as to their uniformity of behaviour: in this sense most Chinamen seem "true to type" to the newcomer.

[21] Homeric *Hymn to Ares.* 5. δικαιοτάτων ἄγε φωτῶν. Compare *Hymn to Aphrodite*, already quoted, note 18.

[22] Il., 8. 431. Compare 1. 541–2, where Hera tells Zeus that he loves κρυπτάδια φρονέοντα δικάζεμεν, to "settle things behind her back."

[23] Il., 23. 574.

[24] Od., 11. 547.

[25] Il., 18. 506. τοῖσιν ἔπειτ' ἤϊσσον, ἀμοιβηδὶς δὲ δίκαζον.

[26] Od., 12. 440. κρίνων νείκεα πολλὰ δικαζομένων αἰζήων.

[27] Od., 11. 570. δίκας εἴροντο ἄνακτα.

[28] Pindar, *Pyth.* 2. 155. ὑποθεύσομαι δίκην λύκου.

[29] Æschylus, *Septem*, 85.

[30] Plato, *Phædrus*, 235D. δίκην ἀγγείου.

[31] Xenophon, *Cyrus*, 8. 3. 38. Aristotle, *Politics*, 2. 3. 9. 1262 a. 25. Sophocles, *Antigone*, 291–2, δικαίως of "well-behaved" horses. Compare Xenophon *Cyrus*, 2. 2. 26.

[32] Empedocles, fragment B. 2. 4. Diels. δίκην καπνοῦ.

[33] Hesiod, *Works and Days*, 263–4.

POLITICAL IDEAS OF THE GREEKS

[34] Hesiod, *Works and Days*, 220–6.

[35] The very ingenious explanation offered by Miss J. E. Harrison, *Themis* Cambridge, 1912, p. 516, does not appear to cover all the circumstances.

[36] Æschylus, *Eumenides*, 433–4. For the meaning of τέλος see p. 159ff.

[37] Hesiod, *Works and Days*, 275–285. For the full significance of νόμος, of which this appears to be the earliest extant mention, see p. 247.

[38] Hesiod, *Works and Days*, 275–285. The whole passage is of the first importance for its parallel treatment of human and biological order.

[39] Hesiod, *Theogonia*, 411–415, 428–430, 434. For τίμη as the recognition of the presence of ἀρχή in a person, see pp. 146. 149. A good example is Od. 14. 117.

[40] "Makes eminent" seems to be the only possible rendering of μετατρέπει in this passage, though the usual meaning of the word is intransitive, "is eminent."

[41] Euripides, *Medea*, 410ff.

[42] Hesiod, *Theogonia*, 901ff.

[43] This primary sense of ὥρα seen in Herodotus, 1. 4, where sensible people do not "regard it seriously" if women let themselves be carried off; compare 9. 8: "at the time they took no notice of it." Compare the compounds θυρωρός, "doorkeeper," and ὀλιγωρός, "inattentive." I owe, however, to Mr. Roderick McKenzie, of St. John's College, Oxford, the warning that the origin of the word ὥρα is obscure, and its connexion with ὥρα disputable, philologically. The personified *Horai* are in Homer gate-warders, Il. 5. 749, 8. 393; ostlers, attending to returning chariots Il. 8. 433; mere reckoners of time as between employer and employed Il. 21. 450. In Homeric *Hymn to Aphrodite* (vi) 5 and 12 they attend to Aphrodite's toilet; in Hesiod, *Works and Days* 75, to that of Pandora. In *Theogonia* 901ff (above quoted) they are daughters of Themis, their names are Eunomia, Dike, and Eirene, and they still have nothing to do with "hours" or other *special* occasions, but are charged with the normal

404

NOTES

course of events in general. On these Hesiodic *Horai* see
F. M. Cornford, *From Religion to Philosophy* (London, 1912),
pp. 168–170, and Miss Harrison, *Themis* (Cambridge, 1912),
pp. 515–518.

[44] Heraclitus fragment 94. Diels.

[45] Heraclitus fragment 100. Diels.

[46] Heraclitus fragment 133. Diels; reputed doubtful, but
ringing true, like so many of that thinker's remains.

[47] The Greek word for "true," ἀληθής, is, literally, "unforgetful," just as the nearest approach to a word for "sin"
in Greek is ἁμαρτία, a "bad shot."

Similarly, if a modern Greek peasant is caught tripping,
his usual excuse is λάθος ἤτονε, κύριε. "It was a slip of memory, sir," however much to his own advantage, if someone
else had not happened to "remember."

[48] Iamblichus, *Vit. Pythag.*, 9. 46.

[49] The ramifications of this allegorical mysticism, on the
borderland between religion and philosophy, are illustrated
in such works as Miss J. E. Harrison, *Themis* (Cambridge,
1912), and F. M. Cornford, *From Religion to Philosophy*
(London, 1912), and, with analogies collected from other
cultures, in the writings of Durkheim and Levy Bruhl, in
R. Hirtzel, *Themis* (Berlin, 1905), and in G. G. A. Murray,
Five Stages of Greek Religion. (Oxford, 1925.)

[50] Even the Hesiodic account of Hecate seems to be out of
place as it stands in our text of the *Theogonia*, and it is also
out of accord with other versions of her origin, which make
her, for example, a daughter of Demeter.

[51] Herodotus, 1. 2.

[52] Herodotus, 1. 115; 6. 129. διδόναι; 5. 83, λαμβάνειν δίκην;
9. 94. ἐλεῖν, γενέσθαι.

[53] Herodotus, 1. 120; 8. 114, δεχέσθαι.

[54] Herodotus, 9. 94.

[55] Herodotus, 9. 64.

[56] Herodotus, 6. 139; 1. 97; 3. 14; 3. 31.

[57] Herodotus, 1. 96, κατὰ τὸ ὀρθόν: 1. 84, Telmessian oracle.

[58] Æschylus, *Choephorœ*, 120. δικαστής.

[59] Herodotus, 1. 100.

[60] Herodotus, 3. 29.

[61] Herodotus, 5. 92. 2.

[62] Herodotus, 1. 89. Croesus; 1. 123 birthdays.

[63] Herodotus, 9. 42.

[64] Pindar, *fragment* 151.

[65] Æschylus, *Agamemnon*, 393.

[66] Sophocles, *Antigone*, 450–1.

[67] Æschylus, *Septem*, 662–671.

[68] Æschylus, *Supplices*, 230–1.

[69] Æschylus, *Choephoræ*, 61–4.

[70] Plato, *Protagoras*, 322 B.-C.

[71] Aristotle, *Politics*, 1. 2. 1252. b. 24.

[72] Aristotle, *Politics*, 1. 2. 1253. a. 1.

[73] I have myself witnessed such a recognition-scene in a San Francisco café between schoolmates from a village in Arcadia.

[74] There was ancient dispute about the precise word at this point; but whether the quarrel was about a man who "had been killed," ἀποκταμένοιο, or "had died," ἀποφθιμένοιο, it is clear that the defendant not only was held responsible but admitted his responsibility and was offering appeasement.

[75] Il., 5. 266; 14. 483; 18. 498.

[76] Il., 13. 659.

[77] Il., 9. 633.

[78] Od., 15. 272–8.   [79] Od., 23. 118ff.

[80] For the Homeric use of δῆμος, see p. 73.

[81] This sense, "had not taken anything," would have required οὐδὲν ἐλέσθαι, not μηδέν. The correct translation is due, I think, to Passow, followed by W. Leaf, *Journal of Hellenic Studies*, VIII, 122, and in his edition of the Iliad, London, 1902, pp. 610–614; by Sir F. Pollock, in his edition of Maine's *Ancient Law*, pp. x, 385ff., 405ff.; and by A. E. Zimmern, *The Greek Commonwealth*. Oxford, 1923, p. 83. How hard it was for the next-of-kin, brought up under the old code of retaliation, to forego his right to take blood for

NOTES

blood, is illustrated both in Celtic society by the behaviour of Orgetorix, who broke up the court which was to try him, Cæsar, *de Bello Gallico*, 4; and in Teutonic, by an exactly parallel incident in early Iceland quoted by G. W. Dasent, *The Story of Burnt Njal*. London, 1861. Introduction, p. lv. "Instead of following up the feud by revenge, the relations of the murdered man had pursued it at law; but when they came to plead at the nearest *thing*" ("mass meeting," like the Homeric *agorá*) "their adversaries, who lived close to the court, mustered in great force and would not allow the trial to come on." The result was a *synœkismos*, as the early Greeks called it; the whole of Iceland was divided into four "quarters," each with its own *thing*, considerably larger than the old local *things* which it superseded; and it was further provided that suits begun in one of the four "Quarter-*things*" should be carried "if need were" to the *Althing*, or mass meeting of all Icelanders, where any single clan which tried to defeat the new conciliatory procedure could be outnumbered and induced to concur in the general will. Even so, the new procedure did not always bring peace. "Thus Illugi, the brother of Grettir, the great outlaw, preferred death at the hands of his [Grettir's] murderers rather than forego the revenge which he was bound to take." Dasent, *l. c.*, p. xxix, note 2.

[82] Il., 23. 486.

[83] Homeric *Hymn*, 32. 2. Hesiod, *Works and Days*, 790; Sophocles, *Electra*, 850; Euripides, *Iphigenia in Tauris*, 1431. Plato, *Cratylus*, 406B.

[84] Cæsar, *de Bello Gallico*, 1. 4. (Orgetorix): see note 81.

[85] G. W. Dasent, *The Story of Burnt Njal*. London, 1861, pp. 197, 202–03, 213–214.

[86] Compare the gestures of a chief with his sceptre. Il., 3. 218.

[87] Il., 23. 579; 1. 542. and p. 174.

[88] Od., 11. 545; 12. 440.

[89] Il., 23. 750–751.

[90] Il., 1. 231, δημοβόρος: Hesiod, *Works and Days*, 263–4. δωροφάγοι.

POLITICAL IDEAS OF THE GREEKS

[91] Od., 9. 335. 369; 10. 204; Il., 1. 252; 11. 63.

[92] A. E. Zimmern, *The Greek Commonwealth*. Oxford, 1923³, p. 83. Our information about these πρυτανεῖα mostly concerns the way in which they were levied from litigants, but it seems necessary, from what is known of the departmental organisation of Athenian finance, to infer that the fund thus accumulated was used for the payments to the *dikastai*; and probably the Athenian practice justifies the inference that the "two talents" in the Homeric scene were provided by the man who was appealing to the elders for a *dikê*.

[93] Aristotle, *Athenian Constitution*, 3. 5.

[94] This vase has been repeatedly figured, e. g., *Encyclopædia Britannica*, 1910, article *Alphabet*, plate at p. 728. Only the last syllables following the hexameter line, ὃς νῦν ὀρχηστῶν πάντων ἀταλώτατα παίζει . . . . . . are blundered and apparently unfinished, as though this unusual effort had been too much for the scribe. They may be τοῦ τόδε, "of him [be] this," or τοῦτο δεκᾶν μιν, "this he [is] to receive."

[95] Aristotle, *Athenian Constitution*, 59.

[96] Since this paragraph was written, Dr. W. A. Heidel has suggested to me the possibility that there was in Attica (as in ancient Israel, and in the Icelandic *althing*) an annual rehearsal of all accepted rules of behaviour; but if the publication of the Attic *thesmoi* by Draco was an innovation, as the ancient account of it suggests, it is difficult to see in what form such a "reading of the law" could have been performed before Draco's time.

[97] Od., 23. 296. λέκτροιο παλαιοῦ θεσμὸν ἵκοντο.

[98] Homer, *Hymn to Ares*, 16.

[99] Quoted by Aristotle, *Athenian Constitution*, 12. 4.

[100] Andocides, 11. 19-26.

[101] Æschylus, *Eumenides*, 389ff. 484.

[102] Sophocles, *Antigone*, 796. 801ff.   [103] Herodotus, 3. 31.

[104] For an instance of Cambyses' ruthlessness, see Herodotus, 5. 25.

[105] Sir P. Vinogradoff, *Historical Jurisprudence*, II. Oxford, 1922, p. 129.

NOTES

[106] So, too, Darius, temporarily installed at Sardis, sat to give justice, ἐν προαστείῳ in the bazaar-suburb just outside the gate of the city or the citadel. Herodotus, 5. 12. On the *Bonkolion* see Harrison and Verrall, *Mythology and Monuments of Ancignt Athens,* London, 1890, pp. 165-6.

[107] Aristotle, *Athenian Constutution,* 3. 3. 56. 3. In 57. 1 the *Basileus* is charged with all "ancestral" festivals.

[108] Aristotle, *Athenian Constitution,* 59.

[109] Aristotle, *Athenian Constitution,* 55. There is no ἄρχων γραμματεύς, that is, as there was (in spite of the contradiction implied) an ἄρχων βασιλεύς.

[110] Collitz-Bechtel, *Griechische Dialektinschriften* III. 2. 4991.

[111] Collitz-Bechtel, *l. c.*: Aptera (in Vol. III, 2), Nos. 4941-8: Delphi (in Vol. II), Nos. 1684ff.

[112] Aristotle, *Athenian Constitution,* 4. 4.

[113] Aristotle, *Politics,* 3. 1. 1275a. 22–32. ἀόριστος ἀρχή, βουλευτικὴ (ἐκκλησιαστοῦ), κριτικὴ (δικαστοῦ).

[114] Aristotle, *Athenian Constitution,* 57. 4.

[115] Aristotle, *Athenian Constitution,* 45. 1.

[116] The date of this challenge of Eumelides is not certain, but the use of the word *dikasterion,* or "place where a *dikastes* works"—like ἐργαστήριον "workshop," βουλευτήριον, "council-hall," φροντιστήριον, "thinking-shop" (for a "college")—suggests that it is not earlier than Solon's establishment of a system of appeal-courts of this popular kind.

[117] Tlepolemus (Il. 2. 661–667) killed a blood-relative, and was expelled by the "sons and grandsons" of Heracles, the namesake of the clan. On the other hand Phœnix (Il. 9. 447–48), though excommunicated by his father, was prevented by his clansmen from going into exile, till he gave them the slip.

[118] Whereas the Athenian *basileus* took off his royal insignia when he was to be considered only as a peer among his peers, so the high priest of Eleusis, when he celebrated the "Mysteries," as a priest-king of the prehistoric kind, wore royal insignia—*strophion* and *stolé*—in token of his "initiative" and competence to "initiate" others into the

POLITICAL IDEAS OF THE GREEKS

local cult; as a reminder also to the men of the rest of Attica that at Eleusis (which had joined the "united states" of Attica very late) they were guests and strangers in the territory of an Eleusinian theocracy, however completely a prehistoric "union of the crowns" had obliterated the political frontier along Mount Ægaleus for administrative purposes; though its defensive masonry was, and is still, conspicuous where the Sacred Way traverses the pass.

[119] Plato, *Euthyphro:* especially 4 B–E,8 A, 15 D. A slave belonging to Euthyphro's father had been killed in a quarrel by a member of Euthyphro's clan. The father arrested this relative and sent to an "expounder" of the laws for advice. Before the answer came the relative died of exposure due to neglect. Euthyphro thought it ὅσιον—in accord with his duty to the gods—to prosecute his father for murder, in the public court of the *Basileus:* but the kinsmen thought this superfluous and improper, the family being competent to deal with domestic offences, even involving the death of a kinsman, for itself; and Euthyphro being in their view not competent to appeal against his father's management of the affair.

NOTES FOR LECTURE V

[1] Od., 9. 233; compare Homeric *Hymn to Hermes,* 188.

[2] Il., 9. 217; 24. 626; Od., 7. 179; 8. 470; 13. 50; 14. 436; 20. 253.

[3] Il., 3. 274, the hair of a sacrificial victim; Od., 20. 210, houses and so forth in distributing an inheritance; Od., 6. 188. Zeus distributes prosperity among men.

[4] Il., 15. 631, oxen; Od., 13. 407, swine; 9. 449, the Cyclops' ram; Il., 5. 777, horses.

[5] Il., 20. 8, nymphs in a grove.

[6] Od., 2. 167.

[7] Il., 6. 195; compare 20. 185; 2. 751 (and regularly in the "Catalogue"); 12. 313; Od., 11. 185; 20. 336.

[8] Il., 23. 177; 2. 780 (passive).

NOTES

[9] Herodotus, 8. 137; 8. 115, and, metaphorically, Sophocles, *Electra*, 176. [10] Herodotus, 4. 191.

[11] Thucydides, 5. 42, μηδετέρους οἰκεῖν τὸ χωρίον ἀλλὰκοινῆ νέμειν.

[12] Æschylus, *Prometheus*, 291–92.

[13] Herodotus, 6. 11. θεῶν τὰ ἴσα νεμόντων; compare 1. 32; 3. 16, and 39; Thucydides, 3. 48.

[14] Herodotus, 1. 59. Persistratus, ἔνεμε τὴν πόλιν; compare 5. 29, 71, 92. Sophocles, *Œdipus Tyrannus*, 237.

[15] Æschylus, *Agamemnon*, 802, οὐκ εὖ πραπίδων οἴακα νέμων. *Septem*, 590 ἀσπίδα; *Agamemnon*, 685, γλῶσσαν; 74, ἰσχύν.

[16] Od., 10. 159, κατήϊεν ἐκ νομοῦ ὕλης.

[17] Hesiod, *Works and Days*, 403, ἀχρεῖος δ' ἔσται ἐπέων νομός.

[18] Hesiod, *Theogonia*, 526, οὐδὲ οἱ ἥλιος δείκνυ νομὸν ὁρμηθῆναι.

[19] Il., 6. 511. ῥίμφα ἑ γοῦνα φέρει μετά τ' ἤθεα καὶ νομὸν ἵππων: compare Il., 2. 474–5, where two flocks of goats have been mixed and are being sorted "at pasture."

[20] Herodotus, 4. 62, 66.

[21] Herodotus, 1. 78, οἱ ἵπποι μετιέντες τὰς νομὰς νέμεσθαι. Xenophon, *Anabasis*, 3. 5. 2. Aristotle, *Hist. Animalium.*, 3. 5. 2.

[22] Plato, *Phaedrus*, 248B. *Laws*, 679A. Demosthenes, 948.10.

[23] Herodotus, 2. 52. Plato, *Protagoras*. 321C.

[24] Herodotus, 3. 38. Cambyses must have been mad; otherwise οὐ γὰρ ἂν ἱροῖσί τε καὶ νομαίοισι ἐπεχείρησε γελᾶν. So, too, in Herodotus, 3. 80, the "monarch" νόμαιά τε κινέει πάτρια; all the more significant because in the same context it is ἰσονομίη, which βουλεύματά τε πάντα ἐς τὸ κοινόν ἀναφέρει, "refers all its resolves to a public" opinion for which the standard is set by those νόμαια πάτρια.

[25] With this aspect of the verb and its substantives go a few poetical compounds, with the accent thrown back. Od., 6. 106, ἀγρόνομοι νύμφαι; Empedocles, fragment 75. Diels. θαλασσονόμων, of shellfish, "ranging the sea-bottom." But the most of the compounds are paroxytone, and have the derivative administrative sense; οἰκονόμος, "householder"; ἀγρονόμος,

411

POLITICAL IDEAS OF THE GREEKS

"farm-overseer"; κληρονόμος, "administrator" and "beneficial owner" of an inheritance. Public magistracies of this type are numerous, such as ἀστυνόμος, "chief constable"; ἀγορανόμος, "clerk of the market"—the Greek nickname of the Roman *aedilis* in that aspect of his work in which itinerant Greeklings chiefly encountered him. Note, however, that ἀστόνομος occurs in contexts where it is doubtful whether it should not be rendered adjectively, and accented proparoxytone: Æschylus, *Agamemnon*, 88, ἀστόνομοι θεοί; Pindar, *Nem.*, 9, 74, ἀγλαΐαι (feasts); but Sophocles, *Antigone*, 355, ὀργαί (sentiments or impulses in regard to public order), is clearly in the administrative sense. Most important of all, αὐτονόμος, "self-administered," describes the classical Greek ideal of government, and ἰσονόμος keeps closely to the primary notion of "equality in apportionment."

[26] Hesiod, *Theogonia*, 66–7, μέλπονται πάντων τε νομους καὶ ἤθεα κεδνὰ | ἀθανάτων κλείουσι; compare Il., 6. 511, μετά τ' ἤθεα καὶ νομον ἵππων. To leave interpretation free, the word νομος is printed here without accent.

[27] Hesiod, *Works and Days*, 276ff.

[28] Hesiod, *Theogonia*, 416–7, ὅτε πού τις . . . | ἔρδων ἱερὰ καλὰ κατὰ νόμον ἱλάσκηται.

[29] Diels,[2] ii, 215, νόμοις πείθου (Chilon); 217, τοῖς μὲν νόμοις παλαιοῖς χρῶ, τοῖς δὲ ὄψοις προσφάτοις (Periander).

[30] Homeric *Hymn to Apollo*, 20, νόμος ὠδῆς; Herodotus, 1. 24; ὁ ὄρθιος νόμος, Æschylus, *Septem*, 954, τὸν ὀξὺν νόμον. The Latin equivalent of νόμος in this sense is *numeri*, while that of νομός, "pasture," is *nemus*, a "clearing" in the forest. See F. M. Cornford, *From Religion to Philosophy*. London, 1912, pp. 31–33.

[31] Herodotus, 8. 89; compare 9. 48, and Æschylus, *Agamemnon*, 802; *Septem*, 590.

[32] Sophocles, *Antigone*, 368ff., νόμους παρείρων χθονὸς | θεῶν τ' ἔνορκον δίκαν | ὑψίπολις.

[33] Euripides, *Supplices*, 526–67, θάψαι δικαίως, τὸν πανελλήνων νόμον | σώζων. Herodotus 7. 104.

[34] Plato, *Apology*, 24B.

412

NOTES

[35] G. G. A. Murray, *The Rise of the Greek Epic.* Oxford, 1907, pp. 80–8.

[36] F. M. Cornford, *From Religion to Philosophy.* London, 1912, pp. 32–33.

[37] Aristophanes, *Knights* 660 (Schol): Compare Thucydides 5. 54–55 διαβατήρια, and Herodotus 6. 76.

[38] Livy, 1. 8, *locus, qui nunc sœptus descendentibus inter duo lucos est, asylum aperuit.* Dionysius of Halicarnassus 2. 15. calls it μεθόριον δυοῖν δρυμῶν, "a boundary-space between two oak-woods."

[39] Pliny, *Natural History,* 12. 1, *Hœc* (trees) *fuere numinum templa, priscoque ritu simplicia rura etiam nunc deo praecellentem arborem dicant.* On this whole topic, compare Sir James Frazer, *The Golden Bough,* I³, ii, 8. and Cornford's essay already quoted in note [36].

[40] Pindar, *Ol.* 8. 86.　　　[41] Hesiod, *Theogonia,* 223.

[42] Plato, *Politicus,* 271D. As the divine "herdsmen" provided for each animal its proper food, there was no need for rapacious food-quest such as the carnivora practise now.

[43] Herodotus, 2. 52. θεοὶ . . . κόσμῳ θέντες . . . πάσας νομὰς εἶχον: see also p. 243.

[44] Pseudo-Timæus, περὶ ψυχῆς κόσμω, 104E.

[45] Plato, *Critias,* 109B.

[46] Od., 10. 302ff., ἐκ γαίης ἐρύσας, καί μοι φύσιν αὐτοῦ ἔδειξεν. ῥίζῃ μὲν μέλαν ἔσκε, γάλακτι δὲ εἴκελον ἄνθος. There is the less need to discuss modern opinions about this passage, as they have been recently collected by J. W. Beardslee, Jr., *The Use of Φύσις in Fifth Century Greek Literature.* Chicago, 1918; to which I have to acknowledge my obligations throughout this section, though without wholly endorsing Doctor Beardslee's conclusions.

[47] Galen, *De.* περὶ φύσιος ἀνθρώπου. *ed. Kuhn,* xv. 3.

[48] Pindar, *Ol.* 1. 67; *Pyth.* 4. 235; *Isthm.* 4. 49; 7. 22.

[49] Pindar, fragment 169 . . . νόμος ὁ πάντων βασιλεὺς . . . ; quoted in Herodotus 3. 38; Plato, *Gorgias,* 484B; *Laws* 690B. 890A; *Protagoras* 337D.

[50] Pindar, fragment 278, ed. Christ.

POLITICAL IDEAS OF THE GREEKS

⁵¹ Pindar, *Nem.*, 6. 5.

⁵² Æschylus, *Supplices*, 496; *Persae*, 441; *Choephoroe*, 281; *Prometheus*, 489; *Agamemnon*, 633, οὐκ οἶδεν οὐδεὶς ὥστ' ἀπαγγεῖλαι τορῶς l πλὴν τοῦ τρέφοντος ἡλίου χθονὸς φύσιν.

⁵³ Plato, *Laws*, 770D.

⁵⁴ Herodotus, 3. 22, τῶν πυρῶν τὴν φύσιν.

⁵⁵ Herodotus, 2. 71. φύσιν ἰδέης τοίησδε. It is worth noting that the word ἰδέα, *idea*, translated "species" here, is used, as in other passages of Herodotus (1. 203; 6. 119; 6. 100) for any distinguishable "kind" of plant, liquid, or policy. It has as yet no abstract or "ideal" implications at all; but corresponds with the φύσις of this or that "kind"; as the achievement of growth-to-completeness stands to the process of growing.

⁵⁶ Herodotus, 2. 38, εἰ κατὰ φύσιν ἔχει πεφυκυίας [τὰς τρίχας].

⁵⁷ Herodotus, 2. 5, Αἴγυπτου γὰρ φύσις ἐστι τῆς χώρης τοιήδε . . . . . . πρόχυσιν τῆς γῆς ἐουσαν.

⁵⁸ Herodotus, 7. 134, φύσι τε γεγονότες εὖ.

⁵⁹ Herodotus, 2. 45, τῆς Αἰγυπτίων φύσιος καὶ νόμων πάμπαν ἀπείρως ἔχειν.

⁶⁰ Herodotus, 3. 38; the word νομίζουσι, translated "are accustomed to think," is strictly "observe as a custom."

⁶¹ Herodotus, 7. 104.

⁶² Herodotus, 7. 102, τῆς Ἑλλάδι πενίη μὲν αἰεί κοτε σύντροφός ἐστι, ἀρέτη δὲ ἔπακτός ἐστι, ἀπό τε σοφίης κατεργασμένη καὶ νόμου ἰσχυροῦ.

⁶³ Heraclitus, fragment 114, Diels, cf. 44. Conversely Heraclitus insists that ὕβριν χρὴ σβεννύναι μᾶλλον ἢ πυρκαϊήν, fragment 43, Diels; where ὕβρις rightly translated *insolentia* in Latin, is that "unaccustomed" breach of normal order, which must be "stamped out," like a bonfire among the close-packed houses of a Greek *polis*. Empedocles, fragment 135, Diels.

⁶⁴ Anaximander, fragment 9, Diels. In the same way, in another striking passage, Heraclitus (fr. 94, Diels) says that "the sun will not overstep his measures," the exact dimensions of his course through the sky, "but if otherwise, the Avengers, auxiliaries of *Dikê*, will find him out."

NOTES

[65] Euripides, *Bacchæ*, 891–96, couples τὸ δαιμόνιον, which has compulsive force in human affairs, with τό τ' ἐν χρόνῳ μακρῷ l νόμιμον ἀεὶ φύσει τε πεφυκός, coupling substantive with cognate verb to make his meaning emphatically clear.

[66] Herodotus, 2. 5; compare 4. 195.

[67] Sophocles, *Œdipus Coloneus*, 1295; *Antigone*, 346. *Œdipus Tyrannus*, 869–70; fragment 515; *Œdipus Tyrannus*, 334–35.

[68] Empedocles, fragment 8, Diels.

[69] Empedocles, fragment 63, Diels.

[70] Hippocrates, *Peri Diaitas*, 1. 11.

[71] On all this aspect of the economic revolution in Greek lands, see P. N. Ure, *The Origin of Tyranny*. Cambridge, 1922, Ch. I; and in his *Greek Renaissance*, Ch. V. London, 1921; and also A. E. Zimmern, *The Greek Commonwealth*. Oxford, 1923³, p. 295ff.

[72] Heraclitus, fragment 1, Diels, διαιρέων ἕκαστον κατὰ φύσιν καὶ φράζων ὅκως ἔχει.

[73] Diogenes Laertius, 9. 5; compare Diels s. v. Heraclitus.

[74] Heraclitus, fragment 41, Diels.

[75] Heraclitus, fragments 112, 113, 116, Diels; his word for "common sense" or the process of "straight thinking" is φρόνησις.

[76] Heraclitus, Diels, A16 (Sextus), τὸ περίεχον ἡμᾶς λογικόν τε ὂν καὶ φρενῆρες. We are reminded of the temperamental Cleomenes in Herodotus, 5. 42, who was οὐ φρενήρης, ἀκρομανής τε, "on the verge of madness and not coherent," his wits "not fitting well together."

[77] Heraclitus, fragment 114, Diels.

[78] Heraclitus fragment 2, Diels; the word λόγος, translated provisionally "reason" here, is, of course, a verbal substantive like νόμος, indicating "what is said"; as νόμος is "what is customarily assigned"; and as most people say things because they, at all events, suppose they have something intelligible to say, λόγος comes to mean "explanation" or "reason given" as well as merely "something said." It was probably only in much later Greek that it came to have

415

any other than this purely verbal sense, and was conceived as something which existed apart from the facts to be explained.

⁷⁹ Heraclitus, fragment 78–79, Diels.

⁸⁰ Diodorus, 9. 26.   ⁸¹ The word used is διασῦραι.

⁸² The principal passage about Archelaus is in Diogenes Laertius, 2. 16–17; Diels³, p. 410.

⁸³ Archelaus, A1, 2, Diels (Diogenes: Suidas).

⁸⁴ Xenophon, *Memorabilia*, 4. 4. 19. The phrase about the gods is θεοὺς οἶμαι τοὺς νόμους τούτους τοῖς ἀνθρώποις θεῖναι; compare Herodotus, 2. 52. θεοὺς . . . ὅτι κόσμῳ θέντες τὰ πάντα . . . For a later view of this "unwritten law" compare Aristotle, *Rhetoric*, 1. 9. 1368B: a "general" or "common" law includes "all those unwritten ones which appear to be admitted by all."

⁸⁵ Aristotle, *Ethics (Nic.)*, 5. 8. 1132B. 32.

⁸⁶ Aristotle, *Rhetoric*, 2. 23. 1398B 18.

⁸⁷ Aristotle, *Metaphysics*, Z. 11. 1037A. 16.

⁸⁸ Aristotle, *Physics*, 2. 7. 198A. 23.

⁸⁹ Aristotle, *de Generatione et Corruptione*, 1. 2. 316A. 10ff.

⁹⁰ Aristotle, *Physics*, 2. 1. 192B. 14.

⁹¹ Aristotle, *Metaphysics*, Λ. 3. 1070A. 6.

⁹² Aristotle, *Politics*, 1. 5. 1254A. 27.

⁹³ Aristotle, *Politics*, 1. 1. 1252B. 34.

⁹⁴ Aristotle, *de Generatione et Corruptione*, 1. 2. 316A. 10ff.

⁹⁵ Aristotle, *Metaphysics*, Λ. 10. 1075A. 11.

⁹⁶ Aristotle, *de Cælo*, 1. 4. 271A. 33; 2. 5. 288A. 2.

⁹⁷ Aristotle, *de Plantis*, 1. 7. 821A. 30. Though not indisputably Aristotle's own work, this essay is in close general accord with his doctrine.

⁹⁸ Aristotle, *Historia Animalium*, 8. 1. 588B. 10.

⁹⁹ Aristotle, *de Partibus Animalium*, 4. 5. 681A. 12ff.

¹⁰⁰ Aristotle, *de Generatione Animalium*, 1. 23. 731A. 32.

¹⁰¹ Aristotle, *Historia Animalium*, 9. 1. 608B. 4.

¹⁰² Aristotle, *Ethics (Nic.)*, 5. 14. 1037B. 26.   Compare *Rhetoric*, 1. 13. 1374A.

¹⁰³ Aristotle, *Ethics (Nic.)*, 5. 8. 1132B. 21.

NOTES

[104] Digest 1. 3. 2. Demosthenes, 774. 16. In this section my debt to that great teacher, the late Sir Paul Vinogradoff, and especially to the second volume of his *Historical Jurisprudence*, Oxford, 1923, will be obvious, and is gratefully acknowledged. I would refer especially to his commentary (Ch. II) on the recently recovered fragment of Antiphon the Sophist, beginning δικαιοσύνη πάντα τὰ τῆς πόλεως νόμιμα, published first in Oxyrrhynchus Papyri XI. 130, and reprinted by Vinogradoff, p. 42.

[105] Note that Isocrates, 15. 82, does not call them παλαιοτάτους "furthest back from now," but ἀρχαιοτάτους, "nearest to the origin" of all law, and most akin to that which is originative in it.

[106] Aristotle, *Rhetoric*, 1. 9. 1366B. 9.

[107] Aristotle, *Rhetoric*, 1. 15. 1376B. 7.

[108] Hesiod, *Works and Days*, 276ff. ἐπεὶ οὐ δίκη ἐστιν ἐν αὐτοῖς.

[109] J. E. G. de Montmorency, *The Natural History of Law*. Inaugural Address as Quain Professor of Jurisprudence in the University of London. Oxford, 1923.

NOTES FOR LECTURE VI

[1] χρήματ' ἀνήρ, cries Alcæus (fragm. 49. Bergk.), "Utilities are the man," not character or upbringing. The trouble was, however, that character and upbringing were inadequate to make use of the utilities now at hand. So, too, though there were no doubt some bad masters in Greece, Aristotle has no hesitation in defining his "free" man as "competent to make use of slaves." The root meaning of χρήματα reappears in such phrases as τοῖς σώμασιν καὶ τοῖς χρήμασιν ὑπηρετεῖν, "to do public service in their persons and with their whole estate," Aristotle, *Athenian Constitution*, 29. 5.

[2] In this sense Aristotle explains and justifies war, as "in the nature of things a way of acquiring wealth, which one is bound to use against wild beasts and against such men as, being of a build to conform to initiative, are reluctant to do so; on the ground that this kind of war is in accord with

417

dikê in the way things actually happen" (*Politics*, 1. 8. 1256B, 24–27). Similarly, and especially, it was in this sense "what happens," when Greeks "exercised initiative" over other peoples. *Politics*, 1. 2. 1252B, 9.

³ Note that the λῃστής probably inherits the function, as well as the name, of the predatory intruders in the migration-period, who "let loose their clans" upon a district and made it desolate: also that the "pirate," πειρατής, is the man who "attempts" adventurous raids, the risks rather than the morality of which deterred people of more ordinary pluck and initiative. It is the boldness, not the badness, of the pirates in fiction, that endears them to the young.

⁴ See, for example, Thucydides' comments (2. 48ff.) on the "unexpectedness" of the Athenian Plague during the Peloponnesian War.

⁵ Just as the Roman *pecunia* for "money" recalls the time when values were reckoned in cattle, so the Greek τόκος, "offspring," for "interest," goes back to a stage when loans were in livestock, and the owner's reward was a share of the increase of the herd while it was in the borrower's possession.

⁶ In the *Persæ* of Æschylus, the Queen reveals to Darius in an instant Xerxes' irretrievable error—ναυτικὸς στρατὸς κακωθεὶς πεζὸν ὤλεσε στρατόν (728), and the phrase seems to have been the popular verdict, for it recurs substantially in Thucydides, 1. 73.

⁷ Pericles goes on to use words which can only mean that he regarded this Athenian "training" as so self-evidently superior as to justify Athenian effort to impose it on those (presumably few and misguided) who did not themselves aspire to it. Thucydides, 2. 41. For the diverse "aims" of Greek states see Aristotle, *Ethics* (*Nic.*), 5. 6. 1131A; democracies aim at "freedom," oligarchies at "wealth," others at "good breeding" and aristocracies at ἀρέτη, "efficiency," without qualification.

⁸ Aristotle, *Politics*, 3. 6. 1278B. 6ff., classifies government into monarchy, minority rule and majority rule; cross-divides between government "in the interest of the gov-

NOTES

ernors" and "in the interest of the whole," and cross-divides again, according as the governors are "richer" or "poorer" than the governed. It is confessedly a research diagram, and the compartment in which a single ruler, himself poor, rules in the interest of the whole, might be as difficult to furnish with historical instances as that discussed in the text.

[9] Thucydides, 1. 27.

[10] Herodotus, 2. 167, ἥκιστα Κορίνθιοι ὄνονται τοὺς χειροτέχνας.

[11] Aristotle, *Politics*, 2. 6. 1265B, 13.

[12] Herodotus, 5. 66. Cleisthenes made the new tribal heroes ἐπιχωρίους, πάρεξ Αἴαντος. τοῦτον δὲ, ἅτε ἀστυγείτονα καὶ σύμμαχον, ξεῖνον ἐόντα, προσέθετο.

[13] Aristotle, *Athenian Constitution*, 55. 3.

[14] Plutarch, *Pericles*, 37; Aristotle, *Athenian Constitution*, 26. 4.

[15] Herodotus, 1. 170.

[16] Demosthenes, *Dionysodorus*, 48 (1297).

[17] Aristotle, *Ethics (Nic.)*, 5. 4. 1131B. 27ff.

[18] For example, in the passage last quoted:—τὸ μὲν γὰρ διανεμητικὸν δίκαιον τῶν κοινῶν ἀεὶ κατὰ τὴν ἀναλογίαν ἐστὶ τὴν εἰρημένην.

[19] Herodotus, 3. 80, ἰσονομίη.

[20] Plato, *Crito*, 51D.

[21] Plato, *Politicus*, 294A.

[22] Aristotle, *Ethics (Nic.)*, 5. 10. 1137B. 12.

[23] Aristotle, *Rhetoric*, 1. 13. 1374A.

[24] Aristotle, *Ethics (Nic.)*, 5. 10. 1137B. 26–29.

[25] Herodotus, 3. 80. πλῆθος ἄρχον. Compare 81. For a striking modern example, *not* in a democracy, see the account of the "judges' crisis" in the Transvaal Republic in 1897 in E. A. Walker, *Lord de Villiers and His Times*. London, 1925, chapter xvii.

[26] Aristotle, *Politics*, 4-4. 1292A. "Such a *demos* is analogous to tyranny among one-man governments; its "habit" is the same, and corresponds to the arbitrariness of "slave-owner"; καὶ τὰ ψηφίσματα ὥσπερ ἐκεῖ τὰ ἐπιτάγματα.

[27] Plato, *Laws*, 690A, in a list of "admitted claims to

POLITICAL IDEAS OF THE GREEKS

initiative," ἀξιώματα τοῦ τε ἄρχειν καὶ ἄρχεσθαι, places "the claim of the thoroughbred to initiate for the mongrel." γενναίους ἀγεννῶν ἄρχειν, only second to the natural initiative of parent over child, and before the claims of age and experience over youth, of master over slave, of stronger over weaker, and of common sense over stupidity and ignorance. That these various claims are soon found to conflict is no qualification of the speaker's appeal to experience, that each is in fact an ἀξίωμα ὀρθὸν πανταχοῦ, a "claim established everywhere" in human affairs.

28 W. Bateson, *Proceedings of British Association for the Advancement of Science* (Presidential Address to the meeting in Australia). London, 1914, p. 33ff., quoting Francis Galton *Hereditary Genius*. London, 1892².

29 Plato, *Meno*. 93C–94E. For Kimon's physical appearance, see Plutarch, *Cimon*, 5.

30 A fifty-century vase at Munich, published by Furtwängler and Reichhold, *Griechische Meisterwerke*. Berlin, 1912.

31 I have dealt with this aspect of Greek family life in an essay on *"The Plot of the Alcestis"* in the *Journal of Hellenic Studies*, xxvii. 195. See especially *Alcestis*, 311–319.

32 Εὔνους, "of a good intelligence," is the regular word; sometimes also φιλόφρων, "thinking thoughts like our own."

33 S. Ferri, *"Inscrizioni di Cyrene"* in Abhandlungen der Berl. Akademie, 1926. What is notable is that while the πολίτευμα, or corporation, which is to carry on the government of the *polis* is reconstituted in elaborate detail, it is left to a more or less expert commission to report upon the νόμοι in accordance with which all business private or public is to be conducted hereafter as before, so completely were the "ancestral customs" outside the scope of a merely "political" reform. I owe this reference to my friend, Professor M. Rostovtseff, of Yale.

34 Plato, *Laws*, 644D. 645A. ἐπὶ δὲ πᾶσι τούτοις λογισμὸς, ὃ τί ποτ' αὐτῶν ἄμεινον ἢ χεῖρον, ὃς γενόμενος δόγμα πόλεως κοινὸν νόμος ἐπωνόμασται.

NOTES

[35] Plato, *Laws*, 657C, χαίρομεν ὅταν οἰόμεθα εὖ πράττειν: and also 673D. "The initiative to this is the fact that every animal, as it grows up, is wont to skip, and man, as we said before, gets a perception of rhythm, and has created dancing," both formal dancing in a "chorus," and the rhythmical games of children. It has been tragic testimony to the results of appropriation by another Mediterranean people, that the Greek women in the Dodecanese ceased after the Italian occupation of these islands in 1912 to teach their children the traditional dancing-games "because they will have no use for them; we are all too sad now." Nor has the Greek ever lost this childlike, almost animal delight in acquiring fresh accomplishments from his neighbours—

> "To do whatever you can do,
> And do it rather better too."

as those most familiar with him in his own haunts, or even in the cities of the gentiles, can testify. As his Roman masters knew, *ad cælum iusseris, ibit.*

[36] Plato, *Laws*, 666. The older men are to do their share in public singing, but not till "after liquor taken," as the Irishman said, to renew their youth and clear their temper. In Greek lands, still, the race is to the swift; it is an obstacle race, for the most part; and many men are "too old at forty" for more than a subordinate part. Nor do the young men make it any too easy for them.

[37] Plato, *Laws*, 642C. μόνοι γὰρ ἄνευ ἀνάγκης, αὐτοφυῶς, θείᾳ μοίρᾳ, ἀληθῶς καὶ οὐ τι πλαστῶς, εἰσὶν ἀγαθοί.

[38] Diogenes Laertius, 9. 15. τὰ δὲ περὶ φύσεως ἐν παραδείγματος εἴδει κεῖσθαι: compare Diels, p. 70.

[39] In the following paragraph I have amplified some phrases of my essay on the "Background of Greek Science," printed the *University of California Chronicle*, XVI, 4, Berkeley, 1914, and also summarized the relevant portions of an address on the "Relations of Anthropology to Political Science," in *Proceedings British Association for the Advancement of Science* (Winnipeg meeting), 1909: reprinted in *Publ. His-*

torical Department, University of California, IV.   Berkeley, 1914.

[40] See note 37, and compare t/h'at epitome of the work of Christ on earth, περιῆλθεν εὐεργετῶν· "He went about doing good." *Acts* 10. 38.

INDEX

INDEX

INDEX

INDEX

INDEX

INDEX